FILM +TV GRAPHICS 2

Edited by Walter Herdeg $ 28.00

This new second edition of Film + TV Graphics provides a thorough—and international—examination of all essential aspects of film and television graphic design. Introduction by John Halas. Sections include: Entertainment Films, introduced by John Hubley; TV Films, by M. Massimino-Garnièr; Sponsored Films, by John Halas; Commercial Films, by Harold Friedman; Titles and Captions, by Louis Dorfsman; Experiments, by Jeffrey Altshuler. Film + TV Graphics 2 is a unique professional and artistic guide in the field of animation.

COMPANION VOLUMES IN THIS SERIES:

GRAPHIS/DIAGRAMS

The Graphic Visualization of Abstract Data

Edited by Walter Herdeg

Selected with the graphic designer in mind, who is often faced with the difficult task of having to present a body of information in diagrammatic form, this international review will serve as an abundant source of inspiration. There are six sections: (1) statistical, comparative diagrams; (2) flow diagrams, organization and time charts; (3) diagrams visualizing functions, processes; (4) tabulations, timetables; (5) cartographic diagrams, decorative maps; (6) diagrams used as design elements. "The book clearly indicates the great possibilities for elegant and creative design in an area that is too often neglected or simply untested. Graphis/Diagrams demonstrates the great potential for message-carrying in charts or diagrams and its design possibilities for the creative graphic designer."—*Art Direction.*

184 pages, 9¼" × 9⅜", 268 illustrations, with 86 in colour.

GRAPHIS/RECORD COVERS

The Evolution of Graphics in Record Packaging

Edited by Walter Herdeg

This comprehensive survey of album art presents a fascinating cross-section from the early stages of record cover design up to the most recent achievements in this field. Arranged in seven sections— the pioneers; the work done in the 1950s; and five music categories: classical music, jazz, light music, pop/rock/beat, miscellaneous records. Detailed captions and indexes of artists, designers, art directors and publishers are also included.

194 pages, 9¼" × 9⅜", 649 illustrations, 64 in colour.

Write for a complete catalogue to :

VISUAL COMMUNICATION BOOKS

Hastings House, Publishers
10 East 40th Street, New York 10016

FILM &

TV GRAPHICS 2

An International Survey of the Art of Film Animation

Ein internationaler Überblick über die Kunst im Animationsfilm

Un panorama international de l'art du film d'animation

Edited by/Herausgegeben von/Réalisé par

Walter Herdeg

The Graphis Press, 8008 Zürich (Switzerland)

Editor, Art Director, Designer: Walter Herdeg
Assistant Editors: Stanley Mason, Dina Lom
Project Managers: Dina Lom, Vreni Monnier
Art Assistant: Otmar Staubli
Cover Design: Raymond Savignac, Paris

Distributed in the United States by

Hastings House

Publishers
10 East 40th Street, New York, N.Y. 10016

PUBLICATION No. 144   [ISBN   8038–2322–3]

Contents Inhalt Sommaire

The Editor would like to express his sincere thanks to all who have contributed to this book. His special gratitude also goes to Bruno Edera and to the ASIFA, who helped to put us in touch with leading film artists all over the world. He would also like to take this opportunity to thank Dina Lom for her valuable cooperation in the compilation of the book.

Der Herausgeber möchte all jenen herzlich danken, die auf irgend eine Weise zum Gelingen dieses Buches beigetragen haben. Spezieller Dank gebührt auch Bruno Edera und der ASIFA, die uns weltweit mit den wichtigsten Künstlern in Verbindung brachten. Bei dieser Gelegenheit möchte er auch Dina Lom für ihre wertvolle Mithilfe bei der Verwirklichung dieses Buches bestens danken.

L'Editeur adresse ses remerciements à tous ceux qui ont contribué d'une manière quelconque à la réalisation de cet ouvrage. Il est particulièrement obligé à Bruno Edera et à l'ASIFA qui nous ont mis en contact avec les artistes les plus renommés dans le monde entier. Il tient à remercier Dina Lom de sa précieuse collaboration dans la réalisation de cet ouvrage.

Editor's Foreword

An illustrated book about the animated film? A static survey of a perpetually moving medium? It is of course very difficult to give a reliable impression of the artistic quality of a film in a few frames or even a short sequence. We were fully aware of this problem, but the success of our first anthology of film and television graphics had proved that there was a real need for such a work, so we proceeded to collect material for a second volume. The items we received were in some cases technically unsatisfactory, but we have done all in our power to attain optimum reproduction and to secure sufficient information for our captions and credits.

Anyone who leafs through the resulting book is likely to be fascinated by the great variety apparent in the personal styles of the contributing artists. Each endeavours in his own way to make use of the great creative potential of the animated film. It is to be hoped that this international survey of the best and most interesting work now being done will encourage other artists to turn their hands to this so important medium of the mass communication age.

Some encouragement in this direction is already being provided by the international festivals of the animated film which are organized at Annecy and Mamaia, Zagreb, Oberhausen, Ottawa, Melbourne and elsewhere. These meetings are of the greatest value in keeping film-makers informed of the work their colleagues are doing and in facilitating the exchange of ideas and experience.

The book of course owes a great deal to all those artists and producers who took the trouble to submit material for it. And a special word of thanks must also go to the six authors whose introductory texts are such a valuable contribution to it.

Vorwort des Herausgebers

Eine Publikation über den Animationsfilm – bewegungslose Bilder eines sich ständig bewegenden Mediums? Es ist ausserordentlich schwierig, in Einzelbildern oder knappen Sequenzen einen zuverlässigen Eindruck über die künstlerische Qualität eines Films zu vermitteln. Wir sind uns dieses Problems voll bewusst. Der Erfolg des ersten Bandes über Film- und Fernsehgraphik hat uns jedoch bewiesen, dass ein echtes Bedürfnis nach einem solchen Werk besteht. Ermutigt durch diese Tatsache haben wir uns an die Realisierung des zweiten Bandes gemacht. Wir waren bemüht, aus dem uns zugesandten Material, das zum Teil technisch unzulänglich war, die bestmögliche Bildwiedergabe zu erzielen und uns genügend Informationen für ausführliche Legenden zu beschaffen.

Wenn man das nun vorliegende Buch aufmerksam durchblättert, ist man fasziniert von der Verschiedenartigkeit der persönlichen Handschriften der darin vertretenen Künstler. Jeder versucht auf seine Art, die dem bewegten Film innewohnenden gestalterischen Möglichkeiten auszuschöpfen. Es ist zu hoffen, dass dieser internationale Überblick der besten und interessantesten Arbeiten diesem so wichtigen Medium der Massenkommunikation neue Talente zuführen wird.

In diese Richtung weist auch der Beitrag der internationalen Trickfilmfestivals, die in Annecy und Mamaia, Zagreb und Oberhausen, in Ottawa und Melbourne organisiert werden und den Filmschaffenden die Möglichkeit geben, sich über die Arbeiten auf diesem Gebiet zu informieren, Anregungen zu sammeln und Erfahrungen auszutauschen.

Wenn das Niveau der in diesem Buch gezeigten Arbeiten erfreulich hoch ist, so ist das auch das Verdienst der vielen Künstler und Produzenten, die sich die Mühe genommen haben, uns ihre besten Arbeiten einzusenden. Besonderer Dank gebührt auch den sechs Autoren, die dieses Werk durch ihre Einführungstexte wesentlich bereichert haben.

Préface de l'Editeur

The Authors of the Introductory Texts
Die Autoren der Einführungstexte
Les Auteurs des textes d'introduction

Un ouvrage illustré consacré au film d'animation? Un panorama figé d'un média pérpetuellement en mouvement? Il est bien vrai qu'il s'avère difficile de donner une impression tant soit peu fiable de la qualité artistique d'un film à travers quelques cases isolées ou même une séquence d'images. Pleinement conscients de ce problème, nous avons pourtant constaté, à travers le succès de notre première anthologie de la création graphique appliquée au cinéma et à la télévision, que ce genre d'ouvrage répondait à un besoin réel. C'est ainsi que nous avons été amenés à réunir les matériaux composant ce second volume. Même si certains travaux reçus étaient peu satisfaisants sur le plan technique, nous avons apporté le plus grand soin à les reproduire avec le maximum de fidélité. Inutile de préciser que nous avons également fait notre possible afin d'obtenir un maximum d'informations pour nos légendes et références.

A feuilleter le présent ouvrage, on découvre avec fascination l'énorme diversité apparente des styles personnels adoptés par les artistes représentés. Il a donc mille et une manières de mettre en forme l'immense potentiel créatif du film d'animation. On peut espérer que ce panorama international d'actualité des meilleures réalisations du genre en termes de qualité et d'intérêt encouragera d'autres artistes à œuvrer pour ce média absolument essentiel à l'âge des communications de masse. A cet égard, les festivals internationaux du film d'animation d'Annecy, de Mamaïa, de Zagreb, d'Oberhausen, d'Ottawa, de Melbourne et autres lieux favorisent très utilement l'échange d'informations, d'idées et d'expériences.

J'aimerais remercier ici très sincèrement tous les artistes et producteurs qui ont bien voulu nous faire parvenir leurs travaux en vue de la présente publication. Mes remerciements vont en particulier aux six auteurs qui, par leurs textes d'introduction, ont singulièrement enrichi les perspectives de l'ouvrage.

JOHN HALAS, born in Budapest, worked in Paris before founding the Halas & Batchelor studios in London. Now President of the ASIFA, he has made numerous top-ranking animated films and written several books on animation.

JOHN HUBLEY, born in Wisconsin in 1914, worked under Walt Disney and later for UPA, creating Mr. Magoo. Some major films on profound human issues made with his wife Faith have won them Oscars and international acclaim.

HAROLD FRIEDMAN has worked for Elektra Films, MPO, Inc., and as President of Savage Friedman, Inc., has made many award-winning films. Now produces films for Directors Circle, Inc. Is a leading figure in American commercials.

MAX MASSIMINO-GARNIÈR, born in Turin in 1924, joined Paul Film in 1954 and won many awards with his films. Now represents Italy in various international bodies and directs the television series "European Fairy Tales".

LOUIS DORFSMAN, born in 1918, was trained at Cooper Union and has long ranked among America's most distinguished designers and art directors. He joined CBS in 1946 and today guides and supervises their entire design policy.

JEFFREY ALTSHULER is a New-York-based producer of television commercials. He is Film and Television Editor of Print magazine and gives a course in the production of television commercials at the New School, New York.

JOHN HALAS, geboren in Budapest, arbeitete in Paris, bevor er in London das Studio Halas & Batchelor gründete. Seine Animationsfilme und verschiedene Publikationen gewannen weltweite Anerkennung. Er ist Präsident der ASIFA.

JOHN HUBLEY, 1914 geboren, arbeitete mit Walt Disney, später für UPA. Seine Filme (mit seiner Frau Faith realisiert) über menschliche Probleme wurden mit mehreren Oscars und internationalen Anerkennungen ausgezeichnet.

HAROLD FRIEDMAN arbeitete für Elektra Films und MPO. Als Präsident von Savage Friedman, Inc. schuf er viele preisgekrönte Filme. Heute – eine führende Persönlichkeit in der TV-Werbung – produziert er für Directors Circle, Inc.

MAX MASSIMINO-GARNIÈR, 1924 in Turin geboren, kam 1954 zu Paul Film und gewann mehrere Preise für seine Filme. Er vertritt Italien in verschiedenen internationalen Gremien und betreut die TV-Serie «Europäische Fabeln».

LOUIS DORFSMAN, 1918 geboren, studierte an der Cooper Union und gehört schon lange zu den bekanntesten amerikanischen Designern und Art Direktoren. Seit 1946 bei der CBS, leitet er heute das gesamte Gestaltungsprogramm.

JEFFREY ALTSHULER ist ein Newyorker Fernsehwerbe-Fachmann und -Produzent. Beim Print-Magazin leitet er das Ressort Film und Fernsehen. An der New School, New York, gibt er Kurse über die Gestaltung von TV-Werbefilmen.

JOHN HALAS, né à Budapest, a travaillé à Paris avant de fonder le studio Halas & Batchelor à Londres. A créé plusieurs films d'animation remarquables et a écrit divers ouvrages sur l'animation. Il est président de l'ASIFA.

JOHN HUBLEY, né en 1914, a travaillé avec Walt Disney, puis pour l'UPA. Quelques-uns de ses longs métrages sur les problèmes humains, créés avec sa femme Faith, ont remporté des Oscars et des distinctions internationales.

HAROLD FRIEDMAN a travaillé pour Elektra Films et MPO. En tant que président de Savage Friedman il a créé plusieurs films couronnés. Réalise à présent des films pour Directors Circle. Est un personnage éminent dans la publicité TV.

MAX MASSIMINO-GARNIÈR, né à Turin en 1924, s'est associé à Paul Film en 1954. Il a remporté plusieurs prix pour ses films. Il représente l'Italie en divers comités internationaux et dirige la série télévisée «Fables Européennes».

LOUIS DORFSMAN, né en 1918, a fait ses études à la Cooper Union. Il est l'un des graphistes et directeurs artistiques les plus renommés aux USA. Depuis 1946 il travaille pour CBS où il dirige et supervise le programme graphique entier.

JEFFREY ALTSHULER est un producteur newyorkais de spots télévisés. Il est rédacteur en chef de cinéma et TV du magazine Print et donne des cours à la New School, New York, sur la production de films publicitaires télévisés.

Film and TV Graphics of Today

There have been four basic periods of development in film and TV graphics since the invention of moving pictures.

The first was the discovery of the technique of continuous projection of images in terms of frame-by-frame animation at the beginning of the century. During that period, which started in Paris in 1904 with Emile Cohl, practically every image which appeared to move on the screen was considered magic. Even at that early time the opportunity for visual humour was very well understood by Emile Cohl.

The second period was devoted to perfecting the technical potential of the invention, experiments with combined live photography and cartoons leading towards smoother animation, colour and sound. It culminated in the work of Walt Disney and achieved a world-wide popularity which it owed to its mass appeal, its entertaining content and technical brilliance. Unfortunately, however, at the colour stage of development the medium lost its early magic, its lightness and its dependence on visual humour, the invention of which lies at the root of this genre. The imitation of natural movement and things that live photography can do better caused a crisis among creative visualizers, and their revolt motivated the third period of development in film graphics.

This set in soon after the war both in Europe and the USA. The progressive treatment of graphics, instead of postcard realism in background design, as well as a functional structure in character design for animated figures and an abstract continuity in story development, opened up some new potential for the medium. England, UPA in Hollywood and Zagreb in Central Europe showed the way. The significance of this period was that the graphic designer for the first time became an equal partner with the animator and the film technician. This balance is still maintained today.

The fourth period of development has been sparked off by the introduction of electronics. Part of the development is due to the emergence of television and video-tape as well as the use of computers as a device for generating moving pictures. Television especially has opened up channels for new applications of graphic design. Titles, announcements, introductions, special effects and continuity bridges have demanded graphic solutions at a constantly high rate and brought into this field a new generation of visualizers capable of solving entirely new problems which did not exist even a decade ago.

The big demand for animated commercials which could be termed miniature feature films brought into this field also a new generation of visualizers both inside advertising agencies—to solve marketing problems in terms of moving pictures—and in production companies—to present these ideas in the most appealing and effective way.

Once again, just as in the early period of film creation at the beginning of the century, the creation of film is in the hands of an individual artist instead of a factory type of organization as during the second and third periods. But the performance requires a knowledge of new tools such as electronic generators, synthesizers and computers. Film designers of today are obliged to work with electronic engineers and TV technicians. Electronic painting, input and output capabilities of monitors, graphic display systems, vector modes, memory storage and the whole range of peripheral and interactive devices are a necessary adjunct to the creation of the contemporary moving images of today.

For the new generation of film designers these additional tools and electronic languages mean enrichment in the medium, additional facilities for expressing themselves so as to reach the vast new audiences which the medium brings them. This new machine intelligence also marks the beginning of the fifth period of development in film and TV graphics.

John Halas

Film- und Fernsehgraphik heute

In der Entwicklung der Film- und Fernsehgraphik hat es seit der Erfindung des bewegten Bildes vier Hauptperioden gegeben.

Die erste nahm ihren Anfang mit der Entdeckung der fortlaufenden Bildprojektion einer von Bild zu Bild erfolgenden Animation zu Beginn des Jahrhunderts. Während dieser Periode, die 1904 in Paris mit Emile Cohl begann, wurde praktisch jedes Bild, das sich auf der Leinwand bewegte, für Zauberei gehalten. Selbst in diesem frühen Stadium wurde die Möglichkeit visuellen Humors von Emile Cohl bereits ausgeschöpft.

Die zweite Periode war der Perfektion des technischen Potentials der Erfindung gewidmet. Experimente, die Live-Aufnahmen und Zeichnungen kombinierten, führten zu flüssigerer Animation mit gekonnter Farb- und Tongebung. Diese Periode gipfelte in der Arbeit Walt Disneys und brachte weltweite Popularität, dank dem unterhaltsamen Inhalt und der technischen Brillanz, die bei den Massen grossen Anklang fanden. Unglücklicherweise verlor das Medium jedoch mit der Einführung der Farbe seine frühere Magie, seine Leichtigkeit und seinen engen Bezug zum visuellen Humor, der ein nicht wegzudenkender Bestandteil des Mediums ist. Die Imitation von natürlichen Bewegungen und Dingen, die durch die Photographie besser bewältigt werden können, führte bei den kreativen graphischen Ideengestaltern zu einer Krise. Ihre Auflehnung löste die dritte Entwicklungsphase in der Filmgraphik aus.

Diese begann kurz nach dem Krieg sowohl in Europa wie auch in den USA. Durch eine progressive graphische Gestaltung, die auf den Postkartenrealismus als Hintergrunddarstellung verzichtete, wie auch durch die funktionelle Strukturierung der Charakterfiguren und einen eher abstrakten Handlungsablauf, wurden neue Möglichkeiten auf diesem Gebiet geschaffen. Ein grosses Verdienst kommt dabei England, der UPA in Hollywood und Zagreb zu, die in dieser Hinsicht wegweisend waren. Das Bedeutende an dieser Periode war, dass der Graphik-Designer erstmals gleichberechtigter Partner des Filmanimators und des Filmtechnikers wurde. Dieses Gleichgewicht ist auch heute noch erhalten.

Die vierte Entwicklungsperiode begann mit der Einführung der Elektronik auf dem Gebiet der Graphik, mit dem Aufkommen des Fernsehens, des Videobandes, wie auch mit dem Einsatz von Computern zur Erzeugung bewegter Bilder. Besonders das Fernsehen hat dem Graphik-Designer neue Wege und Möglichkeiten eröffnet. Titel, Programmankündigungen, Einleitungen, Titelsequenzen, Spezialeffekte und Programmüberleitungen forderten unablässig neue graphische Lösungen. So entstand in diesem Bereich eine neue Generation von graphischen Ideengestaltern, die fähig sind, diese gänzlich neuen Probleme zu lösen, Probleme, die vor einem Jahrzehnt noch nicht einmal existierten.

Mit dem Aufkommen von Animations-Werbespots, die als Miniaturspielfilme konzipiert werden, eröffnete sich dem Künstler ein völlig neuer Gestaltungsbereich – einerseits bei Werbeagenturen, wo Marketingprobleme durch bewegte Bilder gelöst, andererseits bei Produktionsgesellschaften, wo die Ideen in möglichst gefälliger und wirkungsvoller Weise präsentiert werden müssen.

Wie in den Anfängen des Filmemachens um die Jahrhundertwende, wird die Realisierung des Films wieder einem einzelnen Künstler anvertraut, der das Kollektiv, wie es in der zweiten und dritten Phase üblich war, ersetzt. Allerdings muss er die neuesten ihm zur Verfügung stehenden technischen Hilfsmittel – elektronische Generatoren, Synthesizer, Computer – kennen, was natürlich dazu führt, dass sich der Filmschaffende mit einer Equipe von Elektronikern und Fernsehtechnikern umgeben muss, sofern er alle Möglichkeiten ausschöpfen will. Die elektronische Bilderzeugung, die Input- und Output-Möglichkeiten eines Monitors, die graphischen Anzeigesysteme, die Speicherung, sowie der ganze Bereich peripherer und interaktiver Hilfsmittel müssen heute von jedem Filmschaffenden genutzt werden.

Für die neue Generation von Filmdesignern bedeuten diese zusätzlichen Hilfsmittel und elektronischen Sprachen eine Bereicherung des Mediums, zusätzliche Ausdrucksmöglichkeiten, um das riesige neue Publikum zu erreichen. Die gekonnte Einbeziehung dieser Apparate kennzeichnet auch den Beginn der fünften Entwicklungsperiode von Film- und Fernsehgraphik.

John Halas

Où en est la création graphique au cinéma et à la TV?

L'histoire de la création graphique au service du cinéma et de la télévision se divise en quatre grandes périodes depuis la mise au point du cinématographe.

La première s'ouvre lorsqu'est inventée au début du siècle la projection continue d'images sous forme d'une animation case par case. Durant cette période, inaugurée à Paris en 1904 par Emile Cohl, presque chaque image bougeant sur l'écran produisait une sensation de merveilleux. On n'en était alors qu'aux débuts du dessin animé, et pourtant Emile Cohl savait déjà faire appel avec à-propos à l'humour visuel.

La deuxième période a vu se perfectionner l'aspect technique de cette invention; des artistes expérimentant la combinaison prise de vue réelle – cartoon développèrent un style d'animation plus fluide, bientôt doté du son et de la couleur. Cett période culmine avec les créations de Walt Disney, qui durent leur popularité mondiale à l'écho qu'elles éveillaient dans les masses, à leur contenu divertissant et à leur technique parachevée. Il est regrettable qu'en se dotant de la couleur, le nouveau média ait perdu son halo magique, sa légèreté et sa relation étroite avec l'humour visuel indissociable de la formule originale des débuts. L'imitation du mouvement naturel et d'éléments bien mieux saisissables par la photographie fut la cause d'une crise parmi les spécialistes en création visuelle, dont la révolte marque l'avènement d'une troisième tranche d'évolution de la création graphique appliquée au cinéma.

Les débuts de cette troisième période se situent au lendemain de la guerre, tant en Europe qu'aux Etats-Unis. De nouvelles potentialités du média furent révélées à travers le traitement progressif des réalisations graphiques en lieu et place du réalisme banalisé en usage dans l'exécution des décors, en même temps que se développaient la structuration fonctionnelle des personnages des dessins animés et le principe d'une continuité du récit sur le plan abstrait. L'honneur d'avoir tracé la voie dans ces nouvelles directions revient à la Grande-Bretagne, à l'UPA à Hollywood et à Zagreb, en Yougoslavie. Pour la première fois, le graphiste devenait l'égal, l'associé à part entière de l'animateur et du technicien; ce rapport de forces s'est maintenu jusqu'à nos jours.

La quatrième période de développement date de l'introduction de l'électronique dans le domaine du graphisme: télévision, vidéo, emploi de l'ordinateur aux fins de la création de dessins animés. C'est en particulier la TV qui a ouvert à l'artiste graphique de nouveaux domaines de réalisations. La création de titres, d'annonces de programmes, d'introductions, de génériques, d'effets spéciaux, de titres de continuité a nécessité des solutions graphiques sans trêve. C'est ainsi qu'est née une nouvelle génération de spécialistes de la visualisation rompus à solutionner des problèmes totalement nouveaux auxquels on ne songeait même pas il y a à peine une décennie.

La demande croissante de dessins animés publicitaires réalisés sous forme de véritables mini-spectacles filmés a suscité l'apparition d'une nouvelle vague d'artistes attachés soit aux agences de publicité, pour la transposition de problèmes de marketing en termes d'animation, soit aux sociétés de production, pour la présentation de ces idées sous une forme aussi attrayante et efficace que possible.

Nous nous retrouvons dans la situation propre aux débuts de l'art cinématographique au tournant du siècle: la création d'un film est confiée à l'artiste individuel, qui s'est substitué au collectif de création propre aux deuxième et troisième périodes. Il est vrai que la connaissance des outils perfectionnés à disposition, scanners, synthétiseurs, ordinateurs, est devenue indispensable, ce qui fait que le graphiste doit s'entourer d'ingénieurs électroniciens et de techniciens de la télévision s'il veut maîtriser toutes les finesses de son art. La peinture électronique, les possibilités d'opérations d'entrées-sorties à confier aux moniteurs, les systèmes terminaux de visualisation, la mise en mémoire et la gamme entière des équipements péri-phériques et des réseaux informatiques, tous ces moyens doivent aujourd'hui être exploités par qui veut créer des images animées.

Pour la nouvelle génération de graphistes créateurs de films, ces outils supplémentaires et les langages électroniques qui en relèvent représentent un enrichissement réel du média, ainsi que des opportunités d'expression accrues face au vaste nouveau public des téléspectateurs. L'emploi de ces nouvelles machines intelligentes marque en même temps le début de la cinquième période dans l'histoire de l'art graphique au cinéma et à la TV.

John Halas

Index to Artists
Verzeichnis der Künstler
Index des artistes

Index to Directors and Art Directors
Verzeichnis der Régisseure und künstlerischen Leiter
Index des metteurs en scène et des directeurs artistiques

Index to Clients
Verzeichnis der Auftraggeber
Index des clients

Index to Producers
Verzeichnis der Produzenten
Index des producteurs

Index to Agencies and Studios
Verzeichnis der Agenturen
Index des agences et studios

John Hubley

If Walt Disney could return to view current animated film productions, he would probably wonder what has become of the hero-princes, the queen-witches, the pigs and the bunnies, and what has happened to the story. For the animator is moving into an exciting period of change. From a vaudeville and comic-strip childhood, "cartoons" seem to be struggling towards maturity. The films of René Laloux, Karel Zeman and many others are forerunners of what may be a flowering of longer, more personal statements by film artists in this medium. Within the growing aggregate of animated film miles each year, I look for new ideas in the conceptual process, for a move away from comic-strip generalities towards the development of individual, specialized human character, for the presentation of scenes, problems and dilemmas from ordinary life, and narratives that both please and instruct an audience. These aims seem realizable: to increase awareness, to warn, to humanize, to elevate vision, to suggest goals, to deepen our understanding of ourselves and our relationships with each other.

Traditionally, the drawing of animated characters has been stylized and frequently insensitive and unrelated to actual life. Animation artists have too often been content with comic-strip simplicity in terms of drawing and, more important, in terms of characterization. Today's artists are exploring means of delineating rich and complex human capacities and "character" in animation. Given a technological culture that often depersonalizes and dehumanizes, I think that this new vision of the reality of human beings seen as animation characters presents a most urgent and promising prospect.

I can see the day when characters will be conceived and defined beyond the ordinary outer visual aspects as we at present know them. At any given moment we will see a portrayal of two or three of the dramatically relevant inner facets of the character and, at the same moment, the non-visual aspects of the environment. In any case, artists around the world are already defying the old "linear shape" order. Let's hope they also defy the limitations of the fairy tale and confront contemporary issues. May we be fortunate enough to see the development of visuals that are generated by dramatic and psychological imperatives—to continue to reveal human vulnerability and to increase the understanding of human relationships.

Wenn Walt Disney die jüngsten Animationsfilm-Produktionen sehen könnte, würde er sich wahrscheinlich fragen, was aus den heldenhaften Prinzen, den Hexenköniginnen, den Schweinchen und Hasen geworden und wo die Story geblieben ist. Der Filmanimator befindet sich in der Tat auf dem Weg in eine aufregende neue Periode. Seiner Variété- und Comics-Kindheit den Rücken kehrend, scheint der «Zeichentrickfilm» an Reife zu gewinnen. Die Filme von René Laloux, Karel Zeman und vielen anderen sind die Vorläufer einer Periode, die durch engagierte Filme mit persönlichen Aussagen der Künstler gekennzeichnet ist. In der von Jahr zu Jahr wachsenden Animationsfilm-Produktion zeichnen sich vielversprechende Tendenzen ab: neue Ideen im Gestaltungsablauf, eine Bewegung weg von Comic-strip-Gemeinplätzen hin zu individuellen, ausgeprägteren menschlichen Charakteren, die Darstellung von Szenen, Problemen und Sorgen aus dem Alltag, eine neue Erzählweise, unterhaltend und belehrend zugleich. Diese Ziele scheinen realisierbar: Bewusstseinsentwicklung, Warnung vor falschen Entscheidungen, Humanisierung, Horizonterweiterung, neue Zielsetzungen, Vertiefung unseres Selbstverständnisses und der Beziehung zu unserer Umwelt.

In früheren Zeichnungen wurden die Charakterfiguren oft stilisiert und ohne Beziehung zum wirklichen Leben dargestellt. Zu oft gaben sich Trickfilmzeichner mit einem simplifizierten Comicsstil zufrieden und, was noch schwerer wiegt, wählten comics-ähnliche Charaktere. Die Filmanimatoren von heute erforschen die Möglichkeiten, reichere und komplexere menschliche Eigenschaften und «Charaktere» zu schaffen. In einer oft unpersönlichen, unmenschlichen, auf die Technik ausgerichteten Zivilisation halte ich diese Vision einer neuen Realität des Menschen im Trickfilm als sehr vielversprechend.

Ich sehe den Tag kommen, an welchem die gewöhnlichen äusserlichen visuellen Aspekte in den Hintergrund treten und die Figuren so konzipiert und definiert werden, dass einige wichtige innere Werte der Figur, verbunden mit nicht-visuellen Aspekten deren Umwelt, in den Vordergrund treten. Jedenfalls lehnen sich Künstler in aller Welt schon gegen die alte Ordnung der «linearen Form» auf. Hoffen wir auch, dass sie von den Märchen abkommen und zeitgemässe Themen aufgreifen. Vielleicht haben wir das Glück, Zeugen einer durch dramatische und psychologische Beweggründe motivierten Entwicklung zu werden, die die menschlichen Schwächen und das Bedürfnis nach besseren zwischenmenschlichen Beziehungen aufzeigt.

Si Walt Disney revenait parmi nous, il serait bien étonné de voir ce qui, dans la production cinématographique d'animation, est arrivé aujourd'hui à ses jeunes princes, à ses sorcières royales, aux cochons et aux lapins, et au récit lui-même. L'animateur s'est en effet engagé entre-temps dans une période de renouvellement profond du genre. Après une enfance placée sous le signe de la farce et de la bande dessinée, le cartoon semble décidé à conquérir sa maturité. Les films de René Laloux, de Karel Zeman et de tant d'autres annoncent une ère dominée par des moyens et longs métrages empreints de la personnalité de leurs créateurs. Dans la masse des productions animées qui s'accumule d'année en année, j'aperçois des tendances et événements prometteurs: de nouvelles idées quant au processus conceptuel, l'abandon de la typologie généralisatrice du dessin animé en faveur de personnages individualisés au caractère plus spécifique, l'exploration des scènes, problèmes et dilemmes propres à la réalité quotidienne, l'adoption d'un ton narratif à la fois divertissant et instructif. Le tout au service d'objectifs qui proposent d'amener l'homme à une prise de conscience, de le mettre en garde contre ses errements, de le rendre plus humain, d'élever sa vision des choses, de lui suggérer des buts essentiels, de l'aider à mieux se comprendre et à améliorer ses relations avec ses semblables.

Le dessin animé traditionnel stylisait les personnages en les traitant trop souvent avec indifférence et hors du contexte de la vie réelle. Les artistes d'aujourd'hui cherchent par contre à donner expression aux riches et complexes potentialités humaines et à présenter des vrais «caractères». Sur la toile de fond d'une civilisation technologique vouée à la dépersonnalisation et à la déshumanisation, cette vision nouvelle de la réalité des êtres humains dans le cinéma d'animation mérite à mon avis toute notre attention en tant que démarche riche de promesses pour l'avenir.

Je prévois le jour où il sera possible de concevoir et de définir des personnages au-delà du plan de l'apparence visible, en mettant à vif deux ou trois facettes internes essentielles d'un personnage en même temps que les aspects non visuels de son environnement. De toute manière, des artistes du monde entier sont en train de mettre en cause l'ordre consacré de la «vision linéaire». Nous aurons peut-être la chance d'assister à l'avènement d'un art visuel obéissant à des mobiles dramatiques et psychologiques et dévoilant la fragilité de l'homme et son besoin de communication sociale totale.

Entertainment Films
Unterhaltungsfilme
L'Animation-spectacle

1–5 In *L'Arche de Noé* (Noah's Ark) Laguionie employs a style based on primitive art but imbued with the contemporary spirit, which gives it an elegiac quality that is reflected in his enchanted landscapes. A group of explorers in search of Noah's ark up in the frostbound mountains find Noah himself alive and ready to set out again on his journey, persecuted by the unseeing human race. The reference to the tragic condition of man, this time overshadowed by the menace of nuclear destruction, raises this film to new heights of dramatic force.

1–5 Le style que Laguionie s'est créé pour *L'Arche de Noé,* s'inspirant de l'art naïf, est pénétré d'un esprit contemporain d'où l'ambiance élégiaque qui se reflète surtout dans les ravissants paysages de montagnes. Une expédition en quête de l'Arche de Noé dans les montagnes enneigées trouve Noé lui-même qui – poussé par une foule invisible – est prêt à continuer son voyage. Laguionie a réussi à réaliser un film d'une actualité brûlante par la référence au sort tragique de l'humanité, cette fois-ci accentué par la menace d'une destruction nucléaire.

1–5 In *L'Arche de Noé* (Noahs Arche) wird der von Laguionie bewusst auf der naiven Kunst basierende Stil von zeitgenössischem Geist durchsetzt, was der Darstellung, besonders der Landschaft, einen elegischen Anstrich verleiht. Eine Expedition, die in den tiefverschneiten Gebirgen nach Noahs Arche sucht, stösst auf Noah selber, der bereit ist, seine Reise fortzusetzen. Die Anspielung auf das tragische Schicksal der Menschheit – diesmal überschattet von der Atombombe – verleiht dem Film eine erstaunliche Dramatik und Aktualität.

1

2

3

4

5

ARTIST / KÜNSTLER / RÉALISATION:
1–5 Jean-François Laguionie

DIRECTOR / RÉGISSEUR:
1–5 Jean-François Laguionie

PRODUCTION / PRODUKTION:
1–5 Les Films Paul Grimault/O.R.T.F., Paris

6–15 The Beatles' *Yellow Submarine*, an 85-minute animated film produced in the late sixties, created—one might say—a new art form. Heinz Edelmann's happy pop-art style, as if made to go with the new Beatles sound, was the perfect expression of an attitude to life which lasted for a decade or more. The film tells of old Fred, former conductor of Sergeant Pepper's Lonely Hearts Club Band, who is hounded out of his country, Pepperland, by the virulent anti-music campaign of the Blue Meanies ("A world without music is a Blue world"). A friend puts him on to the Yellow Submarine for a last-minute escape. The submarine surfaces in Liverpool, where Old Fred recruits Ringo, John, Paul and George (Fig. 15). Together they head back for Pepperland, but not without various encounters with Shakespeare, Freud, Moses and Napoleon, among many others. A pepper-powdered sneeze finally propels them back to occupied Pepperland, which has been almost completely drained of colour. A fight with the Blue Meanies ensues and must, naturally, end with the Beatles' victory.

6–15 Die friedvolle Monarchie Pfefferland wird während eines Konzertes der Sergeant Pepper's Lonely Hearts Club Band von den Blue Meanies überfallen. Diese sind gekommen, um das ahnungslose Volk der Musik zu berauben und ihm gleichzeitig auch das Glück und die Liebe zu nehmen. Bandleader Old Fred flieht im Gelben Unterseeboot *(Yellow Submarine)* nach Liverpool, wo er die Beatles für die Rückeroberung des Landes engagiert. Mit vier neuen Songs bewaffnet fahren die Pilzköpfe zurück nach Pfefferland. Auf der Überfahrt werden sie in teils bewegte, teils haarsträubende Abenteuer verstrickt; sie verwandeln sich mehrfach und begegnen einer Anzahl Personen aus Vergangenheit und Gegenwart. Zu guter Letzt spült sie ein heftiger Pfeffer-Nieser an die Gestade des besetzten Landes, wo sie ihren musikalischen Kampf mit den Meanies aufnehmen und gewinnen. Heinz Edelmanns froher Pop-Stil, der wie für die Beatles-Musik geschaffen scheint, macht *Yellow Submarine* zum bahnbrechenden Film des Jahrzehnts. Sein Einfluss lässt sich noch heute in hohem Masse spüren.

6–15 *The Yellow Submarine* (Le sous-marin jaune), un film produit vers la fin des années 60, a frayé de nouvelles voies en introduisant le style pop dans le cinéma d'animation. Les illustrations de Heinz Edelmann, créées, semble-t-il, pour accentuer la musique des Beatles, reflètent d'une façon adéquate la conception de la vie de la décennie écoulée. Le film raconte l'histoire du vieux Fred, autrefois directeur du Sergeant Pepper's Lonely Hearts Club Band, qui est chassé de Pepperland par une campagne anti-musique acharnée, lancée par les Blue Meanies. Il les échappe de peu grâce à un ami qui l'embarque à bord du sous-marin jaune. Arrivé à Liverpool, Fred recrute les Beatles (fig. 15). Les cinq bonhommes font route pour Pepperland — odyssée aventureuse au cours de laquelle ils rencontrent divers personnages, tels que Shakespeare, Freud, Moïse, Napoléon. Un fort éternuement poivré les rejette à la côte de Pepperland. Le pays est presque entièrement dénué de couleurs. Une lutte musicale contre les occupants s'engage, lutte qui se termine – naturellement – par une victoire des Beatles.

6–14

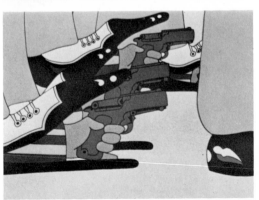

15

ARTIST / KÜNSTLER / RÉALISATION:

6–15 Heinz Edelmann

DIRECTOR / RÉGISSEUR:

6–15 George Dunning, TVC Ltd., London

PRODUCTION / PRODUKTION:

6–15 Apple Films, London/King Features, Los Angeles

ARTIST / KÜNSTLER / RÉALISATION:

16–18 Jan Habarta
19–21 John & Faith Hubley

DIRECTOR / RÉGISSEUR:

16–18 Jan Habarta
19–21 John Hubley

PRODUCTION / PRODUKTION:

16–18 Axel Jahn, München
19–21 The Hubley Studio, New York

16

19

17

18

16–18 Frames from *Zwischen den Träumen* (Between the Dreams). The film in fact depicts states of mind "between dream and reality". Before moving to Germany in 1966, Habarta was a film director in the Miniature Studio in Warsaw. To judge by this film, he is a painter by propensity. His pictures are based on experiences derived from Futurism, Cubism, from the Herwart Walden group and the late Bauhaus.
19–21 Frames from *Of Men and Demons*. They are taken only from the part of the film showing the demons of rain, thunder and lightning which constantly harry man and force him to develop ever new methods of self-defence. The episodes shown, which are simply drawn and easy to understand, lead the viewer directly into the centre of the problem complex created by environmental pollution.

16–18 Images de *Zwischen den Träumen* (Entre les rêves), consacré à l'expression des états intermédiaires entre l'éveil et le sommeil, le rêve et la réalité. Avant de s'installer en Allemagne en 1966, Habarta était metteur en scène au Studio Miniature de Varsovie. Dans son film, il se révèle peintre avant tout et influencé par le futurisme, le cubisme, le groupe Herwart Walden et le Bauhaus dernière manière.
19–21 Images de *Of Men and Demons* (Des Hommes et des Démons), empruntées aux séquences qui montrent l'homme aux prises avec les démons de la pluie, du tonnerre et de la foudre qui l'obligent à inventer des moyens d'autoprotection et de défense. Des épisodes dessinés simplement, de manière à être compris de tous, introduisent le spectateur aux problèmes complexes de la pollution de l'environnement.

16–18 Bilder aus *Zwischen den Träumen*. Der Film zeigt seelische Zustände zwischen Traum und Wirklichkeit. Habarta war, bevor er 1966 nach Deutschland übersiedelte, Regisseur im Studio Miniatur in Warschau. Nach seinem Film zu urteilen, müsste man ihn eher den Malern zuordnen. Seine Filmbilder wurzeln in den Erfahrungen des Futurismus, des Kubismus und der Kreise um Herwart Walden und das späte Bauhaus.
19–21 Bilder aus dem Film *Of Men and Demons* (Über Menschen und Dämonen). Sie zeigen nur den freien Teil des Films, die Dämonen Regen, Blitz und Donner, die dem Menschen auf der Erde stark zu schaffen machen und ihn zwingen, laufend neue Mittel zu seinem Selbstschutz zu entwickeln. Die einfach und verständlich gezeichneten Episoden auf der Erde bringen den Beschauer unvermittelt in den Problemkreis der Umweltverschmutzung.

20

21

22

23

24

25

28

22–25 *L'Empreinte* (The Footprint) is a bitter little story by the cartoonist Cardon who has worked for various newspapers and magazines such as *France Soir*, *Humanité*, *Charlie Hebdo* and *Politique Hebdo*. Its serious theme is that of man's enslavement. A strange prosthesis, the purpose of which is at first unclear, is strapped round the heads and chests of the children after birth. Only when it is removed is the mystery solved: it provides space for the footprint of the child's lord and master. The impact of this film with its moving comment on the fate of certain social classes is heightened by the forceful style of the drawing. The 35-mm, 7½-minute colour film was the first to be shown by Cardon at Annecy (1975) and promptly won first prize.

26–33 *Oiseau de nuit* (Night Bird). The story is about a civil servant who drives from the office every evening. Almost by chance he discovers a woman with wings and a bird's head by the roadside one evening and drives her to a mysterious door. A glimpse of paradise is allowed him, but his own fear of the unknown leads him to destroy what he does not understand. Then he goes back to his daily round. The 35-mm, 8½-minute film is in colour.

22–25 *L'Empreinte* (Der Fussabdruck), eine bitterböse Geschichte des Zeichners Cardon, der seit 1965 für verschiedene Zeitungen und Wochenzeitschriften wie *France Soir*, *Humanité*, *Charlie Hebdo* und *Politique Hebdo* arbeitet. Den Kindern wird gleich nach der Geburt eine seltsame Prothese an den Rücken geschnallt, die mit zwei Spangen um die Stirn und die Brust befestigt wird. Auf den ersten Blick tritt der Sinn dieser Prothese nicht klar zutage – erst nach Entfernen derselben zeigt sich, dass sie Raum lässt für einen Schuhabdruck, für die Stiefel der herrschenden Klasse. Dieser sozialkritische Film zeigt in sehr eindrücklicher Weise das Schicksal gewisser sozialer Schichten, die bereits von Geburt an geprägt sind. Der Film gewinnt sehr durch den kräftigen Strich. Dieser Film – der erste, den Cardon in Annecy zeigte – wurde mit dem ersten Preis ausgezeichnet.

26–33 *Oiseau de nuit* (Nachtvogel). Ein Staatsbeamter fährt Abend für Abend vom Büro nach Hause zurück. Zufällig entdeckt er eines Abends am Strassenrand eine Frau mit Flügeln und Vogelkopf. Er nimmt sie mit und fährt sie bis vor ein geheimnisvolles Tor. Es wird ihm erlaubt, einen Blick ins Paradies zu werfen, dann kehrt er zurück in seinen Alltag.

22–25 *L'Empreinte*, une histoire cruelle du dessinateur Cardon, qui a réalisé depuis 1965 des bandes dessinées pour plusieurs quotidiens et hebdomadaires, tels que *France Soir*, *Humanité*, *Charlie Hebdo* et *Politique Hebdo*. Des enfants se voient affublés dès leur naissance d'une curieuse prothèse attachée dans le dos et maintenue par des sangles sur le front et la poitrine, prothèse qui semble absurde de prime abord. Ce n'est qu'en l'enlevant que l'on s'aperçoit qu'elle y a créé la place pour l'empreinte du soulier du maître. Cette histoire sociocritique vise à manifester d'une façon impressionnante le sort des classes ou groupes désavantagés et exploités dès leur naissance. Ce film, déjà plein d'effet en soi, l'est encore davantage du fait du tracé vigoureux des traits. Cardon a reçu le premier prix pour le tout premier film qu'il a présenté à Annecy en 1975.

26–33 *Oiseau de Nuit*. Un fonctionnaire de Mairie rentre tous les soirs du bureau. Il découvre par hasard, un soir, au bord de la route, une femme ailée à la tête d'oiseau et l'amène jusque devant un portail mystérieux. Il a le droit de jeter un coup d'œil dans un paradis qu'il ne comprend pas avant de retourner à son train-train quotidien. Film couleur de 8 mn. ½.

26–33

ARTIST / KÜNSTLER / RÉALISATION:

22–25 Jacques A. Cardon/Henri Lacam
26–33 Bernard Palacios

DIRECTOR / RÉGISSEUR:

22–25 Jacques A. Cardon
26–33 Bernard Palacios

PRODUCTION / PRODUKTION:

22–25 Marie-Jo Corajoud/International Film Promotion, Paris
26–33 Paul Dopff/Pink Splash Productions, Maisons-Alfort/FRA

34–36

34–36 *Au Fou*. Unworried by fashions and new techniques, the Japanese artist Yoji Kuri has in the last few years turned out a whole series of small masterpieces. His style is inimitable. He draws almost as a child would: a house; a man in the house; a tree. Every leaf and every stone is carefully portrayed. This is the vocabulary he uses to tell his stories of accidents, horror and sex.

37–43 *A Christmas Carol*. This 26-minute film is based on the well-known novel by Charles Dickens. Its powerful drawings tell the story of old Scrooge's Christmastide conversion to a more generous philosophy with artistic gusto. The Richard Williams animation studio was awarded the American Oscar for this production in 1973.

34–36 *Au Fou*. Der Japaner Yoji Kuri schuf im Laufe der letzten sechs Jahre, unberührt von neuen Techniken und Kunstströmungen, eine Reihe kleiner Meisterwerke. Sein Stil ist unverwechselbar. Er zeichnet ähnlich wie ein Kind: ein Haus; einen Mann im Haus; einen Baum. Gewissenhaft wird jedes Blatt und jeder Stein nachgezeichnet. Mit diesem Vokabular erzählt er seine Geschichten von Unfällen, von Horror und Sex.

37–43 *Eine Weihnachtsgeschichte* (A Christmas Carol). Dieser 26 Minuten dauernde Film wurde nach dem berühmten Werk von Charles Dickens gedreht. Die kräftigen Zeichnungen erzählen die Geschichte des alten Scrooge, der sich zu einer grosszügigeren Lebensanschauung durchringt. Richard Williams' Studio erhielt 1973 für diesen Film den amerikanischen Oscar.

34–36 *Au Fou*. Dédaignant les modes et techniques nouvelles, l'artiste japonais Yoji Kuri a produit, ces six dernières années, une série de petits chefs-d'œuvre. Son style est inimitable: il dessine à la manière d'un enfant: une maison, un homme dans la maison, un arbre. Les soins méticuleux qu'il apporte à la description d'une feuille, d'une pierre servent admirablement la présentation de ses scènes d'accidents, de sexe, d'atrocités.

37–43 *Chant de Noël* (A Christmas Carol). Ce film se base sur l'une des œuvres les plus connues de Charles Dickens. Les dessins au trait vigoureux racontent l'histoire du vieux Scrooge qui finit par adopter une philosophie plus généreuse. Le studio d'animation de Richard Williams a reçu en 1973 l'Oscar américain pour cette production.

37–42

  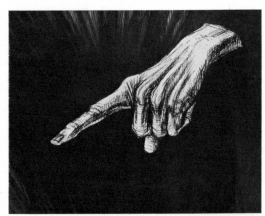

30

43

ARTIST / KÜNSTLER / RÉALISATION:

34–36 Yoji Kuri
37–43 Richard Williams/Ken Harris/Richard Purdum

DIRECTOR / RÉGISSEUR:

34–36 Yoji Kuri
37–43 Richard Williams

PRODUCTION / PRODUKTION:

34–36 Kuri Jikken Manga Kobo, Tokyo
37–43 Chuck Jones/Richard Williams Animation Ltd., London

44

45

46

47

ARTIST / KÜNSTLER / RÉALISATION:

44, 45 Sadao Tsukioka
46, 47 Roberto Gabioli/Paolo Piffarerio
48–63 Seymour Chwast

DIRECTOR / RÉGISSEUR:

44, 45 Sadao Tsukioka
48–63 Len Glasser

PRODUCTION / PRODUKTION:

44, 45 Sadao Tsukioka
46, 47 Gamma Film, Milan
48–63 Harold Friedman/Push Pin Studios, Inc., New York

44, 45 *A Man.* A lion-tamer plays the role of a lion.
46, 47 *Crepuscolo Veneziano* (Venetian Twilight), a film about the passing of Venice. The dramaturgical elements are a reserved use of colour, grand perspectives, theatrical poses of the human figures and a flowing motion that is borrowed from the waters.
48–63 *American Follies.* A short historical analysis of American life from the days of the Pilgrim Fathers to the war in Vietnam. As one head develops out of the last one, Seymour Chwast's dry and ironic humour is displayed in all its usual panache and wit. Versatility, however, is not allowed to become an end in itself. Concentration on the essence of the subject guarantees an ever-fresh resourcefulness and imaginative approach. The figures are drawn right out of our own continuing human comedy, delineated with earthy reason and conceived and executed with exceptional artistic vision. One of the founder members of the Push Pin Studios, Chwast is still at the head of this extraordinarily prolific group of graphic artists which has achieved almost legendary fame all over the world. Despite an overwhelming working day, each task is still approached as a serious and separate problem, and neither complacency of style nor platitudinous thinking is tolerated.

44, 45 Einzelbilder aus *A Man*, der einen Raubtierdompteur in der Rolle des Löwen zeigt.

46, 47 *Crepuscolo Veneziano* (Venezianische Dämmerung) ist ein Film, der dem verfallenden Venedig gewidmet ist. Sparsam verwendete Farben, grosszügige Perspektiven, theatralische Posen der Menschen und das die vielen Kanäle und das Meer symbolisierende Fliessen des Wassers sind die hauptsächlichsten dramaturgischen Elemente dieses Werkes.

48–63 *American Follies* (Die amerikanischen Torheiten). Dieser Film gibt eine kurze historische Analyse Amerikas, von der Zeit der Pilgerväter bis zu den Kriegsgeschehen der letzten Jahre. Seymour Chwasts Ironie und sein trockener Humor zeigen sich deutlich in jener Sequenz, in der sich ein Kopf aus dem vorangehenden entwickelt. Seine Gewandtheit und die Vielfältigkeit seines Stils werden jedoch nicht als Selbstzweck angesehen. Indem er sich auf das Wesentliche des Themas beschränkt, kann er seinen geistreichen Einfällen freien Lauf lassen. Seine Figuren – Darsteller auf der Bühne der menschlichen Komödie – werden mit praktischem Verstand eingefangen und zeugen in ihrer Konzeption und Ausführung von einer aussergewöhnlichen künstlerischen Phantasie. Chwast, Gründermitglied der Push Pin Studios, steht heute noch an der Spitze dieser künstlerisch aussergewöhnlich profilierten Gruppe von Graphikern, die seit ihrem Bestehen beinahe legendären Ruhm erlangt hat. Obwohl die Studios mit Arbeit überhäuft sind, wird jeder Auftrag als ein in sich geschlossenes Problem angegangen, wobei weder stilistische Selbstgefälligkeit noch seichte, abgedroschene Ideen toleriert werden.

44, 45 Images de *A Man* (Un homme). Un dompteur de lions joue le rôle du lion.

46, 47 Images de *Crepuscolo Veneziano* (Crépuscule Vénitien), un film sur la décadence de Venise. L'usage sobre de la couleur, les perspectives grandioses, les attitudes théâtrales des personnages ainsi que le rythme ondoyant symbolisant le courant de l'eau – voilà les éléments principaux de cette mise en scène exceptionnelle.

48–63 *American Follies* (Les Folies américaines). Ce film donne un bref aperçu de l'histoire américaine de la période des Pèlerins jusqu'à l'engagement des Etats-Unis dans la guerre au Viêt-nam. L'ironie et l'humour sec de Seymour Chwast sont mis en évidence particulièrement dans la séquence qui présente des têtes dont chacune se développe de la précédente. Puisque son point de mire est toujours l'essentiel d'un sujet, la souplesse de son style n'est jamais considérée comme étant une fin en soi, mais plutôt comme expression artistique de son imagination. Ses personnages – des acteurs dans la comédie humaine de nos jours – sont dessinés avec logique terre à terre et témoignent quant à leur conception et exécution d'une fantaisie artistique exceptionnelle. Chwast, l'un des co-fondateurs des Push Pin Studios, est encore le chef de fil de ce groupe de graphistes exceptionnellement prolifique, groupe dont l'importance et la renommée sont devenues presque légendaires. Bien qu'ils soient toujours accablés de travail, chaque tâche qui leur est confiée est traitée comme problème singulier, et ils rejettent tout ce qui se révèle être une prétention stylistique ou une idée rebattue.

48–63

64

65

66

67

64–68 Key drawings from a 5-minute animated cut-out sequence in the feature film of Hermann Hesse's *Steppenwolf*. Fig. 68 shows the protagonist Harry as half man, half wolf. The wolf jumps out of Harry's face back into his childhood, where young Harry and the wolf are separate beings constantly fighting each other. Later Harry tries to conform but the wolf inside him enforces the eternal split in the character of things. Fig. 64 symbolizes this inner division, with two armies fighting each other on top of his head. The shell (Fig. 65) stands for Harry as an artist and intellectual above the forces of good and evil. Harry the bourgeois (Fig. 67) is transformed into Harry the armchair while experiencing various symbolic visions. Bradac himself scripted, designed and directed the sequence, Otmar Gutmann did the animation.

64–68 Illustrations clé d'une séquence d'animation de 5 mn., intégrée dans le film *Steppenwolf* (Le Loup des steppes) de Hermann Hesse. Le loup sortant d'un bond du visage de Harry se dirige vers l'enfance, période pendant laquelle Harry et le loup étaient deux êtres indépendants qui se sont battus continuellement. Plus tard, Harry tâche à se conformer, mais le loup qui le domine fait naître en lui une dissension de sentiments. La fig. 64 symbolise son état mental illustré par deux armées qui se battent sur sa tête. La coquille de limaçon (fig. 65) représente Harry en tant qu'artiste et intellectuel flottant au-dessus du bien et du mal. Harry le bourgeois se déguise en fauteuil (fig. 67) pendant qu'il a des visions symboliques. Bradac a écrit le scénario, a dessiné et dirigé la séquence, O. Gutmann a été responsable de l'animation.

64–68 Schlüsselszenen aus einer 5minutigen Trickfilmsequenz, die in die Verfilmung von Hermann Hesses *Steppenwolf* integriert wurde. Abb. 68 zeigt den Hauptdarsteller Harry, aus dessen Gesicht der Wolf in die Kindheit zurückspringt, in eine Zeit, als Harry und der Wolf noch zwei unabhängige Wesen waren, die sich ständig bekämpften. Später versucht Harry sich anzugleichen, aber der ihn dominierende Wolf erzwingt in Harry einen seelischen Bruch. Die zwei sich auf seinem Kopf bekämpfenden Armeen (Abb. 64) symbolisieren seine innere Zerrissenheit. Das Schneckenhaus (Abb. 65) soll Harry als Künstler und Intellektuellen darstellen, der sich jenseits von Gut und Böse befindet. Der Bourgeois Harry (Abb. 67) verwandelt sich in einen Lehnstuhl, während er verschiedene symbolische Visionen hat.

ARTIST / KÜNSTLER / RÉALISATION:

64–68 Jaroslav Bradac

DIRECTOR / RÉGISSEUR:

64–68 Jaroslav Bradac

PRODUCTION / PRODUKTION:

64–68 Peter Sprague, New York

ARTIST / KÜNSTLER / RÉALISATION:

69–71 Jacques Colombat
72–74 Zdzislav Kudla

DIRECTOR / RÉGISSEUR:

69–71 René Laloux
72–74 Bogdan Radkowski

PRODUCTION / PRODUKTION:

69–71 Bernard Legargeant, Paris
72–74 Bohdan Butenko/Studio Filmow
    Rysunkowych, Bielsko-Biala/POL

69–71

72–74

69–71 In René Laloux' musical comedy *La montagne qui accouche* (The Mountain that Brings Forth), a horde of pin-up girls land on a strange planet. The curious inhabitants, at first intent on eating them, are soon beguiled. The encounter between two appetites, greed and sex, is thus won by sex.

72–74 *The Flower*. A man lost in the desert falls in love with a flower, an attraction that is finally to prove fatal. The 16-mm film was made for Polish television.

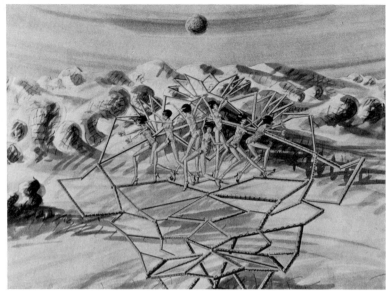

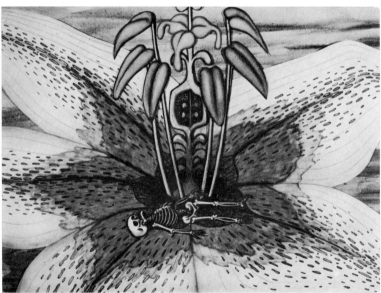

69–71 *La Montagne qui accouche* (Der Berg, der gebar), diese musikalische Komödie von René Laloux, erzählt von einer Horde Pin-up-Girls, die auf einem Planeten landet. Die erstaunten Bewohner, die sie anfangs verzehren wollen, lassen sich umgarnen. Es entspinnt sich alsbald ein Kampf, wobei das Hungergefühl der sexuellen Lust unterliegt.
72–74 *The Flower* (Die Blume). Ein Mensch, verlassen in der Wüste, verliebt sich in eine Blume, eine Zuneigung, die schlussendlich zu seinem Tod führen wird.

69–71 *La Montagne qui accouche.* Dans cette comédie musicale de René Laloux, une bande de pin-up envahit une étrange planète, dont les habitants renoncent bientôt à leur appétit anthropophage en faveur de l'appétit sexuel, grand vainqueur de la joute et de la fable.
72–74 *The Flower* (La Fleur). Un homme perdu dans le désert s'éprend d'une fleur qu'il soigne avec tendresse, un amour qui lui sera fatal finalement. Le film de 16 mm a été tourné pour la télévision polonaise.

75

76

75, 76 *Un* (One). This first film by two graduates of the Ecole des Arts Décoratifs in Paris was made possible by a grant of the Service des Arts Graphiques of the ORTF. It tells the story of a last survivor of a civilization and the nightmarish creature that pursues him.

77–86 Jan Svankmajer's *Jabberwocky* is a film about childhood. It is a film—a game—a dream. It was filmed in a free, improvised way, straight into the camera, just like a game. It is a film about the first revolts of childhood, the part of a child's inner life which, in the interests of "civilization", is nipped in the bud, to be followed by the cruel and repulsive social repression of adult life. As the film ends, so do the dream and the childhood, giving way to an adulthood devoid of fantasy. In place of the child's navy blue dress a dull black social suit now hangs in the wardrobe. The film won the first prize at Oberhausen, 1974.

87, 88 *Butterfly Ball*. In this children's film the frog invites all the animals in the wood to a big ball. Lee Mishkin, veteran of Popeye, Magoo and the Pink Panther, deploys all his tricks in this bright mixture of Tiffany glass and Hollywood.

75, 76 *Un* (Einer). Dieses Erstlingswerk von zwei Absolventen der Ecole des Arts Décoratifs in Paris konnte dank der Unterstützung des Service des Arts Graphiques der ORTF realisiert werden. Die Geschichte: der letzte Überlebende einer Kulturperiode wird von einem Alptraum verfolgt.

77–86 *Jabberwocky* von Jan Svankmajer ist ein Film über die Kindheit, ein Spiel, ein Traum. Er wurde frei improvisiert und direkt in die Kamera gedreht. Er handelt von der ersten Auflehnung der kindlichen Seele gegen die im Interesse unserer Gesellschaft ausgeübte Repression, die zur Aufrechterhaltung der von den Erwachsenen rigoros eingeführten Ordnung jegliche kindliche Regung im Keime erstickt. So wie der Film seinem Ende entgegengeht, endet auch der Traum und mit ihm die Kindheit, um in eine fantasielose Erwachsenenwelt überzuleiten. Anstelle des blauen Kinderkleides hängt nun der schwarze Geschäftsanzug im Schrank. 1. Preis Oberhausen 1974.

87, 88 *Butterfly Ball* (Schmetterlingsball). Ein Kinderfilm. Der Frosch lädt alle Tiere des Waldes zu einem grossen Ball ein. Lee Mischkin, nach Popeye, Magoo und dem rosaroten Panther, zieht hier alle Register, um diese bunte Folge in schillernden Farben zu realisieren.

77–84

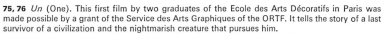

87

88

85

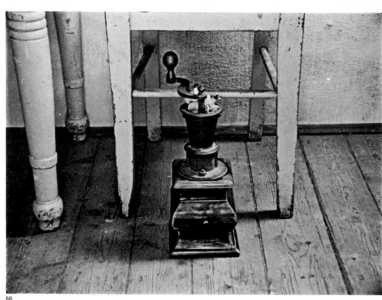

86

75, 76 *Un.* Ce premier film a été réalisé avec le soutien du Service des Arts Graphiques de l'ORTF. Les deux réalisateurs, anciens élèves de l'Ecole des Arts Décoratifs y présentent un personnage de cauchemar qui poursuit le dernier représentant d'une civilisation disparue.

77–86 *Jabberwocky* de Jan Svankmajer est un film consacré à l'enfance. C'est un film – un jeu – un rêve. Il a été enregistré directement par la caméra – librement improvisé afin de souligner son caractère de jeu. L'enfance, le sujet principal de ce film, n'est pas mise en lumière sous l aspect – vie heureuse sans problèmes – qu'on associe souvent à cette période. L'âme enfantine se révolte contre la répression qui, dans l'intérêt de notre société, étouffe tout sentiment afin de garantir l'ordre social rigoureusement instauré par les adultes. Le moment où le film touche à sa fin, le rêve et l'enfance s'effacent et à leur place surgit un monde des adultes dépourvu d'imagination. Le vêtement bleu de l'enfant est remplacé par le complet noir de l'homme d'affaires. Ce film a remporté le 1er prix à Oberhausen en 1974.

87, 88 *Butterfly Ball* (Le Bal des Papillons). Un film pour enfants. La grenouille invite tous les animaux de la forêt à participer à un grand bal. Mishkin, qui n'a pas oublié Popeye, Magoo et la panthère rose, fait de ce mélange de verre Tiffany et de Hollywood un véritable feu d'artifice.

ARTIST / KÜNSTLER / RÉALISATION:

75, 76 Paul & Gaëtan Brizzi
77–86 Jan Svankmajer
87, 88 Alan Aldridge

DIRECTOR / RÉGISSEUR:

75, 76 Paul & Gaëtan Brizzi
77–86 Jan Svankmajer
87, 88 Lee Mishkin

PRODUCTION / PRODUKTION:

75, 76 Paul & Gaëtan Brizzi, Paris
77–86 Kratky Film, Prague
87, 88 Halas & Batchelor, London

89

90

93

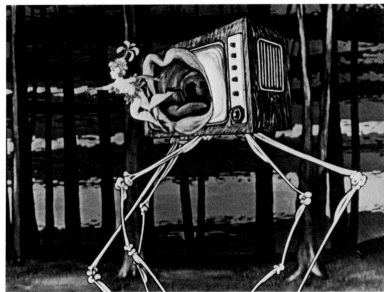

94

ARTIST / KÜNSTLER / RÉALISATION:

89–92 Bruno Bozzetto
93 Piotr Kamler
94 Zdzislav Kudla
95 John Leach
96 Paul Driessen

DIRECTOR / RÉGISSEUR:

89–92 Bruno Bozzetto
93 Piotr Kamler
95 John Leach
96 Paul Driessen

PRODUCTION / PRODUKTION:

89–92 Bruno Bozzetto, Milan
93 Les Films de la Rivière, Paris
94 Studio Filmów Rysunkowych, Bielsko-Biala/POL
95 Leach & Rankin, Toronto
96 Gaston Sarault/National Film Board of Canada

89–92 *Opera.* An ideal subject for the bright ideas of Bruno Bozzetto, who here presents a number of short episodes centring upon musical compositions in which Bach, Beethoven, Wagner, Paganini, Rossini and Puccini are all involved. The film won prizes both in Annecy (1973) and in New York (1974).

93 *Cœur de Secours* (A Spare Heart). J. Kamler worked for years for the research department of French television, where he was able to try out techniques, materials and effects to his heart's content. Today his possibilities seem unlimited. Here he presents a poetic tale of two small chessplayers in a world of filigree wheels. Special Jury Prize, Annecy 1973.

94 *Sounds of the Forest.* A man in the sinister woods. Only when he gets back to his production line, where cans are being filled with fresh woodland air, does he feel safe again. A tale about the dehumanization of society.

95 Frame from *Evolu* (Evolution), a student's 7-minute colour film about a man's personal evolution. Coloured faces are shown developing and changing.

96 Frame from *Cat's Cradle,* a 10¼-minute colour film on the interdependence of things. Paul Driessen's string-like creatures tell a story of flight, pursuit and escape.

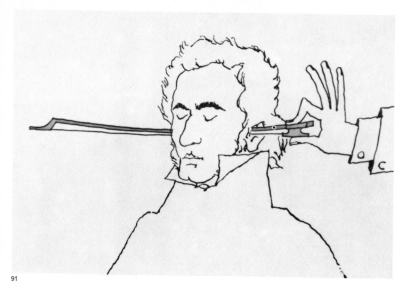

91

92

95

96

89–92 *Opera.* Ein ideales Thema für den einfallsreichen Bozzetto: eine Reihe von kurzen Episoden rund um musikalische Werke, in welche Bach, Beethoven, Wagner, Paganini, Rossini und Puccini verwickelt sind. Dieser Film wurde 1973 in Annecy und 1974 in New York mit einem Preis ausgezeichnet.

93 *Cœur de Secours* (Sicherheitsherz). Beim Service de la Recherche des ORTF konnte Kamler jahrelang ungehindert Techniken, Materialien und Effekte ausprobieren. Nichts scheint ihm heute unmöglich. Hier zeigt er eine poetische Geschichte von zwei kleinen Schachspielern inmitten von Filigranrädchen. Der Film erhielt den speziellen Jury-Preis von Annecy 1973.

94 *Sounds of the Forest* (Das Rauschen im Wald). Ein Mensch im Walde, der ihm ganz unheilvoll vorkommt. Erst wenn er wieder an seinem Fliessband steht und frische Waldluft in Dosen abfüllt, fühlt er sich wieder sicher. Ein Film über unsere entmenschlichte Gesellschaft.

95 Bild aus *Evolu* (Entwicklung), einem 7minutigen Studenten-Farbfilm über die persönliche Entwicklung eines Mannes. Farbige Gesichter entwickeln und verändern sich.

96 Einzelbild aus *Cat's Cradle* (Fadenabnehmen), einem 10¼minutigen Film über die gegenseitige Abhängigkeit der Dinge.

89–92 *Opéra.* Un sujet qui se prête à merveille aux idées brillantes de Bruno Bozzetto: une série d'épisodes sur des œuvres musicales qui ont affaire avec Bach, Beethoven, Wagner, Paganini, Rossini et Puccini. Ce film a remporté des prix à Annecy en 1973 et l'année prochaine, en 1974, à New York.

93 *Cœur de Secours.* Pendant des années, Kamler a pu essayer les techniques, les matériaux et les effets les plus divers au Service de Recherche de l'ORTF. Aujourd'hui rien ne lui semble impossible. Il présente ici l'histoire poétique de deux petits joueurs d'échecs entourés de roues filigranées. Prix Spécial du Jury d'Annecy 1973.

94 *Sounds of the Forest* (Le Bruissement de la Forêt). Un homme dans une forêt inquiétante. Il ne se ressaisit qu'une fois retourné à la chaîne où il remplit des boîtes d'air frais de la forêt. Le thème est la dénaturation de l'homme dans la société.

95 Image d'*Evolu*, un film couleur de 7 mn. traitant de l'évolution personnelle d'un homme. Les visages multicolores se développent et se transforment.

96 Image de *Cat's Cradle* (Au Bout du Fil), film de 10 mn. ¼ sur l'interdépendance des choses. Les créatures crispées de Paul Driessen racontent une histoire de fuite et de poursuite.

97

98

99

100

97–100 *A String of Tales.* Four Hungarian folk tales are blended in this film. The hero of the story goes on a reconnoitring visit prior to a marriage proposal. The farmer tells his wife to go down to the cellar to fetch some wine. Later he sends his daughter after her mother and finally goes down to the cellar himself. To pass the time, the revellers tell tales. The master story is one about the stupidity of the rich peasant farmer, and the three stories within a story are all about the triumph of brain over brawn.
101, 102 *That is Not True.* The main story of these four folk tales, all spectacularly animated by Hungarian neo-primitive painters, is about a king who promises to give his daughter in marriage to the man who can tell a story so unlikely that even the king himself will not believe it. A peasant lad passes the test and wins his reward.

97–100 *A String of Tales* (Volkstümliche Geschichten). Vier ungarische Märchen wurden in diesem Film zusammengefasst. Er erzählt von einem jungen Burschen, der, bevor er seinen Heiratsantrag stellt, auf eine Schnuppervisite geht. Der Vater schickt die Mutter in den Keller, Wein zu holen. Darauf schickt er seine Tochter nach der Mutter zu sehen und folgt den beiden dann selber nach. Um sich die Zeit zu vertreiben, erzählen die Wartenden Geschichten. Die eine berichtet von der Dummheit eines reichen Bauern, die andern handeln alle vom Sieg des Geistes über den Körper.
101, 102 *That is not True* (Das ist nicht wahr). Die Rahmengeschichte dieser vier ungarischen Märchen, alle von naiven Malern farbenprächtig dargestellt, erzählt von einem König, der seine Tochter und die Hälfte seines Königreiches an denjenigen Freier verschenken will, der eine so unwahrscheinliche Geschichte erzählen kann, dass selbst der König sie nicht glaubt.

97–100 *Contes en fil.* Quatre contes hongrois ont été réunis dans ce film, qui raconte l'histoire d'un jeune homme en train de faire une visite exploratoire avant de demander une jeune fille en mariage. Le père de la fille, un paysan, dit à sa femme d'aller chercher du vin à la cave. Plus tard, il envoie la fille chercher sa mère, puis il descend lui-même. Afin de faire passer le temps, les visiteurs se racontent des histoires. Le récit principal traite des sottises d'un paysan nouveau riche. Les autres ont pour sujet le triomphe de l'esprit sur la force.
101, 102 *That is not True* (Ce n'est pas vrai). Le récit encadrant quatre contes hongrois est l'histoire d'un roi qui est prêt à faire cadeau de sa fille et de la moitié de son royaume au prétendant qui lui raconte une histoire aussi étrange que même le roi ne peut y croire. Un jeune paysan y réussit et prend la fille pour femme. Style naïf.

101

ARTIST / KÜNSTLER / RÉALISATION:

97–100 Emma Heinzelmann
101, 102 Kati Macskassy/Max Massimino-Garnièr

DIRECTOR / RÉGISSEUR:

97–100 Peter Szoboszlay
101, 102 Kati Macskassy

PRODUCTION / PRODUKTION:

97–102 Pannonia Filmstudio, Budapest

102

ARTIST / KÜNSTLER / RÉALISATION:

103 Paul Grimault
104–109 Manfredo Manfredi
110–112 Ferran Gallart

DIRECTOR / RÉGISSEUR:

103 Paul Grimault
104–109 Manfredo Manfredi
110–112 Ferran Gallart

PRODUCTION / PRODUKTION:

103 Les Films Paul Grimault, Paris
104–109 Corona Cinematografica S.r.l., Rome
110–112 Ferran Gallart/Films d'Animation, Avully/SWI

103

103 *Le Diamant* (The Diamond). In this film Paul Grimault satirizes colonial history in the story of a rich traveller whose flying machine one day lands on an oasis inhabited by a primitive tribe. They own nothing but a sacred diamond which the visitor tries to acquire by making rain and donating a few umbrellas to the delighted natives. When this barter trade fails, he tries to steal the jewel. But his spacecraft conks out in the desert, punishing him for his greed.
104–109 Movement sequence from *L'Uva Salamanna* (The Salamanna Grapes), a fairy tale of a king whose youngest daughter can only be won by a suitor who chooses the correct gift. The king's wisdom is challenged, for he has forgotten the gift of love.
110–112 The theme of *Quand la paix joue avec les hommes* (When Peace Plays with Men) is that of the earth being destroyed by the ironical and unconscious mutation of peace itself. A dove plays at being a nuclear bomber, is transformed into one and destroys both the world and itself.

103 *Le Diamant*. Paul Grimault ironisiert die Kolonialgeschichte am Beispiel eines reichen Reisenden, der in einer von einem primitiven Volksstamm bewohnten Oase landet. Sie besitzen nur einen heiligen Diamanten, den der Eindringling haben will. Er lässt es regnen und schenkt den erfreuten Eingeborenen einige Regenschirme. Der Tauschhandel kommt nicht zustande, und so will er den Diamanten stehlen. Er wird für seine Gier bestraft, denn der Motor seines Raumschiffes versagt mitten in der Wüste.
104–109 Bewegungsablauf aus *L'Uva Salamanna* (Die Salamanna-Trauben). In diesem Märchen will der König seine Tochter nur dem Freier geben, der das richtige Geschenk wählt. Des Königs Weisheit wird in Frage gestellt – er vergisst das Geschenk der Liebe.
110–112 *Quand la paix joue avec les hommes* (Wenn der Friede mit den Menschen spielt). Thema dieses Films ist die Zerstörung der Erde durch eine ironische und unbewusste Veränderung des Friedens. Eine Taube spielt Atombomber, verwandelt sich daraufhin in einen solchen und zerstört die Welt und sich selber.

103 *Le Diamant*. Paul Grimault se moque de l'histoire coloniale. Un riche voyageur atterrit dans une oase habitée par une tribu primitive qui ne possède qu'un diamant sacré. Le visiteur, désireux de l'avoir, fait venir de la pluie et présente un nombre de parapluies aux indigènes enchantés. Lorsque ce troc faillit il décide à voler le diamant. Son navire spatial tombe en panne au milieu du désert, le punissant ainsi de sa cupidité.
104–109 Séquence de mouvement de *L'Uva Salamanna* (Les raisins de Salamanna). Dans ce conte, un roi est prêt à donner sa fille cadette au prétendant qui choisit le bon cadeau. Cependant, sa sagesse est mise en question car il n'a pas pris en considération le cadeau de l'amour.
110–112 *Quand la paix joue avec les hommes*, un film ayant pour thème l'anéantissement de la terre par la mutation ironique et inconsciente de la paix elle-même. Une colombe joue à être bombardier nucléaire; par la suite, elle est transformée en bombardier, et de cette façon elle passe à détruire la terre et elle-même.

113

114

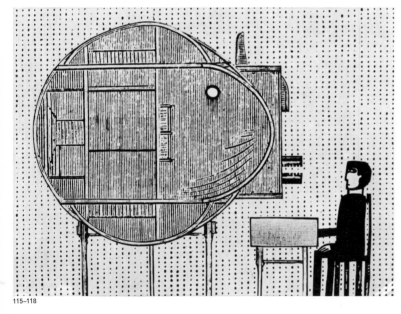

115–118

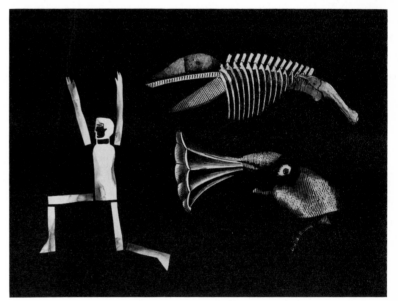

113–118 *Adam II.* After his Polish period, when he made several films with Walerian Borowczyk, Jan Lenica was increasingly influenced by Ionescu, Kafka and Sartre. His philosophy is convincingly expressed in his 80-minute film *Adam II,* made in Germany in 1969. Solitude of the individual in a dehumanized world is the theme. Civilization has destroyed the equilibrium between man and nature, between man and his social surroundings. What remains is scientific and mechanical, a mysterious and frightening vision. Lenica's rigorous style is always in search of the essential rather than the spectacular, and his narrative devoid of easy drama. This purity of purpose is a rare quality and outside of Lenica's work is found only in films such as *La Planète Sauvage* and some of Borowczyk's pieces.

113–118 *Adam II.* Après avoir quitté la Pologne, où il a tourné plusieurs films avec Walerian Borowczyk, Jan Lenica s'est inspiré de plus en plus de Ionescu, Kafka et Sartre. Sa nouvelle philosophie se reflète de façon convaincante dans *Adam II,* un long métrage réalisé en Allemagne en 1969. Il y résume les problèmes de la civilisation moderne – la solitude de l'individu dans un monde impitoyable détruisant les relations entre l'homme et la nature, entre l'homme et la société dont il fait partie. L'homme n'est plus qu'un être scientifique et méchanique. Cette vision, mystérieuse et effrayante en soi, l'est encore davantage du fait du style vigoureux. Il tend à saisir l'essentiel plutôt qu'à obtenir un effet spectaculaire et dramatique. Cette qualité ne se retrouve que dans *La Planète Sauvage* et dans quelques films réalisés par Borowczyk.

113–118 *Adam II.* Nach Verlassen Polens, wo Jan Lenica mit Walerian Borowczyk mehrere Filme realisierte, wurde ein wachsender Einfluss Ionescus, Kafkas und Sartres spürbar. Seine neue Philosophie bringt er in seinem Film *Adam II,* den er 1969 in der Bundesrepublik drehte, deutlich zum Ausdruck. Thema dieses Films ist die Vereinsamung des Menschen in einer entmenschlichten Welt, in einer Zivilisation, die jede Beziehung des Menschen zur Natur und zu seiner sozialen Umgebung zerstört. Der Mensch wird zu einem rein mechanischen, wissenschaftlich erfassbaren Wesen – eine furchterregende Vision. Lenicas kräftiger Stil zielt auf das Wesentliche ab, nicht auf spektakuläre und dramatische Effekte. Ausser in Lenicas Werken findet sich ein ähnlich sauber herausgearbeitetes Thema höchstens in *La Planète Sauvage* und in einigen Filmen von Borowczyk.

ARTIST / KÜNSTLER / RÉALISATION:

113–118 Jan Lenica

DIRECTOR / RÉGISSEUR:

113–118 Jan Lenica

PRODUCTION / PRODUKTION:

113–118 Boris von Borresholm/Lux Film, München

47

119–125 *Ubu Roi* is Jan Lenica's most recent production, a 50-minute film in colour. It is drawn by himself throughout, and he directed and co-produced it. *Ubu Roi* is based on the macabre comedy by Alfred Jarry which was first performed in Paris in 1896 and immediately banned until thirty years after the death of the *poète maudit*. Since then it has been performed in the theatre (the Paris première in 1937 characteristically had a set designed by Max Ernst), as a puppet play, even as an opera—and now in Lenica's interpretation as a film. One may wonder what Jarry's absurd poetry has to do with Lenica's delightfully malicious vein. Lenica believes that Jarry's persiflage, which inspired Aragon, Breton, Cocteau, Tzara, Apollinaire and Ionescu, can be put over more effectively in animated form, and gestures and voices have been manipulated to this end. *Ubu Roi* has many affinities with *Macbeth*, hence Lenica's characters are Shakespearean figures who have come down in the world and now strike puppet poses. But a collection of poses would be merely a sort of misdirected world theatre. Lenica, while reducing the size of the stage, has enlarged the perspectives. That is the new aspect of his work: after his short films and his first feature film *Adam II*, he has here adopted a new style—the seizing of the character merely in the outline of the drawing.

119–125 *Ubu Roi* ist Jan Lenicas neuester 50-Minuten-Farbfilm. Er hat alle Zeichnungen geschaffen, führte selbst auch Regie und zeichnete als Ko-Produzent. *Ubu Roi* basiert auf der makabren Komödie von Alfred Jarry, die im Jahre 1896 in Paris uraufgeführt und nach einem Theaterskandal sofort abgesetzt wurde. Dreissig Jahre nach dem Tod des *poète maudit* wurde sie 1937 in Paris neu inszeniert (Bühnenbild von Max Ernst) und wird seither als Theaterstück, als Puppenspiel, ja sogar als Oper immer wieder zur Aufführung gebracht. Jetzt sehen wir Lenicas Interpretation – als Trickfilm. Man kann sich fragen, was Jarrys absurde Poesie mit Lenicas anmutiger Bosheit zu tun hat. Lenica glaubt, Jarrys Persiflage, welche Dadaisten und Surrealisten inspiriert hat, in getrickter Form am eindrücklichsten darstellen zu können, und hat seine ganzen Mittel darauf abgestimmt. *Ubu Roi* hat viele Affinitäten mit *Macbeth*, deshalb sind Lenicas Figuren auch Shakespeare-Gestalten, die in der Welt heruntergekommen sind und nun als Marionetten ihre Posen einnehmen. Eine Ansammlung von Posen wäre jedoch ein Welttheater verfehlter Schöpfung. So verkleinert denn Lenica die Szene, vergrössert aber die Perspektive. Nach seinen Kurzfilmen und dem ersten Langfilm *Adam II* führt er hier einen neuen Stil ein – die Erfassung des Charakters allein im Umriss der Zeichnung.

119–125 *Ubu Roi*, dont tous les cels ont été exécutés par Jan Lenica lui-même, est la dernière création qu'il vient d'achever. Il a assuré la réalisation ainsi que la coproduction de ce film de 50 min. *Ubu Roi*, basé sur la comédie macabre d'Alfred Jarry, fut mis au ban dès sa première présentation à Paris en 1896. Ce n'était que trente ans après la mort du poète maudit, en 1937, que la pièce fut reprise à Paris avec des décors réalisés par Max Ernst. Depuis sa redécouverte, *Ubu Roi* a conquis les planches sous forme de pièce de théâtre, de spectacle de marionnettes et même d'opéra. La plus récente interprétation – la voici, un film d'animation de Jan Lenica. On se demande ce que la poésie absurde de Jarry a à voir avec la malice pleine de charme de Lenica. Il est persuadé pouvoir mieux mettre en évidence le persiflage de Jarry, qui a influencé les dadaïstes ainsi que les surréalistes, par le dessin animé en adaptant les gestes et les voix en conséquence. *Ubu Roi* est très proche de *Macbeth* d'où les personnages shakespeariens clochardisés qui adoptent des poses de marionnettes. L'ensemble de ces poses équivaut à un jeu grinçant qui résumerait tous les ratés de la Création. Chez Lenica, la diminution de la scène entraîne un agrandissement des perspectives. Après les courts métrages et depuis *Adam II* un nouveau style s'affirme qui tend à saisir un caractère sur le vif rien que par les contours du personnage.

120

123

119

48

121

122

124

125

ARTIST / KÜNSTLER / RÉALISATION:

119–125 Jan Lenica

DIRECTOR / RÉGISSEUR:

119–125 Jan Lenica

PRODUCTION / PRODUKTION:

119–125 Jan Lenica & Boris von Borresholm/Lux Film,
        München/ZDF, Mainz

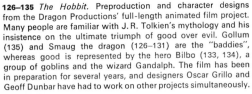

126–135 *The Hobbit.* Preproduction and character designs from the Dragon Productions' full-length animated film project. Many people are familiar with J. R. Tolkien's mythology and his insistence on the ultimate triumph of good over evil. Gollum (135) and Smaug the dragon (126–131) are the "baddies", whereas good is represented by the hero Bilbo (133, 134), a group of goblins and the wizard Gandalph. The film has been in preparation for several years, and designers Oscar Grillo and Geoff Dunbar have had to work on other projects simultaneously.

126–135 *The Hobbit.* Charakterstudien für ein Trickfilmprojekt der Dragon Productions. Vielen ist J. R. Tolkiens Mythologie bekannt, ebenso seine mit Nachdruck vertretene Theorie, dass das Gute letztlich über das Böse siegt. Gollum (135) und Smaug der Drache (126–131) sind die «Bösewichte», das Gute wird durch Bilbo (133, 134), eine Gruppe von Kobolden und den Zwerg Gandalph vertreten. Die Vorarbeiten zu diesem Film ziehen sich bereits über mehrere Jahre hin, da die Designer, Oscar Grillo und Geoff Dunbar, gleichzeitig an andern Projekten arbeiten.

126–135 *The Hobbit.* Etudes de caractère pour un long métrage projeté par Dragon Productions. La mythologie de J. R. Tolkien est connu ainsi que l'importance qu'il attache au fait que le bien triomphe en fin de compte du mal. Gollum (fig. 135) et Smaug le dragon (fig. 126–131), les deux méchants, personnifient le mal tandis que le bien est représenté par Bilbo (fig. 133, 134), un groupe de lutins et le sorcier Gandalph. Les travaux préparatoirs s'étendent déjà sur plusieurs années, car les artistes Oscar Grillo et Geoff Dunbar réalisent simultanément d'autres projets.

132

ARTIST / KÜNSTLER / RÉALISATION:
126–135 Oscar Grillo/Geoff Dunbar

DIRECTOR / RÉGISSEUR:
126–135 James R. Nurse

PRODUCTION / PRODUKTION:
126–135 Dragon Productions, London

133

134

135

150458

136–141 *Who are we?* The Yugoslav animator Zlatko Grgiç, visiting the National Film Board of Canada, created this amusing short pageant of Canadian history for entry at Annecy 1975.

142–147 Frames from the colour film *The Further Adventures of Uncle Sam.* This film shared the Grand Prix of Annecy, 1971. It tells a wild tale of the abduction of the Statue of Liberty. It employs sugary colours combined with elements of pop art, comic strip, features borrowed from modern advertising and even Mickey Mouse. It is in fact the sort of contemporary film that might well be deposited in a foundation stone for the edification of posterity.

136–141 *Who are we?* (Wer sind wir?). Während eines Besuchs bei der Kanadischen Filmkommission schuf der jugoslawische Trickfilmer Zlatko Grgiç diesen amüsanten Abriss der kanadischen Geschichte für Annecy 1975.

142–147 Aus *The Further Adventures of Uncle Sam* (Die weiteren Abenteuer von Onkel Sam). Der Film wurde mit dem Grossen Preis von Annecy 1971 ausgezeichnet. Eine wilde Geschichte von der Entführung der Freiheitsstatue von New York, in zuckersüssen Farben, durchsetzt mit Pop-Elementen und Mickey Mouse, mit Werbegags und Comic Strips. Ein Film, den man als Ausdruck unserer Zeit für die Nachwelt bewahren sollte.

136–141 *Who are we?* (Qui sommes-nous?). Zlatko Grgiç, un cinéaste yougoslave, a créé ce dessin animé pendant un séjour auprès de l'Office national du film au Canada. Ce spectacle amusant fait passer en revue l'histoire canadienne.

142–147 *The Further Adventures of Uncle Sam* (Nouvelles Aventures de l'Oncle Sam). C'est l'histoire rocabolesque de l'enlèvement de la statue de la Liberté. Production typique de notre temps, qui mériterait d'être scellée dans une pierre de fondation pour l'édification de la postérité. Il utilise des couleurs mielleuses, le pop, le dessin d'humour, divers éléments publicitaires et même le personnage de Mickey.

136–141

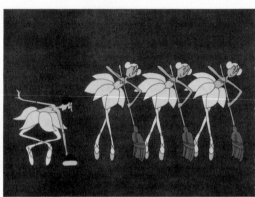

142–146

165

ARTIST / KÜNSTLER / RÉALISATION:

155–157 Sue Butterworth/Michael Mills
158–160 Bohdan Butenko
161–164 Graham Percy
165 John R. Gaug

DIRECTOR / RÉGISSEUR:

155–157 Michael Mills
161–164 William Feigenbaum
165 John R. Gaug

PRODUCTION / PRODUKTION:

155–157 Michael Mills/Potterton Productions, Inc., Montreal/The Reader's
           Digest Association, Inc., New York
161–164 Brut Productions, New York/Pannonia Filmstudio, Budapest
165 John R. Gaug/Michael Mills Productions Ltd., Montreal

166

167

169

170

172   173

166–168 *Le chien mélomane* (The Music-Loving Dog). After a long pause during which he had done some very fruitful work as a producer, Paul Grimault presented this new film at the Annecy 1973 festival. It tells the story of a dog's successful resistance to a diabolical inventor who operates with an ultrasonic violin.
169–171 Full-length animated feature films have always had enormous technical and financial problems which were only overcome by drawn figures of the Disney type. In his *Théâtre de Monsieur et Madame Kabal* Walerian Borowczyk has cleared away all the obstacles and created a genuine film for adults, full of sombre poetry in its story and its images.
172–174 *Bigger Is Better.* Cut-out shapes and moving drawings are here used to depict the transition from the individual to mass society and the consequences it entails.

166–168 *Le chien mélomane* (Der musikliebende Hund). Nach einer Pause, in der Grimault vor allem als Produzent wertvolle Arbeit leistete, präsentierte er an den Filmfestspielen 1973 in Annecy diesen seinen neuen Film. Es ist die Geschichte eines Hundes, der sich erfolgreich gegen einen teuflischen Erfinder zur Wehr setzt, der die Welt mit einer Ultraschall-Violine bedroht.
169–171 Abendfüllende Zeichentrickfilme hatten schon immer mit enormen technischen und finanziellen Problemen zu kämpfen. Die einzige Möglichkeit war bis vor kurzem das Erzählen einer Geschichte mit gezeichneten Figuren à la Disney. Mit seinem *Théâtre de Monsieur et Madame Kabal* fegte Walerian Borowczyk alle Hindernisse hinweg und schuf einen echten Film für Erwachsene, voll schwarzer Poesie in Bild und Erzählung.
172–174 *Bigger Is Better* (Grösser ist besser). Mit ausgeschnittenen Formen und bewegten Zeichnungen wird hier der Übergang vom Einzelnen zur Massengesellschaft und dessen Folgen gezeigt.

166–168 *Le chien mélomane.* Après un long silence où il s'était surtout affirmé comme directeur, Paul Grimault a présenté un nouveau film à Annecy en 1973. Le sujet, c'est d'un chien mélomane qui résiste victorieusement à la sournoise entreprise du diabolique inventeur d'un violon à ultrasons.
169–171 Les longs métrages animés ont toujours eu des problèmes énormes quant au financement et à la production technique. Dans son *Théâtre de Monsieur et Madame Kabal*, Walerian Borowczyk a balayé d'un coup de main toutes ces difficultés et nous offre un vrai film pour adultes, remarquable par la sombre poésie qui se dégage de l'histoire et de l'image.
172–174 *Bigger Is Better* (Le plus gros sera le mieux). Au moyen de papiers découpés et de dessins animés, on nous montre ici le passage de la cellule individuelle à la société de masse et ses conséquences.

ARTIST / KÜNSTLER / RÉALISATION:

166–168 Paul Grimault
169–171 Walerian Borowczyk
172–174 Derek Phillips

DIRECTOR / RÉGISSEUR:

166–168 Paul Grimault
169–171 Walerian Borowczyk
172–174 Derek Phillips

PRODUCTION / PRODUKTION:

166–168 Les Films Paul Grimault, Paris
169–171 Cinéastes Associés, St. Maurice
172–174 Derek Phillips Films, Hounslow/GBR

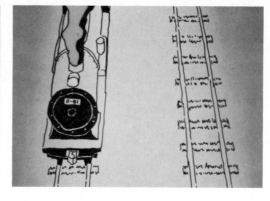

175–177

175–177 *GT 2*, a 5½-minute pop-art animated film by the Japanese artist Hal Fukushima, tells the story of a little boy who loves trains, the strange scenery that is revealed to him, and the nice fellow passengers he meets.
178–183 *This is Not a Museum.* A man makes the acquaintance of modern art in an unconventional museum. The film is beautifully painted, in some cases directly on the film-strip. The sculpture in Fig. 181 is borrowed from Magritte.
184–192 Sequence from *Calaveras.* The film is based on the illustrations of the Mexican artist Guadalupe Posada who lived from 1852 to 1913 and is now being rediscovered. His work shows certain parallels with Bruegel, Goya and Hokusai. Colombat studied the remaining traces of the artist and his art in Mexico The film depicts a life beyond in which each person goes on playing his earthly part.

175–177 *GT 2*, ein Zeichentrickfilm mit Popelementen, der von Hal Fukushima, einem japanischen Künstler, realisiert wurde. Die Geschichte dreht sich um einen kleinen Jungen, einen Eisenbahn-Liebhaber, der auf seiner Reise durch fremdartige Landschaften mit netten Menschen Bekanntschaft macht.
178–183 *This is Not a Museum* (Dies ist kein Museum). In einem unkonventionellen Museum lernt ein Mann die moderne Kunst kennen. Der Film ist sehr schön gemalt, teilweise direkt auf den Filmstreifen. Abb. 181 zeigt eine Magritte entlehnte Plastik.
184–192 Sequenz aus *Calaveras.* Der Film basiert auf den Illustrationen des mexikanischen Künstlers Guadalupe Posada (1852–1913). Das Werk dieses wiederentdeckten Künstlers zeigt gewisse Parallelen zu Bruegel, Goya und Hokusai. Colombat folgte seinen Spuren in Mexiko. Der Film zeigt ein Leben im Jenseits, in dem jeder seine irdische Rolle weiterspielt.

175–177 *GT 2*, film d'animation, créé par l'artiste japonais Hal Fukushima. C'est l'histoire d'un gamin et des trains qu'il adore. Pendant qu'il est emmené à travers d'étranges paysages, il fait la connaissance de gentilles personnes voyageant avec lui.
178–183 *This is Not a Museum* (Ceci n'est pas un Musée). Dans un musée peu conventionnel, un homme fait connaissance avec l'art moderne. Les belles peintures sont en partie appliquées sur la pellicule même. Fig. 181: sculpture empruntée à Magritte.
184–192 Séquence de *Calaveras*, film basé sur les illustrations d'un artiste mexicain que l'on vient de redécouvrir, Guadalupe Posada (1852–1913). Posada évoque à maints égards Breughel, Goya et Hokusai. Le réalisateur, Colombat, est allé au Mexique étudier l'œuvre et la biographie de son modèle. Le film décrit la vie dans l'au-delà où rien en somme n'est changé, chacun continuant à tenir le rôle qu'il avait sur terre.

178–183

ARTIST / KÜNSTLER / RÉALISATION:

175–177 Hal Fukushima
178–183 John E. Haugse
184–192 Jacques Colombat

DIRECTOR / RÉGISSEUR:

175–177 Hal Fukushima
178–183 John E. Haugse
184–192 Jacques Colombat

PRODUCTION / PRODUKTION:

175–177 Hal Work Shop, Tokyo
178–183 John E. Haugse, Santa Barbara/USA
184–192 Les Films Armorial, Paris

193, 194 *Wir sind viele* (We Are a Crowd). Borislav Sajtinac is a painterly creator of strong dramatic stories which he is inclined to bring, in a style sometimes reminiscent of Topor, to a sad if not tragic end. His irony is apparent in this bitter little tale of a cat conjuring with mice. The tricks become ever more cruel, but the public continues to applaud.
195–197 *Befreiung der Hauptperson* (Liberation of the Main Person), made in West Germany in 1973, is the tale of a lonely man in the midst of an arid land who kills himself on a millwheel. The style develops into a desperately pessimistic symbolic realism.
198 *Nicht alles, was fliegt, ist auch ein Vogel* (Not All that Flies is a Bird). The threatening city serves as a background for the increasing isolation of man. A little man is prevented from rebuilding his house by a monster bird, symbolizing politics and brute force.

193, 194 *Wir sind viele* (Nous sommes nombreux). Les histoires extrêmement dramatiques de Borislav Sajtinac, où l'élément pictural est très prononcé et dont le style évoque à maints égards Topor, prennent presque sans exception une fin triste, sinon tragique. Cette histoire cruelle d'un chat prestidigitateur respire une ironie au fond assez mordante.
195–197 *Befreiung der Hauptperson* (Libération du Personnage Principal), tourné en Allemagne en 1973. C'est l'histoire d'un homme solitaire qui ne supporte plus la monotonie et met fin à sa vie sur la roue du moulin. Le style évoque un réalisme symbolique désespérément pessimiste.
198 *Nicht alles, was fliegt, ist auch ein Vogel* (Tout ce qui vole n'est pas Oiseau). Une ville effroyable – voici le symbole de l'isolement progressif de l'homme. Un monstre volant, représentant la politique et la cruauté, empêche le petit homme à reconstruire sa maison.

193, 194 *Wir sind viele*. Borislav Sajtinacs äusserst dramatische Geschichten, die alle auf sehr malerische Weise dargestellt werden – sein Stil erinnert teilweise an Topor –, nehmen nahezu ausnahmslos ein trauriges, wenn nicht tragisches Ende. Seine Ironie kommt in dieser bitterbösen Geschichte zum Ausdruck, in welcher eine Katze ihre Zaubertricks an Mäusen versucht.
195–197 *Befreiung der Hauptperson*, 1973 in der Bundesrepublik gedreht, erzählt die Geschichte eines einsamen Mannes, der es in seiner öden Umgebung nicht mehr aushält und sich auf dem Mühlrad umbringt. Der Stil mündet in einen hoffnungslos pessimistischen symbolischen Realismus.
198 *Nicht alles, was fliegt, ist auch ein Vogel*. Eine furchterregende Stadt dient als Kulisse, um die fortschreitende Isolierung des Menschen zu illustrieren. Ein fliegendes Monster, das Politik und Grausamkeit symbolisiert, hindert einen kleinen Mann am Wiederaufbau seines Hauses.

193

194

195

196

198

197

ARTIST / KÜNSTLER / RÉALISATION:

193–198 Borislav Sajtinac

DIRECTOR / RÉGISSEUR:

193–198 Borislav Sajtinac

PRODUCTION / PRODUKTION:

193, 194 Oase Film, Essen
195–197 V. Majic KG, München
198 Neoplanta Film, Zagreb

199

200

ARTIST / KÜNSTLER / RÉALISATION:
199–214 Nedeljiko Dragiç

DIRECTOR / RÉGISSEUR:
199–214 Nedeljiko Dragiç

201–212

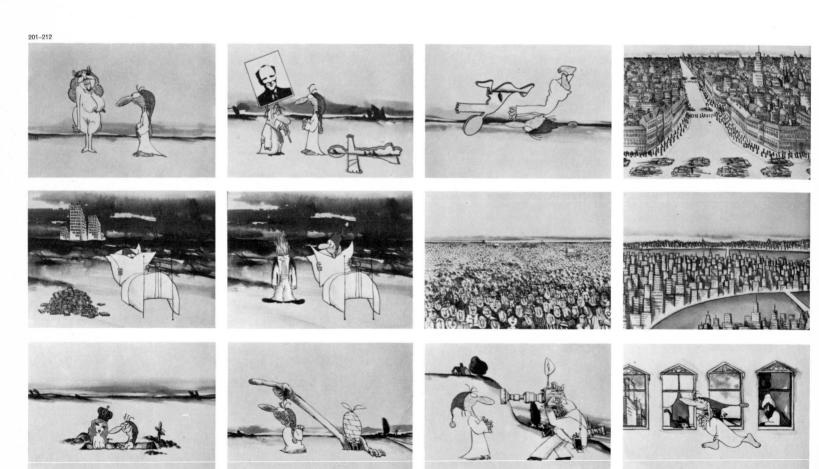

199, 200 *Diary*. Frames from a film by the Yugoslav artist Nedeljko Dragic, director of the Zagreb School, which won the Grand Prix at Zagreb in 1974. Full of ideas and striking imagery, it is a spirited 8½-minute colour recording of his impressions of New York.
201–212 *Tup-Tup*. Another prizewinner (Melbourne 1973). A man wants to read the paper in the privacy of his own home when a mysterious noise begins to irritate him. In his fight against the noise he is driven to destroying things. A desperate cry against the distortion of our times.
213, 214 *Tamer of Wild Horses,* made in 1966, is an ambitious film about man's courage and will-power in dominating the forces of nature.

199, 200 *Diary* (Tagebuch). Ein geistreicher und fantasievoller Farbfilm über die New-Yorker-Impressionen des jugoslawischen Künstlers Nedeljko Dragic: er ist Direktor der Zagreber Schule, die 1974 den grossen Preis am Trickfilm-Festival in Zagreb erhielt.
201–212 *Tup-Tup*, ein weiterer preisgekrönter Film Dragics (Melbourne 1973). Ein Mann, der in der Zurückgezogenheit seines Heims seine Zeitung lesen will, wird durch einen mysteriösen Lärm irritiert. Im Kampf gegen diesen Lärm schlägt er alles kurz und klein. Ein Protest gegen die Zerrüttung des Menschen in unserer Zeit.
213, 214 *Tamer of Wild Horses* (Bändiger wilder Pferde), 1966 gedreht, ist ein ehrgeiziger Film über den Willen des Menschen, die Naturkräfte zu beherrschen.

199, 200 *Diary* (Journal intime). Cases d'un film réalisé par Nedeljko Dragic, artiste yougoslave et directeur de l'Ecole de Zagreb qui a remporté le Grand Prix de Zagreb en 1974. Ce film, plein de fantaisie et d'idées spirituelles, retrace ses impressions de New York.
201–212 *Tup-Tup*. Lauréat de Melbourne 1973. Un homme se met à lire le journal dans l'intimité du foyer lorsqu'un bruit assez bizarre commence à l'irriter. La bagarre qu'il entraîne pour étouffer ce bruit débouche dans la destruction de tout ce qui lui tombe sous la main. C'est la lutte désespérée contre l'ébranlement nerveux de l'homme dans le monde actuel.
213, 214 *Tamer of Wild Horses* (Dompteur de chevaux sauvages), tourné en 1966. Un film traitant de l'ambition et des efforts de l'homme de dominer les forces naturelles.

213

PRODUCTION / PRODUKTION:
199–214 Zagreb-Film, Zagreb

214

215

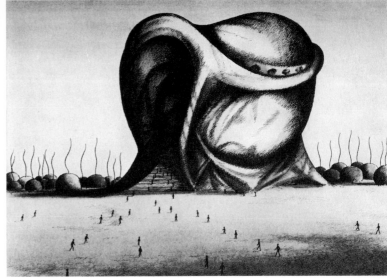

216

217

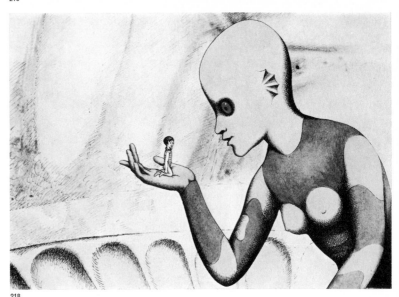

218

215–219 *La Planète Sauvage* (The Wild Planet) is a feature film in colour, the first full-length animated picture ever to be entered in the Cannes Film Festival (1973), where it won a Special Award. Based on a science fiction novel by Stefan Wul published in 1957, it tells the story of the Draags, inhabitants of the planet Ygam, androids 40 ft. tall with blue skins and red eyes. They have organized their welfare state on the basis of their complete scientific knowledge. Their spare time is spent in meditation. Their pets are the Oms, smaller creatures rather like human beings, who are killed when their number increases unduly or when they begin asking awkward questions. Terr, a young Om who is kept as a pet, still has emotions and the ability to reflect on his and his fellows' paralysing dependence on their dehumanized masters. Together with a group of wild Oms no longer protected by the benevolence of the rulers, he rebels against this civilization of cold reason and unlimited progress, succeeds in building a rocket and in making his escape to the Wild Planet. The secret energy supply of the Draags is now discovered by the group of rebel Oms, and by putting it out of action they succeed in forcing their erstwhile masters to accept a true partnership for the first time, though the two cultures continue to lie far apart. The film thus ends on a note of cautious optimism.
220 A sketch for *La Planète Sauvage*.

215–219 *La Planète Sauvage* (Der wilde Planet) ist ein abendfüllender Film in Farbe und der erste gezeichnete Film, der an den Filmfestspielen in Cannes gezeigt wurde, wo er 1973 einen Spezialpreis erhielt. Der Film erzählt von den Draags, Androiden von 12 Metern Höhe mit blauer Haut und roten Augen, die den Planeten Ygam bewohnen. Aufgrund ihrer vollendeten wissenschaftlichen Kenntnissen errichteten sie einen Wohlfahrtsstaat; ihre Freizeit verbringen sie in Meditation. Statt Haustieren halten sie sich menschenähnliche Wesen, die Oms. Sobald deren Zahl jedoch zu stark anwächst oder sie beginnen, unangenehme Fragen zu stellen, so werden sie mit einer Art Insektizid unschädlich gemacht. Terr, ein junger Om, der als Haustier verhätschelt wird, hat seine Fähigkeiten zu fühlen und zu denken beibehalten. Seine lähmende Abhängigkeit von den unmenschlich gewordenen Gebietern ist ihm voll bewusst. Mit einer Gruppe von wilden Oms, die nicht mehr unter dem Schutz ihrer Herren stehen, erhebt sich Terr gegen dieses Regime von kalter Vernunft und unerbittlichem Fortschrittsstreben und flieht auf den Wilden Planeten. Er entdeckt dort die geheimen Energiequellen der Draags und droht, sie zu zerstören. Damit erzwingt er einen dauernden Frieden mit seinen früheren Herren – die Kultur der beiden Partner bleibt jedoch weiterhin verschieden. So endet der Film dennoch auf einer optimistischen Note.
220 Skizze zu *La Planète Sauvage*.

219

ARTIST / KÜNSTLER / RÉALISATION:

215–225 Roland Topor

DIRECTOR / RÉGISSEUR:

215–225 René Laloux

PRODUCTION / PRODUKTION:

215–225 Les Films Armorial/O.R.T.F., Paris/
Czech Filmexport, Prague

220

215–219 *La Planète Sauvage.* Un long métrage en couleur, le premier film d'animation jamais montré au Festival de Cannes (1973) d'où il a remporté un prix spécial. C'est l'histoire des Draags, habitants du planète Ygam, qui sont des androïdes mesurant 12 m, à la peau bleue et aux yeux rouges. Ils ont constitué un état social qui se base sur leurs connaissances scientifiques parfaites. Pendant les heures de loisirs, ils s'adonnent de préférence à la méditation. Au lieu d'animaux, ils ont domestiqué des Oms, de petites créatures d'apparence humaine. Ils se mettent à décimer les Oms sauvages en les aspergeant d'insecticide dès que leur nombre s'accroît ou dès qu'ils commencent à poser des questions peu commodes. Terr, un jeune Om domestiqué, qui n'a pas perdu ses facultés intellectuelles, est conscient de la dépendance paralysante des maîtres inhumains, dépendence dont souffrent ses camarades. Avec un groupe d'Oms sauvages qui ne profitent plus de la protection bénévolante des dirigeants, il se soulève contre cette civilisation froidement calculatrice et ambitieusement progressiste. Ils réussissent à construire une fusée. Ils atterrissent sur la Planète Sauvage où ils découvrent les sources d'énergie secrètes des Draags; la menace de les détruire leur permet de conclure une paix entre les Oms et les Draags. Mais les deux civilisations subsistent, aussi disparates qu'elles soient, telles qu'elles étaient auparavant.
220 Esquisse pour le film *La Planète Sauvage*.

221–225 *La Planète Sauvage* (The Wild Planet) is a co-production of Les Films Armorial, the ORTF of France and Czech Filmexport. The writer/director René Laloux and the fabulously inventive artist Roland Topor have together created a film which is outstanding in its plastic perspectives and its surrealist atmosphere. The peculiar chill Topor instills into his apocalyptic pictures forces the spectator to stand at a distance. Only thus does the theme of the film attain its full impact. The fear of a dehumanized brave new world is powerfully conveyed.

221–225 *La Planète Sauvage* (Der wilde Planet) ist eine Koproduktion von Les Films Armorial, Frankreichs ORTF und dem Tschechischen Filmexport. In enger Zusammenarbeit zwischen dem Autor/Regisseur René Laloux und dem fantastisch erfinderischen Künstler Roland Topor ist ein Film mit aussergewöhnlich plastischen Perspektiven und surrealistischer Atmosphäre entstanden. Die merkwürdige Kälte, die Topors apokalyptische Figuren ausströmen, zwingt den Betrachter zur Distanz. Nur so kann sich das Thema des Films in seiner vollen Macht entfalten. Die Furcht vor einer unmenschlichen, kalten und technisierten Zukunft jedoch bleibt.

221–225 *La Planète Sauvage* est une co-production des Films Armorial, de l'ORTF et du Filmexport tchèque. L'auteur-directeur René Laloux et Roland Topor, un artiste d'une imagination sensationnelle, ont créé un film tout à fait extraordinaire quant aux perspectives plastiques et à l'atmosphère surréaliste qu'il respire. Une impression de froideur que répandent les figures apocalyptiques force le spectateur à reculer d'un pas afin d'observer ce film d'une certaine distance. C'est ainsi que l'effet du film est pleinement mis en évidence. La crainte d'un monde inhumain, froid, dominé par les sciences et la technique reste omniprésent.

Credits on previous page
Künstlerlisten auf vorangehender Seite
Liste d'artistes à la page précédente

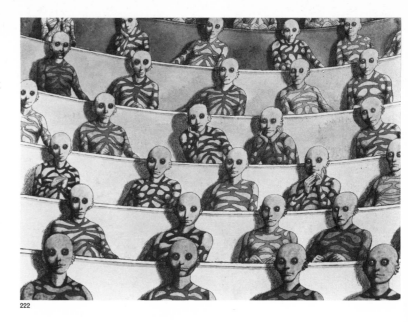

222

221

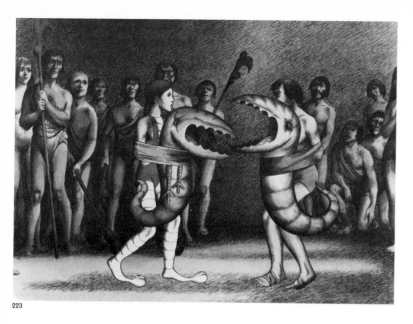

223

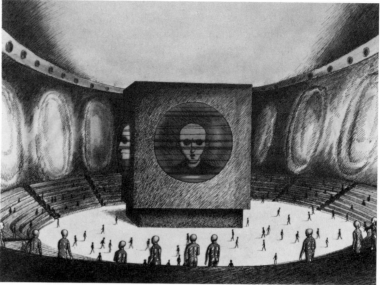

224

225

ARTIST / KÜNSTLER / RÉALISATION:

226 Vaclav Bedrich
227–232 Leszek Komorowski
233–235 Seppo Suo-Anttila

DIRECTOR / RÉGISSEUR:

226 Vaclav Bedrich
227–232 Leszek Komorowski
233–235 Max Masimino-Garnièr

PRODUCTION / PRODUKTION:

226 Kratky Film, Prague
227–232 Studio Miniatur Filmowych, Warsaw
233–235 Seppo Suo-Anttila, Helsinki/
         Corona Cinematografica, Rome

226

226 *The Cleansing Bath,* the grotesque and humourous story of the beautiful Zéa, who is rescued from the clutches of an evil-minded scientist. Bédrich has taken up a tradition already established by Karel Zeman in his own ironical series *The Deadly Scent,* of which this film forms part.

227–232 *Those Cruel Ruffians,* a 10-minute colour satire for older children and adults. Its theme: the useless and unnecessary shooting in modern films. By their senseless gun bravado Bill and John endanger the life of their home town, getting on their neighbours' nerves and causing grave accidents.

233–235 *The Man and the Snake* the Finnish contribution to the series of *European Fables* which is being assembled in Italy for eventual showing in theatres and on television. The film is based on a Finnish folk tale, its style being influenced by mediaeval art and murals from old stone churches.

226 *The Cleansing Bath* (Das reinigende Bad), eine groteske und humorvolle Geschichte der schönen Zéa, die aus den Händen eines bösen Wissenschafters gerettet wird. Bédrich führt die auf Karel Zemans Serie *Das tödliche Parfum* zurückreichende Tradition weiter. Dieser Film ist ein Teil dieser Serie.

227–232 *Those Cruel Ruffians* (Diese grausamen Raufbolde), eine Satire für Jugendliche und Erwachsene über die unnötigen Schiessereien in modernen Filmen. Durch ihren prahlerischen Umgang mit Waffen gefährden Bill und John das Leben anderer, strapazieren die Nerven der Nachbarn und verursachen Unfälle.

233–235 *The Man and the Snake* (Der Mann und die Schlange), ein finnischer Beitrag zur Serie *Europäische Sagen,* die in Italien für eine mögliche TV-Sendung zusammengestellt wird. Der Film basiert auf einem finnischen Volksmärchen. Der Stil geht auf mittelalterliche Kunst und frühe Wandmalereien zurück.

226 *The Cleansing Bath* (Le bain purifiant), une histoire grotesque de la belle Zéa sauvée miraculeusement des griffes d'un savant détraqué. Un film fondé sur la tradition qui remonte à Karel Zeman et sa série *Le parfum qui tue,* dont il fait partie.

227–232 *Those Cruel Ruffians* (Ces bandits cruels), un film satirique destiné aux jeunes et aux adultes. Thème: les fusillades inutiles dans les films modernes destinées à créer une atmosphère de suspense. Par leurs fanfaronnades de révolver, Bill et John portent atteinte à la sécurité de leur ville, énervent leurs voisins et causent un nombre de graves accidents.

233–235 *The Man and the Snake* (L'Homme et le serpent), contribution finlandaise pour une série intitulée *Fables Européennes* réunie à l'heure actuelle en Italie pour une éventuelle série télévisée. Il reprend un conte populaire finlandais. Le style évoque l'art médiéval et les anciennes peintures murales.

236

236–239 *Frank Film,* a funny and intimate autobiographic collage with an offhand monologue by the director reflecting on his youth and upbringing, illustrated and counterpointed by the thousands of bits and pieces he has collected and cut out over the years: all the noses, eyes, cats, sausages, girls, soup cans, etc., he has ever seen in his young life. The film won the Grand Prix at Annecy in 1973, the Academy Award for Best Cartoon Short in 1974 and several other prizes into the bargain.
240–242 *The Shell.* Drawings from a film produced by Studio Miniatur Filmowych in 1975. The artist Kalina keeps them in a satirical, grotesque key.
243–245 *The Candy Machine* depicts the struggle between a subway rider and a vending machine which refuses to deliver the goods. A drama borrowed from everyday life on the theme of man versus machine.

236–239 *Frank Film,* une amusante collage autobiographique – au fond assez intime – accompagnée d'un monologue spontané du directeur qui fait passer en revue son enfance et son éducation. Il y livre le contenu de sa vie composé de milliers de morceaux qu'il a collectionnés et découpés au cours des années: les nez, les yeux, les chats, les saucisses, les filles, les potages en conserve etc. qui ont défilés devant lui. Le Grand Prix d'Annecy 1973 est revenu à *Frank Film,* ainsi que l'Academy Award for Best Cartoon Short et nombre d'autres prix.
240–242 *The Shell* (La Coquille). Dessins d'un film produit par le Studio Miniatur Filmowych en 1975. L'artiste Kalina réussit à leur donner un air satirique et grotesque.
243–245 *The Candy Machine* (Le Distributeur automatique). Un voyageur lutte contre un appareil refusant de distribuer les bonbons. Un thème pris sur le vif: la lutte entre l'homme et la machine.

236–239 *Frank Film,* eine amüsante autobiographische Collage mit einem ungezwungenen Kommentar des Regisseurs über seine Jugend und seine Erziehung. Aus Hunderttausenden von Elementen zusammengeklebt, die er im Laufe der Jahre sammelte, lässt er sein Leben Revue passieren: alle Nasen, Augen, Katzen, Würste, Mädchen, Suppenbüchsen etc., kurz alles, was Frank in seinem Leben bis jetzt sah. Der Film wurde 1973 mit dem Grossen Preis von Annecy ausgezeichnet, gewann 1974 den Academy Award for Best Cartoon Short und mehrere andere Preise.
240–242 *The Shell* (Die Muschel). Zeichnungen aus einem Film, der 1975 vom Studio Miniatur Filmowych produziert wurde. Der Künstler Kalina gab ihm eine satirische und groteske Note.
243–245 *The Candy Machine* (Der Automat). Ein Reisender kämpft gegen den Automaten, der nicht funktioniert. Ein Thema aus dem Alltag: der Kampf zwischen Mensch und Maschine.

237–239

ARTIST / KÜNSTLER / RÉALISATION:

236–239 Frank Mouris
240–242 Jerzy Kalina
243–245 George Griffin

DIRECTOR / RÉGISSEUR:

236–239 Frank Mouris
240–242 Jerzy Kalina
243–245 George Griffin

PRODUCTION / PRODUKTION:

236–239 Caroline Ahlfors Mouris, New York
240–242 Studio Miniatur Filmowych, Warsaw
243–245 George Griffin/Metropolis Photoplays, New York

240–242

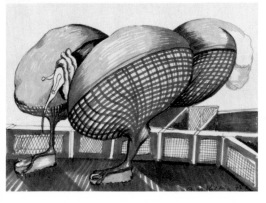

243–245

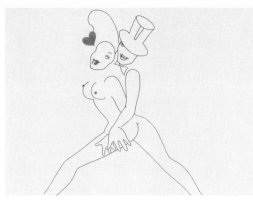

246–250

246–250 Detail and frames from *Putting on the Ritz*, a 3¼-minute colour film to the accompaniment of Gershwin music. In this cartoon cabaret the characters create themselves out of a dancing, ever-changing line.
251–256 *Seven Little Flames.* In a clearing in a forest a grandfather and his grandsons live peacefully, keeping alight the fire in the hearth for the protector of the house. A cunning witch succeeds in destroying their home, but a newly-lit fire brings the protector back and gets rid of the witch.
257–265 *Arès contre Atlas* (Ares against Atlas) is a work of sable humour. An episode will illustrate its approach: an immense bomb is constructed and dropped behind the enemy lines. It falls in a village but does not explode. The whole population of the village thereupon gathers in the church to give thanks. Their hallelujah is so full-throated that it sets the belfry rocking, the big bell crashes down and kills all the villagers. Some of the episodes express anti-war convictions.

246–250 Detail und Bilder aus dem 3¼-Minuten-Farbfilm *Putting on the Ritz* (Wir machen auf luxuriös) mit Musik von Gershwin. Die Charaktere dieses Streifens entstehen fortwährend aus einer tanzenden, sich ständig verändernden Linie.
251–256 *Sedam Plamencica* (Sieben kleine Flammen). In einer Waldlichtung wohnt ein Grossvater mit seinen Enkeln. Sie unterhalten das Feuer für den Hausbeschützer. Eine listige Hexe bringt es fertig, ihr Heim zu zerstören, doch ein neuentfachtes Feuer bringt den Beschützer zurück und verjagt die Hexe.
257–265 *Arès contre Atlas* (Ares gegen Atlas). Der schwarze Humor wird am besten an einer Episode illustriert: eine immense Bombe wird gebaut und hinter die feindliche Linie geschossen. Sie geht auf ein Dorf nieder – jedoch als Blindgänger. Die Bevölkerung versammelt sich zu einem Dankgebet in der Kirche. Ihr Hallelujah bringt sogar den Glockenturm ins Wanken; die Glocke stürzt hinunter und erschlägt die Bewohner. Einige Episoden drücken eine engagierte Anti-Kriegshaltung aus.

246–250 Détail et images du *Putting on the Ritz*, un film couleur de 3 mn. ¼ sur la musique de Gershwin. Dans cette émission de music-hall, les personnages surgissent au détour d'une ligne dansante, en transformation permanente.
251–256 *Sedam Plamencica* (Sept Petites Flammes). Dans une clairière, le grand-père et ses petits-fils entretiennent le foyer pour le protecteur de la maison. Mais une sorcière réussit à détruire leur maison. Ils rallument le feu et c'est ainsi que le protecteur revient pour chasser la sorcière.
257–265 *Arès contre Atlas* révèle un humour macabre, qu'illustre l'épisode suivant: Une énorme bombe est larguée tant bien que mal en pays ennemi. Elle tombe sur un village, sans exploser. Là-dessus, Te Deum solennel qui réunit dans l'église toute la population. L'alléluia chanté à pleins poumons fait branler le clocher, et la grosse cloche dégringole, écrasant tous les villageois. Quelques-uns des épisodes sont d'inspiration nettement pacifiste.

251–256

ARTIST / KÜNSTLER / RÉALISATION:

246–250 Antoinette Starkiewicz
251–256 Pavao Stalter
257–265 Manuel Otéro

DIRECTOR / RÉGISSEUR:

246–250 Antoinette Starkiewicz
251–256 Pavao Stalter
257–265 Manuel Otéro

PRODUCTION / PRODUKTION:

246–250 Antoinette Starkiewicz, London
251–256 Zagreb-Film, Zagreb/
         Corona Cinematografica, Rome
257–265 Cinémation, Pantin/FRA

257–265

266

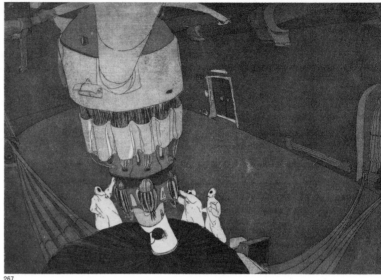

267

266, 267 *Operation X-70* (1971) describes a world infiltrated by a gas which reduces men to a state of somnambulism. This is Servais' rather bitter view of the world, and he develops it with frightening dramatic intensity. The realistic science-fiction-type graphic style—reminiscent of much contemporary art—combined with the skilful use of sound and movement gives the picture a haunting reality.
268–270 Frames from *Vrijeme Vampira* (The Time of the Vampire). Little masterpieces have long emerged with reassuring regularity from the Zagreb studio. This one tells of the merry tipplers from a tavern who congregate in a graveyard to be alone with their girls and are not a bit disturbed by the midnight visits of friendly vampires. Shown at Annecy in 1971.

266, 267 *Operation X-70* (1971) décrit un monde intoxiqué d'un gaz qui réduit l'homme à un être vivant dans un état somnambule. Servais évoque un monde cruel dépeint avec une intensité dramatique et effroyante. Les éléments empruntés à la science-fiction et son style qui rapelle à maints égards l'art contemporain ainsi que la musique et les mouvements subtilement introduits créent une atmosphère qui frappe par sa réalité.
268–270 Cases de *Vrijeme Vampira* (Le temps des Vampires), l'un des petits chefs-d'œuvres qui sortent régulièrement du Studio de Zagreb. On y raconte l'histoire des ivrognes ayant fréquentés une auberge qui se trouve tout près du cimetière du village. Après leur beuverie ils s'y rendent avec leurs amies – la visite nocturne des vampires ne les dérange pas du tout.

266, 267 *Operation X-70* (1971). Die Welt, die hier beschrieben ist, wurde von einem Gas verseucht, das die Menschen in einen schlafwandlerischen Zustand versetzt. Diese bitterböse Zukunftsvision wird von Servais mit einer furchterregenden dramatischen Intensität dargestellt. Die typischen Science-fiction-Elemente und sein an zeitgenössische Kunst erinnernde Stil, die Vertonung und die gekonnten Bewegungsabläufe verleihen diesem Film eine erschreckende Realität.
268–270 Bilder aus *Vrijeme Vampira* (Die Zeit der Vampire). Mit schöner Regelmässigkeit kommen aus dem Zagreber Studio kleine Meisterwerke. Dieses hier erzählt von den leicht angeheiterten Gästen einer Kneipe, die sich mit ihren Freundinnen im benachbarten Friedhof treffen, ohne sich dabei von den mitternächtlichen Besuchen von neugierigen Vampiren stören zu lassen.

268

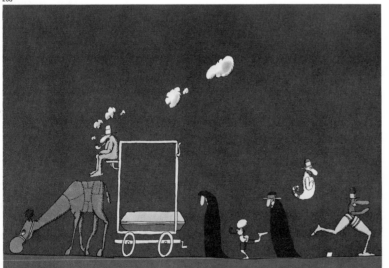

269

270

ARTIST / KÜNSTLER / RÉALISATION:

266, 267 Raoul Servais
268–270 Nicola Majdak

DIRECTOR / RÉGISSEUR:

266, 267 Raoul Servais
268–270 Nicola Majdak

PRODUCTION / PRODUKTION:

266, 267 Pen-Film & Ministry of Culture of Belgium, Bruxelles
268–270 Zagreb Film, Zagreb/Dunav Film, Belgrad

271

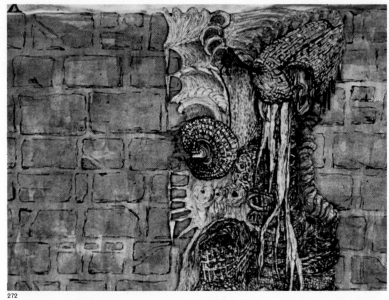

272

273

274

ARTIST / KÜNSTLER / RÉALISATION:

271–278 Leo Hofmann

DIRECTOR / RÉGISSEUR:

271–278 Leo Hofmann

PRODUCTION / PRODUKTION:

271–278 Karel Schmeink, Amsterdam

271–274 *Falling Monuments.* This eight-minute colour film depicts the visitation of a town by a mysterious, destructive force. Architecture in dissolution, peopled by strange forms and machines. A knowledge of the rediscovered Ctulhu stories of the Englishman Lovecraft is essential to a complete understanding of this film, which was shown at Annecy in 1973.

275–278 *Renaissance.* A music pavilion stands in a deserted square around which are located several buildings in different styles. A procession appears carrying a veiled statue and proceeds to an old temple, where religious symbols are exhibited. They all undergo a curious metamorphosis and crumble into dust. The last religious symbol is a phallus-like mushroom. A ten-minute film in colour.

275

276

277

278

271–274 *Falling Monuments* (Untergang der Monumente). Dieser Kurzfilm zeigt eine Stadt, die von einer geheimnisvollen, destruktiven Macht heimgesucht wird. Eine in vollkommener Auflösung begriffene Architektur, bevölkert von fremdartigen Formen und Maschinen. Nur wer die neuentdeckten Ctulhu-Geschichten des Engländers Lovecraft kennt, kann diesen Film voll verstehen.

275–278 *Renaissance.* Ein Musikpavillon steht auf einem verlassenen Platz, um den herum sich Gebäude aus verschiedenen Epochen erheben. Eine Prozession, die eine verhüllte Statue mit sich führt, bewegt sich über den Platz auf einen Tempel zu, wo alte Religionssymbole aufbewahrt werden. Sie alle haben eine merkwürdige Metamorphose durchgemacht und liegen nun in Schutt und Asche. Das letzte Symbol entpuppt sich als ein phallusartiger Pilz.

271–274 *Falling Monuments* (La Chute des Monuments). Ce film en couleur de 8 minutes montre une mystérieuse force destructrice s'acharnant sur une ville. Une architecture qui se dissout, peuplée de formes et machines étranges. Il faut connaître les histoires de Ctulhu de l'Anglais Lovecraft, redécouvertes de nos jours, pour saisir le message profond du film.

275–278 *Renaissance.* Un pavillon de musique est situé dans une place déserte entourée de plusieurs bâtiments construits en différentes époques. Une procession suivant une statue voilée se dirige vers un vieux temple où des symboles religieux sont exposés. Ceux-là ont subi une métamorphose tout à fait bizarre – ils se sont transformés en poussière. Le seul symbole qui reste ressemble à un champignon de forme phallique. Un film couleur de 10 minutes.

ARTIST / KÜNSTLER / RÉALISATION:

279–281 Stanislava Prochazkova
282–285 Miroslav Stepanek

DIRECTOR / RÉGISSEUR:

279–281 Pavel Prochazka
282–285 Miroslav Stepanek

PRODUCTION / PRODUKTION:

279–285 Kratky Film Studio, Prague

279–281 *The Chimney.* A puppet film based on an old Czech opera. A couple of vagabonds offer to rebuild an old farmer's chimney. Their work leaves a lot to be desired, the chimney collapses and the two vagabonds run away with the farmer's money.
282–285 *The Shooting Gallery.* In a shooting gallery, a soldier fires at the targets, mechanically setting each group of characters in motion. For a moment one dancing couple is set free and floats upwards in celebration of its newly-discovered freedom—only to be brought down again by the soldier's gun and forced into mechanical obedience once more. A telling allegory.

279–281 *The Chimney* (Der Kamin). Dieser Puppenfilm basiert auf einer alten tschechischen Oper. Zwei Vagabunden bieten sich an, den Kamin eines alten Bauern wieder aufzubauen. Die Arbeit wird jedoch sehr liederlich ausgeführt, der Kamin fällt zusammen und die beiden Burschen machen sich mit dem Geld des Bauern aus dem Staub.
282–285 *The Shooting Gallery* (Der Schiessstand). Ein Soldat zielt auf die in einer Schiessbude ausgestellten Gruppen und bringt eine nach der anderen in Bewegung. Für einen Augenblick befreit sich eine der Gruppen – ein Bursche und sein Mädchen – und schwebt glücklich über die neuerrungene Freiheit aufwärts. Ein weiterer Schuss holt die beiden wieder herunter und zwingt sie in ihre mechanische Bewegung zurück. Eine sehr sprechende Geschichte.

279–281 *The Chimney* (La Cheminée). Un spectacle de marionnettes fondé sur un opéra tchèque. Deux vagabonds sont prêts à refaire la cheminée d'un vieux paysan. Le travail terminé, il s'avère être un bousillage – la cheminée s'écroule et les deux vagabonds filent avec l'argent du paysan.
282–285 *The Shooting Gallery* (Le stand de tir). Lors d'un tir forain un soldat vise aux groupes exposés qui se mettent en marche l'un après l'autre. Ce n'est que pour un instant qu'un couple – un garçon et sa fille – se détache du groupe et s'envole lentement, enchanté de la liberté regagnée. Mais un coup de fusil du soldat les renvoie à leurs places et les force à l'ancienne obéissance méchanique. Une allégorie assez éloquente.

279

280

281

282

283

284

285

286–291 *Utopia.* In a delightfully fluid style, really making use of the "magic" of animation, Boris Kolar tells the story of a little fellow pestered by the domestic objects around him which have taken on a life of their own.

292–298 *Amateurs Night.* Thalma Goldman, a young Israeli, studied animation in London for two years. This is her third film. On an "amateurs night", a number of amateurs do a strip-tease on the stage. The film shows not only the performers themselves, but also the reactions of an enthusiastic audience that is really "with it".

286–291 *Utopia.* In seinem flüssigen Stil, der die «Magie» des Trickfilms voll ausnützt, erzählt Boris Kolar die Geschichte eines kleinen Mannes, in dessen Haus die Möbel und häuslichen Gegenstände ihr Eigenleben zu führen beginnen.

292–298 *Amateurs Night* (Nacht der Amateure). Die junge Israelin Thalma Goldman lernte zwei Jahre in London Animation und stellt hier ihren dritten Film vor. Darin führen Amateure auf der Bühne einen Strip-Tease vor. Der Film zeigt nicht nur die Darsteller, sondern vor allem das begeisterte Publikum, das das Geschehen auf der Bühne mitverfolgt und mitmacht.

286–291 *Utopia.* Par son style aisé, Boris Kolar a su évoquer la «magie» du dessin animé. Il situe son film dans une maison mystérieuse où les meubles et autres objets inanimés sont possédés d'une vie propre.

292–298 *Amateurs Night* (Nuit des Amateurs). La jeune Israélienne Thalma Goldman a étudié l'animation à Londres pendant deux ans. C'est son 3e film. Des amateurs font du strip-tease sur scène. Le film ne montre pas seulement les personnages principaux, mais aussi et surtout le public enthousiaste, ses réactions et commentaires face à ce qu'il voit sur la scène.

ARTIST / KÜNSTLER / RÉALISATION:

286–291 Boris Kolar
292–298 Thalma Goldman

DIRECTOR / RÉGISSEUR:

286–291 Boris Kolar
292–298 Thalma Goldman

PRODUCTION / PRODUKTION:

286–291 Zagreb Film, Zagreb
292–298 Thalma Goldman, London

298

299–304 Sequence from *Chow Fun* a colour film of 3½ minutes. The artist has tried to recapture the "slithery, oozing motion" of the cartoons of the thirties. Her images form a complex chain in one continuous space. Her choice of colours was inspired by Chinese food packaging.

305–309 In his usual Picasso-like fluid line, Foldes explores in his long work *Daphnis and Chloe* a mobile world of fantasy, where his much admired drawings move and develop against a coloured background. Born in Hungary in 1924, Foldes emigrated to England and later settled in France. Whilst Picasso, Cocteau and the Surrealists have influenced him, he has now become involved, through his work at the Service de la Recherche of the ORTF, with computer techniques, which he has further extended at the National Film Board of Canada. Avoiding mathematical abstraction, he retains his poetic and narrative power and thus creates a unique style of his own.

299–304 Sequenz aus *Chow Fun*, einem 3½-minutigen Farbfilm. Die Künstlerin versuchte, die «schlüpfrige, dahinsickernde Bewegung» der Comics der dreissiger Jahre nachzuahmen. Ihre Bilder formen eine lange Kette in einem unbegrenzten Raum, ihre Farben sind chinesischen Verpackungen entnommen.

305–309 In seiner üblichen Picasso-ähnlichen flüssigen Linie erkundet Foldes in seinem langen Werk *Daphnis und Chloe* eine Welt der Fantasie, in der seine bewunderten Zeichnungen sich vor einem farbigen Hintergrund entfalten. Foldes, 1924 in Ungarn geboren, emigrierte nach England und liess sich später in Frankreich nieder. Picasso, Cocteau und die Surrealisten beeinflussten sein Werk. Durch seine Arbeit beim Service de la Recherche des ORTF, später beim NFBC in Kanada, begann er sich mit der Computertechnik zu befassen. Er vermied jedoch Whitneys mathematischen Abstraktionen und behielt seine poetische und dramatische Aussagekraft.

299–304 Séquence de *Chow Fun*, film couleur de 3 mn. ½. L'artiste a essayé d'y évoquer le «mouvement fluide, glissant» des cartoons des années 30. Ses images s'enchaînent dans un espace continu. Son choix des couleurs s'inspire des emballages de denrées alimentaires chinoises.

305–309 *Daphnis et Chloé.* Les dessins, en fait beaucoup admirés, que Foldes a créés pour cette œuvre importante évoquent à maints égards Picasso. Ils font surgir un monde de fantaisie, dans lequel Foldes s'avance pas à pas. Né en Hongrie en 1924, il a quitté son pays pour s'établir en Angleterre, puis en France. Picasso, Cocteau et les Surréalistes l'ont beaucoup influencé. Par son travail auprès du Service de la Recherche de l'ORTF, puis auprès de l'Office National du Film au Canada, il s'est orienté de plus en plus vers l'ordinateur, tout en évitant les abstractions mathématiques d'un Whitney. Ses dessins respirent une force poétique grâce à son style qu'il a su conserver.

299–304

ARTIST / KÜNSTLER / RÉALISATION:

299–304 Sally Cruikshank
305–309 Peter Foldes

DIRECTOR / RÉGISSEUR:

299–304 Sally Cruikshank
305–309 Peter Foldes

PRODUCTION / PRODUKTION:

299–304 Sally Cruikshank, Berkeley, Ca.
305–309 C. Soissons/Société Française
de Productions, Paris

305–308

309

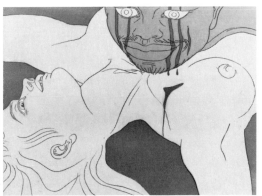

310–312

310–312 *Adelaide Village*. Frames from a film drawn in pastels on location in the Bahamas. Original tin drum music underlines the colour and *joie de vivre* of the local people.

313–319 *Where the Wild Things Are.* Gene Deitch has transferred Maurice Sendak's meticulous drawings to the moving screen. The small sequence of Max's bedroom turning into a jungle illustrates how the animators, Gene Deitch at their head, had to reproduce and create anew—with painstaking effort— the master's carefully thought-out models. The fact that the film looks as if Maurice Sendak had himself been responsible for the millions of sketches is a high tribute to Deitch's craftsmanship. This is indeed a true adaptation of Sendak's book in the film medium, with none of the original flavour lost. These film adaptations of children's books are mostly made for distribution in American schools.

310–312 *Adelaide Village*. Ein auf den Bahamas entstandener Film, in Pastellfarben. Die Untermalung mit Originalmusik verleiht dem Film eine südländische Atmosphäre und wiederspiegelt die Lebensfreude des Volkes.

313–319 *Wo die wilden Kerle wohnen*. Gene Deitch hat Maurice Sendaks Zeichnungen «belebt» und auf den Filmstreifen gebannt. Die kurze Szene, in welcher sich das Schlafzimmer in einen Dschungel verwandelt, zeigt deutlich, mit welch ausgeklügelter Genauigkeit die von Sendak sorgfältig erdachten Modelle wiedergegeben wurden. Die Tatsache, dass der Film den Anschein erweckt, als ob Sendak die Tausenden von Skizzen selber ausgeführt hätte, ist ein schlagender Beweis für Deitchs Können. Nicht die kleinste Spur seiner ursprünglichen Atmosphäre ging bei dieser wohl getreuesten Wiedergabe des Buches verloren. Solche Verfilmungen sind für Schulen bestimmt.

310–312 *Adelaide Village*, un film consacré aux Bahamas. Ce dessin animé en couleurs pastel a été réalisé sur place et sonorisé de musique originale – il évoque ainsi l'atmosphère particulière de l'île, les couleurs et la joie de vivre du peuple.

313–319 *Max et les Maximonstres*. Gene Deitch a converti en dessins animés les créations méticuleuses de Maurice Sendak. La scène où la chambre se transforme en jungle révèle avec quel soin minutieux Gene Deitch et ses animateurs ont reproduit et recréé les modèles inventés par Sendak. Les milliers et milliers d'esquisses semblent à première vue avoir été réalisées par Sendak lui-même – en fait une preuve éclatante du talent et de la finesse artistique de Deitch. C'est l'adaptation la plus véridique de ce livre – pas la moindre nuance n'ait été perdue. La plupart des adaptations cinématographiques de livres d'enfants sont destinées à la distribution aux écoles américaines.

313–318

319

ARTIST / KÜNSTLER / RÉALISATION:

310–312 Pierre L'Amare
313–319 Maurice Sendak/Gene Deitch

DIRECTOR / RÉGISSEUR:

310–312 Pierre L'Amare
313–319 Gene Deitch

PRODUCTION / PRODUKTION:

310–312 Pierre L'Amare/National Film Board of Canada, Montreal
313–319 Morton Schindel/Weston Woods Studios, Weston, Con.

320

321–324

ARTIST / KÜNSTLER / RÉALISATION:

320–324 Daniel Suter
325–330 Manuel Otéro/Daniel Suter/Claude Luyet/
         Gérald Poussin/Georges Schwizgebel

DIRECTOR / RÉGISSEUR:

320–324 Daniel Suter
325–330 Manuel Otéro

PRODUCTION / PRODUKTION:

320–324 G.D.S., Carouge-Genève
325–330 Cinémation, Pantin/FRA

320–324 *Un Jour comme un autre* (A Day Like Another). Frames from a five-minute colour film painted in watery inks. It describes a day from sunrise to sunset on which people live their everyday lives: a man raises his hat, a woman smokes a cigarette and a girl amuses herself on the beach.

325–330 *Patchwork*. Five artists contributed to this film, which is group work with no surrender of individuality. Although the idea is difficult to carry out in practice, it can be recommended. The old master, Manuel Otéro in this case, gave four young Genevese artists a break—and every one of them, although some of them still work together, has gone his own way and found his own style.

320–324 *Un Jour comme un autre* (Ein Tag wie jeder andere). Bilder aus einem 5minutigen Farbfilm, in heller Tusche gemalt. Er beschreibt einen Tag von Sonnenaufgang bis Sonnenuntergang, an dem die Leute ihr Alltagsleben leben: ein Mann hebt den Hut, ein Mädchen amüsiert sich am Strand …

325–330 *Patchwork*. Fünf Künstler machen einen Film – eine Kollektivarbeit ohne Verlust an Individualität. Die Idee einer solchen Zusammenarbeit mag schwierig auszuführen sein, zur Nachahmung sei sie jedoch empfohlen. Hier verhalf Manuel Otéro vier jungen Genfer Nachwuchsleuten zum Durchbruch. Wenn auch einige von ihnen weiterhin zusammenarbeiten, so ging doch jeder einen eigenen Weg und fand einen eigenen Stil.

320–324 *Un Jour comme un autre*. Images d'un film couleur de 5 mn.: un jour du lever au coucher du soleil, où les gens vaquent à leurs occupations: un homme soulève son chapeau, une femme fume une cigarette, une jeune fille s'amuse à la plage …

325–330 Cases de *Patchwork* (Mosaïque). Cinq artistes collaborent à un film sans abandonner leur individualité. L'idée d'une telle collaboration n'est pas facile à réaliser, mais elle est d'autant plus digne d'être imitée. Le vieux maître du film d'animation, Manuel Otéro, a donné ici leur chance à quatre jeunes artistes genevois. Bien que quelques-unes continuent à réaliser des projets communs, chacun d'entre eux suit son chemin à lui et a su se créer son propre style.

325–330

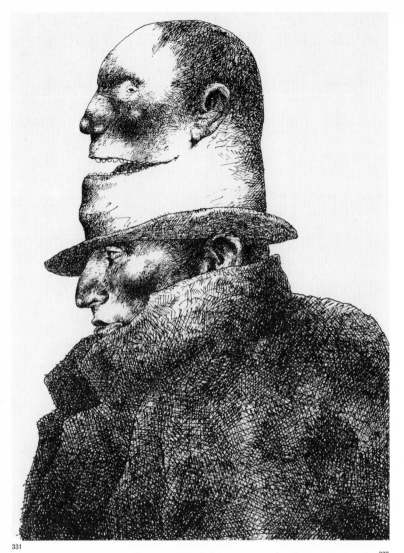

331

333

332

331–334 Drawings for an adult entertainment film project, *Pecos Bill, or The Liars' Club*. Pecos Bill, seen in Fig. 334 riding a cyclone slick-heeled, without a saddle, is a mythical cowboy whose prodigious and lawless deeds have been sung in the folktales of the Wild West for a hundred years and more. The film will be the artist's highly personal interpretation of his deeds. Growing up with the coyotes along the Pecos River in Texas, Bill is baptized by the Preacher, a gold-prospector and seldom encountered Baptist circuit orator. He falls in with a wild bunch and, sinking lower and lower, finally becomes a cowboy.

331–334 Zeichnungen zu einem projektierten Unterhaltungsfilm für Erwachsene, *Pecos Bill, or The Liars' Club* (Pecos Bill, oder der Klub der Lügner). Pecos Bill ist eine mythologische Cowboy-figur, deren kühne und verwegene Taten während langer Zeit die Gemüter der Bewunderer des Wilden Westens bewegte. Der Film zeigt des Künstlers eigene Interpretation dieses Lebens. Bill wächst mit den Coyoten am Pecos-Fluss in Texas auf und wird von einem Prediger, einem Gold-gräber und Wanderpriester der Wiedertäufer, nach allen Ritualen getauft. Er lässt sich jedoch mit einer Gruppe von Abenteurern ein und endet schliesslich als wilder Cowboy.

331–334 Dessins du long métrage projeté *Pecos Bill, or the Liars' Club* (Pecos Bill, ou Le Club des menteurs). Pecos Bill, qui enfourche un cyclon (fig. 334), est un cowboy mythique et ses actes illégaux mais d'autant plus audacieux ont été le motif préféré de contes populaires du Far West pendant plus d'un siècle. Ce film reflétera en fin de compte l'interprétation personnelle de l'artiste. Bill ayant passé son enfance avec des coyotes au bord de la rivière Pecos au Texas a été baptisé par un chercheur d'or et prédicateur itinérant des Anabatistes rarement vu dans les parages. Bill s'accointe avec un groupe d'aventuriers, et, tombant de plus en plus bas dans l'illégalité, en vient à mener une vie de cowboy.

334

335

335 *Legenda Lodzka* (Legend of an Industrial Town) is a moral tale about a town full of factories where a devil has made his abode. He does not like human beings and plays all kinds of tricks on them. He makes their lives unbearable, smokes and soils everything in the town; and eventually all the factory chimneys rebel and run away to the woods. The devil, enraged because he can no longer do any harm, sinks underground and never again appears in the town.

336, 337 *The Mad, Mad, Mad World* is a film created by one of the students of the enterprising Teheran Institute for the Intellectual Development of Children and Young Adults. It shows the changing territories of the world expanding until they gobble each other up.

338–351 Frames from *Smile 1, 2 and 3*. The first part is about peace, which all men are forever seeking; yet even though some of them come near peace for a while, does peace really exist? The second part is about Oedipus, who decides to shake off his complex, to take life and death into his own hands—and discovers his beginnings. The third part is about the Virgin Mother and her disintegration and was inspired by a tale from *The Arabian Nights*.

335 *Legenda Lodzka* (Legende einer Industriestadt), ist eine moralische Geschichte über eine Stadt voller Fabrikgebäude, in welcher sich ein Teufel niedergelassen hat. An menschlichen Wesen findet er keinen Gefallen und spielt ihnen deshalb alle Arten von bösen Streichen. Er bereitet ihnen ein unerträgliches Leben, indem er die Stadt verraucht und verschmutzt; doch alle Fabrikkamine beginnen zu rebellieren und rennen in den nahegelegenen Wald. Der Teufel, wütend über seine Niederlage, versinkt im Boden und wird seither nie mehr gesehen.

336, 337 *The Mad, Mad, Mad World* (Die totalverrückte Welt), wurde von einem Studenten des Teheraner Instituts für die intellektuelle Entwicklung von Kindern und Jugendlichen realisiert. Er zeigt die sich verändernden Territorien, die sich erweitern bis sie einander «auffressen».

338–351 Bilder aus *Smile 1, 2 und 3*. Der 1. Teil ist dem Frieden gewidmet, der, von allen Menschen angestrebt und von einigen beinahe erreicht, eventuell gar nicht existiert. Der 2. Teil handelt von Oedipus, der, entschlossen, seinen Komplex abzuschütteln, von nun an über sein Leben und seinen Tod selber entscheidet. Der 3. Teil endlich ist der heiligen Jungfrau und dem Zerfall ihres Mythos gewidmet; er basiert auf einer Geschichte aus *Tausend und einer Nacht*.

ARTIST / KÜNSTLER / RÉALISATION:

335 Andrzej Piliczewski
336, 337 Noureddin Zarrinkelk
338–351 Ernest & Gisèle Ansorge

336

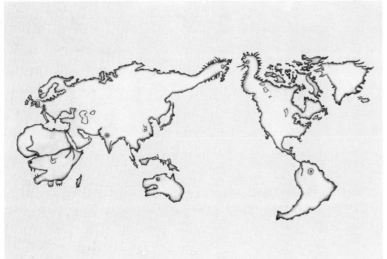

337

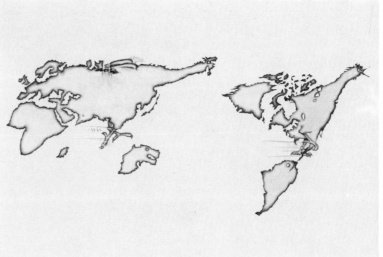

DIRECTOR / RÉGISSEUR:

335 Andrzej Piliczewski
336, 337 Noureddin Zarrinkelk
338–351 Ernest & Gisèle Ansorge

PRODUCTION / PRODUKTION:

335 Featurette Film Studio SE-MA-FOR, Lodz
336, 337 Institute for the Intellectual Development of Children and Young Adults, Teheran
338–351 NAG-Film, Etagnières/SWI

335 *Legenda Lodzka* (La Légende d'une ville industrielle), un conte moral d'une ville pleine d'usines, ville où un diable a élu domicile. Il déteste les êtres vivants et joue toutes sortes de vilains tours afin de rendre leur vie insupportable – il enfume et souille la ville entière; en fin de compte, toutes les cheminées des usines se soulèvent et filent vers les bois. Enragé de sa défaite, le diable s'engloutit et n'a plus été revu depuis.

336, 337 *The Mad, Mad, Mad World*. C'est un film qui a été réalisé par un étudiant de l'Institut pour le développement intellectuel d'enfants et de jeunes gens à Téhéran. Il représente les territoires du monde qui, s'étendant continuellement, se dévorent en fin de compte.

338–351 Cases du film *Smile 1, 2, 3* (Sourire 1, 2 et 3). La première partie est consacrée à la paix que tous désirent, que quelques-uns ont approchée, peut-être même possédée. Mais existe-t-elle vraiment? La seconde partie est consacrée à Œdipe qui pour mettre fin à son complexe décide lui-même de sa naissance et de sa mort. La troisième partie, enfin, est consacrée à la Sainte Vierge et sa désagrégation. Cette partie s'inspire d'un conte des *Mille et une Nuits*.

350

351

352–356 Frames and drawings from *Lautrec,* Geoff Dunbar's widely acclaimed colour short. It received the Grand Prix for shorts at the 1975 Cannes Film Festival. An impression of Toulouse-Lautrec's work, it took eighteen months to produce and it runs approximately 7 minutes.
357, 358 Two frames from *Das Gestohlene Glück* (Stolen Happiness), which shows the indifference of capitalist societies to their artistic patrimony. While a small group is unscrupulously piling up these works of art it deprives a large number of those who love art of an important part of their life and enjoyment.
359 A frame from Katja Georgi's *Spindel, Weberschiffchen und Nadel* (Spinning Wheel, Shuttle and Needle). The design clearly reflects the subject matter.

352–356 Bilder und Zeichnungen aus *Lautrec,* Geoff Dunbars begeistert aufgenommenem Kurzfilm. Er wurde 1975 an den Filmfestspielen in Cannes mit dem Grossen Preis für Kurzfilme ausgezeichnet. Die Realisierung dieser Impression über Toulouse-Lautrecs Werk nahm achtzehn Monate in Anspruch – für eine Spieldauer von ungefähr 7 Minuten.
357, 358 Zwei Bilder aus dem Film *Das Gestohlene Glück,* der die Gleichgültigkeit der kapitalistischen Gesellschaft gegenüber ihren Kulturgütern aufzeigen soll. Diese werden von einer kleinen Schicht aufgekauft und so der breiten Öffentlichkeit unzugänglich gemacht.
359 Bild aus Katja Georgis *Spindel, Weberschiffchen und Nadel.* Das Thema dieses Films kommt in diesem Bild deutlich zum Ausdruck.

352

353

357

358

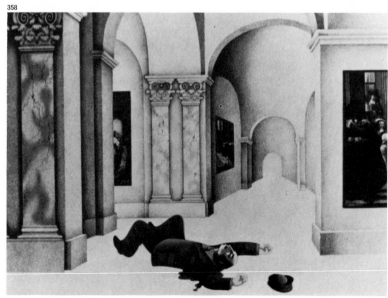

352–356 Cases et dessins de *Lautrec*, un court métrage de Geoff Dunbar qui a été accueilli avec enthousiasme. Le Grand Prix des courts métrages du Festival de Cannes 1975 est revenu à ce film. Cette «impression» sur l'œuvre de Toulouse-Lautrec, produit au cours de dix-huit mois, ne dure que sept minutes environ.
357, 358 Deux cases de *Das Gestohlene Glück* (Le bonheur volé), un film sur l'indifférence des sociétés capitalistes à l'égard de leur patrimoine artistique. Pillé par un groupe assez restreint, ces œuvres d'art sont devenus presque inaccessibles au grand public.
359 Case du film *Spindel, Weberschiffchen und Nadel* (Quenouille, navette et aiguille) de Katja Georgi. Le dessin reflète clairement le sujet.

356

354

355

359

ARTIST / KÜNSTLER / RÉALISATION:

352–356 Geoff Dunbar
357, 358 Klaus Georgi
359 Katja Georgi

DIRECTOR / RÉGISSEUR:

352–356 Geoff Dunbar
357, 358 Klaus Georgi
359 Katja Georgi

PRODUCTION / PRODUKTION:

352–356 Dragon Productions, London
357–359 VEB Defa-Studio für Trickfilme, Dresden

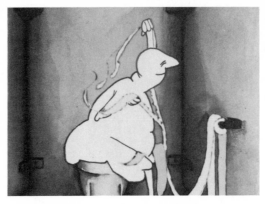

360–362

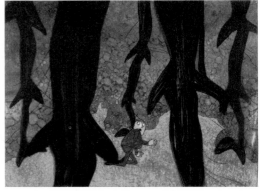

363–365

360–362 Frames from a student production entitled *Da Da Da*. It was made by a group of six second-year students and runs 1 min. 39 sec. It took three months to make.

363–365 *Muha* (The Fly). The Yugoslavs have repeatedly found subjects that offer them freedom of treatment and technique and yet permit them to make serious, adult statements. Their dramaturgy has a depth which must be sensed by the viewer. Their films call forth no enthusiastic admiration (except perhaps for the brilliance of their technique), but they make us think. *Muha* is a film of dimensions, ringing the changes on the relative size of man and fly. Thus in Fig. 365 man is dwarfed by the insect.

366–369 Stills from *Captain Incredible*, an animated film insert in a stage musical to be shown in London and New York. The comics style employed here is in keeping with the subject of the show, whose hero is endowed with superhuman strength.

360–362 Bilder aus dem Film *Da Da Da*, der von sechs Studenten im 2. Studienjahr realisiert wurde. Der Film ist im Laufe von drei Monaten entstanden; Spieldauer 1 Min. 39 Sek.

363–365 *Muha* (Die Fliege). Die Jugoslawen haben wiederholt Sujets gefunden, die vom Material und der Technik her jegliche schöpferische Freiheit zulassen, gleichzeitig aber eine anspruchsvolle Aussage verlangen. Die durch ihre Dramaturgie erzielte geistige Tiefe muss vom Betrachter gefühlsmässig erfasst werden. Die Filme rufen keine Begeisterung hervor (höchstens der brillanten Technik wegen), sie stimmen nachdenklich. *Muha* ist ein Film über die Verhältnismässigkeit, über die sich ändernde relative Grösse von Mensch und Fliege.

366–369 Aus *Captain Incredible*, einer Trickfilmsequenz, die in ein in London und New York gezeigtes Musical integriert werden soll. Der typische Comics-Stil passt zum Thema des Musicals, dessen Held übermenschliche Kräfte besitzt.

360–362 Cases d'un film intitulé *Da Da Da*. Il a été réalisé au cours de 3 mois par un groupe d'étudiants à la deuxième année d'études. Durée du film 1 mn. 39 sc.

363–365 *Muha* (La mouche). Les Yougoslaves sont assez chanceux pour trouver régulièrement des sujets qui leur offrent toute liberté technique et d'interprétation tout en se prêtant à une affabulation sérieuse à l'usage des adultes. Leur dramaturgie excelle à sonder les profondeurs. Leurs films n'éveillent guère l'enthousiasme (sauf, peut-être, leur technique brillante), mais ils font réfléchir. *Muha* interprète par la comparaison de l'homme et de la mouche la pensée pascalienne de l'homme et du ciron.

366–369 Images de *Captain Incredible*, un dessin animé intégré dans une comédie musicale qui sera présentée à Londres et à New York. Le style a été emprunté à la bande dessinée afin de mieux s'accorder avec la comédie, dont le héro est doué de forces et de confidence surhumaines.

366–368

369

ARTIST / KÜNSTLER / RÉALISATION:

360–362 Ian Bell/Greg Miller/Jack Mongovan/Dennis Neil/
   Charles Macrae/Peter Hudecki
363–365 Aleksander Marks/Vladimir Jutrisa
366–369 Jim Fitzpatrick

DIRECTOR / RÉGISSEUR:

360–362 Peter Hudecki
363–365 Aleksander Marks/Vladimir Jutrisa
366–369 Ron Inkpen/Jim Fitzpatrick

PRODUCTION / PRODUKTION:

360–362 Sheridan College, Oakville, Ont
363–365 Zagreb Film, Zagreb
366–369 G.T.O. Productions, London

370

ARTIST / KÜNSTLER / RÉALISATION:

370–374 Ronald Searle

DIRECTOR / RÉGISSEUR:

370–374 Bill Melendez

PRODUCTION / PRODUKTION:

370–374 Bill Melendez Prod. Ltd., London

370–374 *Dick Deadeye*. One of the best-liked artists and cartoonists is Ronald Searle, who designed the animation for this feature-length rock opera based on characters and music by Gilbert & Sullivan. A rascally Sorcerer steals the Ultimate Secret from the powers that be in early Victorian England. Dick Deadeye, the hero of the story, is commissioned to recapture the Ultimate Secret. His adventures take him in and around London, to the wharfs and aboard Her Majesty's Ship Pinafore. The chase of the pirate ship, the Sorcerer and the Ultimate Secret end on the island of Utopia, where beautiful maidens eventually reveal to Dick Deadeye and the other characters involved that the Ultimate Secret is really and only love. The drawings are carried out in a subtly ironic style, recalling a by-gone age with slight nostalgia as well as with detached sarcasm. A book on Searle's work in the film was published by Entercom Productions Ltd., London. A selection of Searle's original drawings for the film are reproduced on these pages.

370–374 *Dick Deadeye.* Ronald Searle, zweifellos einer der beliebtesten Künstler und Karikaturisten, hat die Zeichnungen für diese abendfüllende Rock-Oper geschaffen, deren Musik und Charaktere Opern von Gilbert & Sullivan entnommen wurden. Die Geschichte spielt in der frühen viktorianischen Zeit: ein ruchloser Zauberer stiehlt das Allerletzte Geheimnis. Dick Deadeye, der Held dieser Geschichte, wird mit der Rückeroberung des Geheimnisses beauftragt. Seine abenteuerliche Suche in und um London herum führt ihn schliesslich in den Hafen, wo er sich an Bord der Pinafore begibt. Die Verfolgungsjagd des Piratenschiffes, auf welchem sich der Zauberer mit seiner Beute befindet, endet auf der Insel Utopia, wo wunderschöne Mädchen den Verfolgern und Verfolgten enthüllen, dass das Geheimnis letztendlich die Liebe und nur die Liebe sei. Die in einem leicht ironischen Stil gehaltenen Zeichnungen beschwören eine vergangene Zeit, eine nostalgische Atmosphäre, die gleichzeitig aber einen verhaltenen Sarkasmus ausstrahlt. Ein Buch über Searles Zeichnungen zu diesem Film wurde von den Entercom Productions Ltd., London, herausgegeben. Eine Auswahl seiner Originalzeichnungen wird hier reproduziert.

370–374 *Dick Deadeye.* Ronald Searle, sans doute l'un des artistes et caricaturistes les plus appréciés, a créé les dessins pour ce long métrage – un opéra rock dont les caractères et la musique s'inspirent des opéras de Gilbert & Sullivan. L'histoire est située à l'ère victorienne et retrace l'enlèvement de l'Ultime Secret par une crapule de sorcier. Dick Deadeye, le héro du conte, est chargé de la récupération de l'Ultime Secret. Au cours de ses recherches hasardeuses entreprises à Londres même et aux alentours, il découvre une trace qu'il suit jusqu'au port, où il s'embarque enfin à bord du «Pinafore». La chasse du bateau pirate sur lequel se trouve le sorcier avec l'Ultime Secret prend fin sur l'île d'Utopia. Les ravissantes jeunes filles qui attendent Dick Deadeye et ceux qu'il a pourchassés leur dévoilent que l'Ultime Secret, c'est l'amour et rien que l'amour. Les dessins d'une subtilité exceptionnelle respirent une fine ironie tout en évoquant un temps passé, une atmosphère nostalgique mais aussi un sarcasme subliminal. Les Entercom Productions Ltd. à Londres ont publié un livre contenant les dessins pour ce film. Une sélection des dessins originaux est reproduite ici.

371

372

373

374

375

376

ARTIST / KÜNSTLER / RÉALISATION:

375, 376 Borislav Sajtinac
377, 378 Bob Godfrey
379, 380 Hal Fukushima
381, 382 Vaclav Mergl

DIRECTOR / RÉGISSEUR:

375, 376 Borislav Sajtinac
377, 378 Bob Godfrey
379, 380 Hal Fukushima
381, 382 Vaclav Mergl

PRODUCTION / PRODUKTION:

375, 376 Neoplanta Film, Novi-Sad/YUG
377, 378 Bob Godfrey Films Ltd., London
379, 380 Hal Fukushima, Tokyo
381, 382 Kratky Film, Prague

375, 376 *Iskusenje* (Temptation). Borislav Sajtinac is first and foremost a draughtsman. Another of his films, *Nevesta* (The Young Bride), was among the three winners of the Grand Prix at Annecy, 1971. Both films are about people who would like to influence fate.

377, 378 *Great*, Bob Godfrey's new film, won the 1976 American Academy Award. It is an animated musical on the life and work of the Franco-British engineer I. K. Brunel who was responsible for some extraordinary engineering feats at the height of Queen Victoria's reign. Yet, he discovered that the Victorian era was stubbornly resistant to progress.

379, 380 *The Door*. The Japanese artist Hal Fukushima paints a door in glowing colours, makes it a central object of his story and tells us, sometimes in almost abstract pictures, about its surroundings, its "inside" and "outside".

381, 382 *Laokoon*. Vaclav Mergl, who is primarily a painter, shows us a world of strange technical structures and monstrous carnivorous plants in which a spaceship from the earth alights. He uses a collage technique. The film received a Jury mention at Annecy in 1971.

379

380

377

378

375, 376 *Iskusenje* (Versuchung). Borislav Sajtinac ist vor allem Zeichner. Ein anderer von ihm gezeichneter Film, *Nevesta* (Die junge Braut), errang ex aequo den dreigeteilten Grossen Preis von Annecy 1971. Beide Filme erzählen von Menschen, die das Schicksal beeinflussen möchten.

377, 378 *Great* (Gross). Bob Godfreys neuer Film gewann den American Academy Award 1976. Es ist ein Musical über das Leben und Werk des francobritischen Ingenieurs I. K. Brunel, der während der Regierungszeit Königin Victorias einige aussergewöhnliche Projekte realisierte. Bald wurde ihm jedoch klar, dass sich die viktorianischen Machthaber stur jedem Fortschritt widersetzen.

379, 380 *The Door* (Die Tür). Der japanische Künstler Hal Fukushima malt in prächtigen Farben eine Tür, stellt diese in den Mittelpunkt seiner Erzählung und zeigt uns, manchmal in nahezu abstrakten Bildern, ihre Umgebung, ihr «Innen» und «Aussen».

381, 382 *Laokoon.* Vaclav Mergl, der eigentlich Maler ist, zeigt eine Welt aus sonderbaren technischen Gebilden und monströsen fleischfressenden Pflanzen, auf der ein von der Erde gestartetes Raumschiff landet. Als Technik verwendet er die Collage. Juryhinweis in Annecy, 1971.

375, 376 *Iskusenje* (Tentation). Borislav Sajtinac est avant tout dessinateur. Co-lauréat du Grand Prix d'Annecy 1971 avec son autre film *Nevesta* (La Jeune Mariée), il met en scène, dans ses deux films, des personnages désireux d'influencer le destin.

377, 378 *Great* (Grand). Ce nouveau film de Bob Godfrey a remporté l'American Academy Award en 1976. Il raconte l'histoire de l'ingénieur franco-britannique I. K. Brunel – sa vie et son œuvre. En tant qu'ingénieur responsable de quelques grands projets techniques, il a de maints démêlés avec les représentants d'une ère victorienne obstinément réfractaire au progrès.

379, 380 *The Door* (La Porte). L'artiste japonais Hal Fukushima peint une porte en couleurs éclatantes, en fait le centre de son récit et nous parle en termes parfois presque abstraits de son «intérieur» et «extérieur».

381, 382 *Laokoon.* Vaclav Mergl nous présente dans ce film d'étranges structures techniques et de monstrueuses plantes carnivores accueillant un vaisseau cosmique venu de Terre. Il a recours à la technique du collage. Le film a été mentionné du Jury d'Annecy en 1971.

381

382

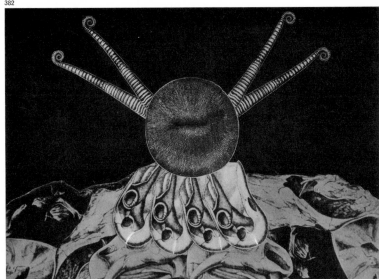

383–388 *People, People, People* is a 4-min. recapitulation of the settlement of North America between 17760 BC and 1976. The original wilderness magnetically attracts the various peoples, and the film suggests the tremendous energy of the migration movements that have finally produced today's dense population. Jazz background music underlines the quickening pace.
389–391 *The Legend of John Henry*, 10¾ minutes, in colour. John Henry is a black American folk hero who here pits his strength against the new-fangled steam-engine drill in Big Ben Tunnel, driving his steel bit into the rock with an iron hammer. A new technique used in this film is the superposition of the action on computer images of electric spark forms. It won the 2nd prize for films of over 3 minutes in Zagreb, 1974.
392–394 *Crocus.* Suzan Pitt Kraning's meticulous drawings evoke an almost Magritte-like atmosphere. An artist's family life: seeing to baby, going to bed, making love. 7 minutes, colour.
395–400 *A Poet's Life.* A piece of filmed literature from Japan, about a poet who is the hope of an oppressed working class.

383–388 *People, People, People,* ein historischer Abriss über die Bevölkerungsentwicklung Nordamerikas von 17760 v. C. bis heute, die soziale und technische Entwicklung, die Migration und die Entwicklung hin zur städtischen Gesellschaft. Jazz-Musik betont noch den beschleunigten Wandel – von den ersten mongolischen Einwanderern zur ersten Mondlandung.
389–391 *The Legend of John Henry*. John Henry, ein schwarzer amerikanischer Volksheld, protestiert gegen einen neuen, dampfbetriebenen Bohrer, indem er sein Bohreisen mit einem Hammer in den Fels treibt. Eine neue Methode der Bilderzeugung durch Umsetzung der Handlung mittels elektrischer Lichtimpulse in Computerbilder. 2. Preis für Filme über 3 Min., Zagreb 1974.
392–394 *Crocus.* Suzan Pitt Kranings Zeichnungen beschwören eine magrittehafte Atmosphäre. Das Leben einer Künstlerfamilie: man besorgt das Kind, man geht zu Bett, man liebt sich.
395–400 *A Poet's Life.* Ein Stück verfilmter Literatur aus Japan über die Bewusstseinsentwicklung eines Dichters, der die Hoffnung der unterdrückten Arbeiterklasse wird.

383–388 *People, People, People,* une récapitulation serrée du peuplement de l'Amérique du Nord de 17760 av. J.-C. jusqu'à 1976, du développement social et technique, des migrations et de l'évolution successive vers une société urbaine. Le fond musical – le jazz – accentue l'évolution accélérée, des premières immigrations mongoles jusqu'au premier atterrissage sur la lune.
389–391 *The Legend of John Henry*. John Henry est un héro populaire des Noirs d'Amérique que l'on voit mesurer sa force à celle d'un nouvel outil de forage à vapeur. Une technique nouvelle de création d'images est utilisée: on superpose l'action sur des images électroniques d'étincelles électriques.
392–394 *Crocus.* Les dessins de Suzan P. Kraning évoquent une atmosphère qui rappelle Magritte. Ils retracent la vie d'un artiste: dire bonne nuit au bébé, aller au lit, faire l'amour.
395–400 *Une vie de Poète.* Un morceau de littérature filmé du Japon. On nous y raconte la prise de conscience et l'évolution d'un poète en qui se concentrent les espoirs de la classe ouvrière.

389–391

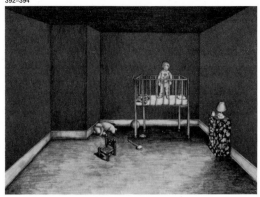

ARTIST / KÜNSTLER / RÉALISATION:

383–388 Faith & John Hubley
389–391 Gary Luno/Sam Weis
392–394 Suzan Pitt Kraning
395–400 Kihachiro Kawamoto

DIRECTOR / RÉGISSEUR:

383–388 John Hubley
389–391 Sam Weis
392–394 Suzan Pitt Kraning
395–400 Kihachiro Kawamoto

PRODUCTION / PRODUKTION:

383–388 The Hubley Studio, Inc., New York
389–391 Nick Bosustow & David Adams, Santa Monica, Ca.
392–394 Suzan Pitt Kraning
395–400 The Kawamoto Production, Tokyo

ARTIST / KÜNSTLER / RÉALISATION:

401–409 Joseph Barbera/William Hanna
410, 411 George Dunning
412–423 Paul Brühwiler
424 Pavao Stalter

DIRECTOR / RÉGISSEUR:

401–409 Charles A. Nichols/Iwao Takamoto
410, 411 George Dunning
412–423 Paul Brühwiler
424 Pavao Stalter

PRODUCTION / PRODUKTION:

401–409 Hanna-Barbera-Sagittarius Production
         for Paramount, New York
410, 411 T.V. Cartoons Ltd., London
412–423 Paul Brühwiler, Zürich
424 Zagreb Film, Zagreb

401–409

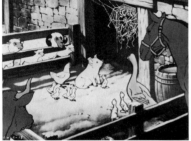

410

411

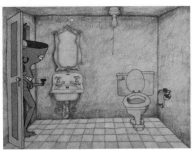

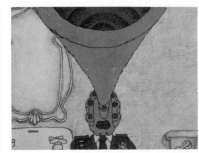

424

401–409 *Charlotte's Web*. A full-length 35-mm entertainment film in colour, based on E. B. White's children's classic. Little piglet Wilbur would have been slaughtered hat not Little Fern got him sold to a neighbouring farm, where he meets a stuttering goose, Templeton the rat, but above all Charlotte the spider who weaves words into her webs.
410, 411 *The Maggot* by George Dunning, a powerful warning against drug-pushing, was awarded the best prize for information at Annecy, 1973.
412–423 *The Party*. Six-minute 16-mm colour film, 1st prize winner at Soleure, 1974.
424 *The Horse* becomes man, a technique borrowed from Dunning's prototype *The Ladder*.

401–409 *Charlotte's Web*. Ein abendfüllender Farbfilm, der auf E. B. Whites klassischem Kinderbuch beruht. Das Schweinchen Wilbur wäre geschlachtet worden, hätte es Little Fern nicht auf einen Nachbarhof verkauft. Dort machte es Bekanntschaft mit der stotternden Gans, mit der Ratte Templeton, vor allem aber mit Charlotte, der Spinne, die Worte in ihr Netz webt.
410, 411 *The Maggot* von George Dunning ist ein eindrücklicher Aufruf gegen den illegalen Drogenhandel. Er gewann 1973 in Annecy den Preis für den besten Informationsfilm.
412–423 *The Party* gewann an den Solothurner Filmtagen den ersten Preis. 6-Minuten-Farbfilm.
424 *The Horse*. Das Pferd wird zum Mann. Die Technik entspricht Dunnings Prototyp *Die Leiter*.

401–409 *Charlotte's Web* (La Toile d'araignée), un long métrage de 35 mm en couleurs, fondé sur le conte pour enfants de E. B. White. Wilbur, le porcelet, aurait été abattu si Little Fern ne l'avait pas vendu à un paysan voisin. Là il rencontre une oie bredouillante, Templeton, le rat, mais avant tout Charlotte, l'araignée, qui tisse des mots dans sa toile.
410, 411 *The Maggot*, réalisé par George Dunning. Il lance un cri d'alarme contre le trafic des stupéfiants. A gagné le prix pour le meilleur film d'information à Annecy en 1973.
412–423 Séquence de *The Party* (La Fête). 1er Prix des Journées du Cinéma Suisse, Soleure 1974.
424 *The Horse*. Le Cheval devient homme. Technique empruntée au prototype de Dunning, *L'Echelle*.

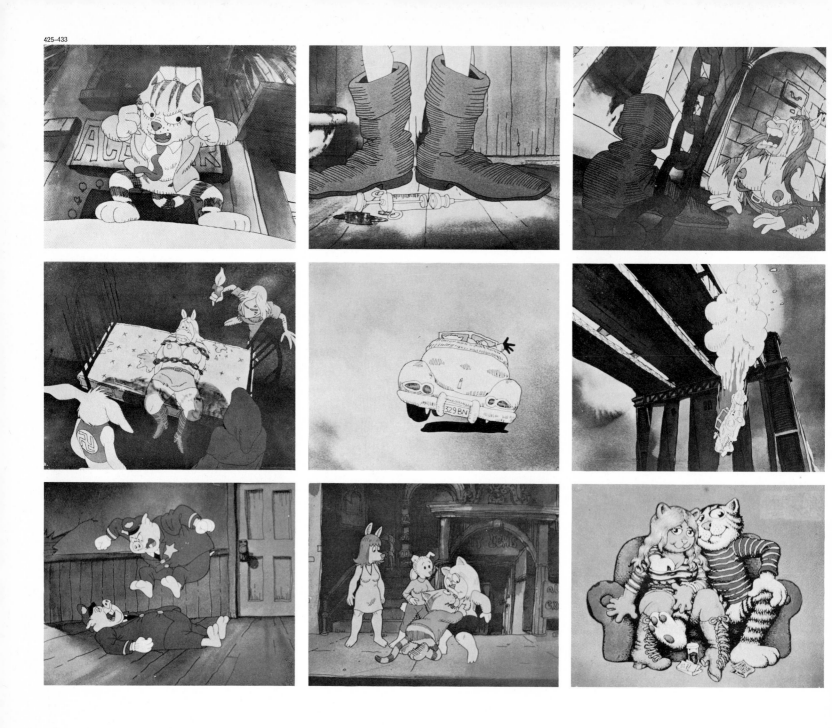

425–434 *Fritz the Cat.* This highly successful full-feature film is based on the ferocious designs of comic-strip artist and caricaturist Robert Crumb. It is a savage satire of present-day American society, with its greed, its drug addiction, its bigotry and its never-to-be-stilled sex hunger. Humans are portrayed as animals, thus underlining the bestiality of life. Fritz, at first the conformist son of a bourgeois family, becomes the world's dirtiest and most depraved cat who falls in with all the insidious ideas and actions of the American subculture of the sixties. He is conscious of his bourgeois background, and his encounters with the various groups, the Blacks and the Whites, the Jews and the Catholics, the revolutionaries and the Fascists, the police "pigs" (Fig. 431) are distorted into mere phrases and clichés. In his sometimes Pacifist, sometimes revolutionary declarations, Fritz never comes to grips with reality; he remains a pseudo-hippie and a pseudo-rebel. He is always on top of the latest trend or fashion, an apparent anarchist and yet nothing but an opportunist. Only sex interests him, sex in all its aspects, sex en masse.

425–434 *Fritz the Cat* ist ein erfolgreicher, abendfüllender Unterhaltungsfilm. Robert Crumb, bekannt als Karikaturist und Comics-Künstler, hat die Zeichnungen für diese brutale Satire über die amerikanische Gesellschaft geschaffen, die ihre Habgier, ihre Drogenprobleme, ihren Fanatismus und nicht zu stillenden Sexhunger anprangert. Tiere übernehmen die Rolle der menschlichen Darsteller, um die Bestialität noch hervorzuheben. Fritz, Konformist bourgeoiser Abstammung, wird zur schmutzigsten und pervertiertesten Katze der Welt, die in der amerikanischen Unterwelt der 60er Jahre ihr Unwesen treibt. Sein bourgeoises Bewusstsein führt in all seinen Begegnungen, mit Weissen und Schwarzen, Juden und Katholiken, Revolutionären und Faschisten, mit den Polizeischweinen, zur clichéhaften Phrasendrescherei. Seine teils faschistischen, teils revolutionären Erklärungen entsprechen in keiner Weise seinem eigenen Ich, er ist und bleibt ein Pseudo-Hippie, ein Pseudo-Revoluzzer. Wie immer auch der Trend, Fritz macht mit – ein scheinbarer Anarchist, in Wirklichkeit ein schmutziger Opportunist. Nur Sex interessiert ihn, in all seinen Aspekten.

425–434 *Fritz the Cat*, un long métrage d'un énorme succès. Robert Crumb, créateur de bandes dessinées et caricaturiste, a réalisé les dessins pour cette satire brutale de la société américaine d'aujourd'hui, dénonçant sa cupidité, ses problèmes de la drogue, son fanatisme et sa lascivité débordante. Les êtres humains ont adopté des traits de bête ce qui souligne encore davantage la bestialité de l'homme. Fritz, le fils conformiste d'une famille bourgeoise, se fait petit à petit le chat le plus répugnant et dépravé du monde entier, s'adonnant à toutes les idées et actions sournoises des bas-fonds américains des années 60. Il est bien conscient qu'il est d'extraction bourgeoise et les rencontres qu'il a avec les divers groupes de la société – les Blancs et les Noirs, les Juïfs et les Catholiques, les révolutionnaires et les fascistes, avec les cochons policiers – elles se réduisent à des phrases vides de sens. Ses déclarations, parfois pacifistes, parfois révolutionnaires, sont loin de refléter ses vraies idées – il reste un pseudo-hippie et un pseudo-révolutionnaire. Quelle que soit la tendance en vogue, Fritz joue toujours un rôle prédominant – un anarchiste à ce qu'il semble, mais en vérité un opportuniste pur et simple. Ce n'est que le sexe qui l'intéresse, les divers aspects du sexe, bref, le sexe en masse.

ARTIST / KÜNSTLER / RÉALISATION:
425–434 Robert Crumb

DIRECTOR / RÉGISSEUR:
425–434 Ralph Bakshi

PRODUCTION / PRODUKTION:
425–434 Steve Krantz Productions, San Francisco

434

441

ARTIST / KÜNSTLER / RÉALISATION:

435–440 Gary Jackson
441 Giulio Gianini/Emanuele Luzzati
442–444 Giuseppe Laganà
445–450 Philippe Fausten

DIRECTOR / RÉGISSEUR:

435–440 Gary Jackson
441 Giulio Gianini
442–444 Giuseppe Laganà
445–450 Philippe Fausten

PRODUCTION / PRODUKTION:

435–440 Gary Jackson/Datafilm, Sydney
441 Giulio Gianini/Emanuele Luzzati, Rome
442–444 Corona Cinematografica S.r.l., Rome
445–450 Phar 3, Reims/FRA

435–440 *Mother's Little Helper.* A sequence from an 8-minute film in colour about an Australian tea lady and her trials and tribulations. She works in an exaggerated, capitalistic environment, and her little dog accompanies her on her tea rounds.
441 *Ali Baba.* Gianini and Luzzati have produced a number of good films together. Gianini is a film man, Luzzati an artist specializing in illustration, ceramics and décors. Their films are all rich in colour with something of the glow of stained glass. Movement is reduced to a minimum.
442–444 *L'Om salbadg* (The Wild Man), by Giuseppe Laganà, writer of children's books, makes skilful use of stylistic elements borrowed from Art Déco. A story of a bogey-man who steals a child, the film was made with movable, cut-out figures.
445–450 *Tyranny,*a film about a man who finds himself confronted with tyranny. It consists wholly of pen drawings done frame by frame. Six months of unbroken work was needed to complete it. Jury's Special Prize in Zagreb, 1974.

435–440 *Mother's Little Helper* (Mutters kleiner Gehilfe). Sequenz aus einem 8-Minuten-Farbfilm über eine australische Kantinenfrau und die Belästigungen, die sie in ihrer täglichen Arbeit in einer übertrieben kapitalistischen Gesellschaft erfährt. Sie hat nur ihren kleinen Hund als treuen Gefährten.
441 *Ali Baba.* Den beiden Realisatoren Gianini und Luzzati verdanken wir eine Reihe guter Filme. Ersterer kommt vom Film, letzterer von der Kunst. Die leuchtenden Farben erinnern an buntes Glas. Die Bewegungen sind auf ein Minimum beschränkt.
442–444 *L'Om salbadg* (Der wilde Mann). Der Kinderbuchautor Laganà verwendet geschickt Art-Déco-Elemente für seine Geschichte vom wilden Mann, der ein Kind stiehlt. Der 11minutige Film besteht aus sich bewegenden, ausgeschnittenen Figuren.
445–450 *Tyrannie,* ein Schwarzweissfilm über einen einfachen Mann, der tyrannisiert wird. Der Film wurde Bild für Bild mit der Feder gezeichnet; seine Herstellung erforderte sechs Monate. Er erhielt den Jury-Sonderpreis in Zagreb 1974.

435–440 *Mother's Little Helper* (Le Petit Chien à sa Mémère). C'est la triste histoire d'une cantinière australienne cruellement éprouvée par un capitalisme poursuit à outrance. Elle n'a que son petit chien qui l'accompagne jour après jour.
441 *Ali Baba.* On doit déjà à Gianini et à Luzzati une série de films de qualité. Gianini est cinéaste, Luzzati illustrateur, céramiste et décorateur. Leurs films se caractérisent par un minimum de mouvement et une abondance de couleurs qui rappellent parfois le chatoiement des vitraux d'églises.
442–444 *L'Om salbadg* (L'Homme Sauvage). L'auteur de livres d'enfants, Laganà, utilise adroitement des éléments d'art déco pour raconter l'histoire de l'homme sauvage qui kidnappe un enfant. Il emploie des personnages animés en papier découpé.
445–450 *Tyrannie,* 8 mn. ¼, est l'histoire d'un homme confronté à la tyrannie. Il s'agit de dessins à la plume assemblés image par image au cours d'un travail qui a duré six mois. Ce film a remporté le prix spécial du jury à Zagreb en 1974.

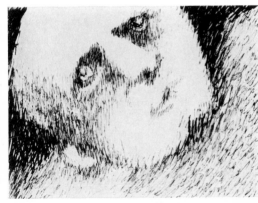

109

Max Massimino-Garnièr

If we are to believe the statement of that master of animation Norman McLaren to the effect that animation is the art of drawn movement, not of drawings that move, yet to agree at the same time with Marshall McLuhan that television is a medium demanding a high degree of participation that cannot be treated merely as a background (the same is true of cartoons, which put only a very limited amount of information at the disposal of the spectator), it may appear surprising that industrial animation for television (as in serials) contradicts all this by providing fare that is poor in movement yet rich in verbal information. Yet in effect the partial or planned animation of the United States has initiated a socio-cultural process by which the public is encouraged to participate in the non-visual or audio-tactile world of the spoken language. In Europe, by contrast, animation, even in the television field, has always paid more attention to the invention of moving characters, to the creation of visual moods, so that we have the inverse phenomenon: Europe, by tradition audio-tactile, is increasing its powers of visual appreciation through television.

In view of the interdependence of these two contrary situations, we can foresee that animation, thanks to its intrinsic capacity for synthesis (the Rumanian animator Ion Popescu said in 1966 that animation enters the head of the spectator almost without being analysed), will become more and more the most suitable form of expression for the electronic medium (TV as an aphorism and almost an extension of the sense of touch), especially if we consider that half a minute of television is equal to three minutes of theatre.

After the "implosion" caused by the electronic media, it is essential to find new contents which will restore the alphabetic and visual equilibrium of the spectator. The animated film can make a large contribution in television to the identification and formulation of these new contents, for it has already proved its maturity as a means of expression. In this way it may help to assuage the complaint of the President of the Association Internationale du Film d'Animation (ASIFA), John Halas, who in the Animation Manifesto at the end of 1975 noted, not without bitterness, that on a global scale "the animated film is still waiting for better recognition of its own contribution by the television industry, which still looks upon animation as an adolescent medium".

Der Meister des Zeichentrickfilms, Norman McLaren, definiert den Animationsfilm als Kunst der gezeichneten Bewegung und nicht als Kunst der bewegten Zeichnung. Marshall McLuhan sieht im Fernsehen ein Medium, das ein hohes Mass an Teilnahme fordert, also nicht als reine Kulisse verwendet werden kann, eine Feststellung, die auch auf Cartoons zutrifft, die dem Zuschauer nur beschränkte Information liefern. Der industriell hergestellte Trickfilm für das Fernsehen (besonders für Serien) widerspricht nun den Feststellungen beider Autoren, da er eher bewegungsarm aber mit verbaler Information reich befrachtet ist. Tatsächlich hat der Animationsfilm in Nordamerika einen soziokulturellen Prozess ausgelöst, wodurch das Publikum vermehrt gezwungen wird, sich mit dem nicht-visuellen, auditiven Charakter der gesprochenen Sprache abzugeben. Im Gegensatz dazu hat sich das Interesse beim europäischen Animationsfilm, sogar im Fernsehen, von Anfang an mehr auf die Erfindung von bewegten Figuren und die Schaffung visueller Stimmungen konzentriert, so dass wir hier das umgekehrte Phänomen beobachten können: das traditionell eher auditive Europa tendiert zu einer Aufwertung der visuellen Aspekte.

Angesichts der Interdependenz dieser konträren Situationen können wir bereits heute voraussehen, dass sich der Animationsfilm dank seiner Fähigkeit zur Synthese (der rumänische Trickfilmer Ion Popescu sagte 1966, dass der Trickfilm vom Zuschauer beinahe ohne Analyse aufgenommen wird) mehr und mehr als die geeignetste Form für das elektronische Medium herauskristallisiert, besonders wenn man bedenkt, dass einer halben Minute Fernsehen 3 Minuten Theater entsprechen.

Nach der von den elektronischen Medien bewirkten Implosion ist es heute dringend notwendig, neue Inhalte zu finden, um das alphabetisch-visuelle Gleichgewicht des Zuschauers wiederherzustellen. Der Zeichentrickfilm kann im Fernsehen einen grossen Beitrag zur Identifizierung und Formulierung dieser neuen Inhalte leisten, denn als Ausdrucksmittel hat er seine Reife bereits bewiesen. Dies würde auch die heutige Stellung des Animationsfilms aufwerten, der, wie John Halas, Präsident der ASIFA, im Ende 1975 erschienenen «Animation Manifesto» nicht ohne Bitterkeit bemerkt, im internationalen Rahmen «immer noch auf Anerkennung seines Beitrags durch die Fernsehindustrie wartet, die den Animationsfilm auch heute noch als ein im Reifeprozess steckendes Medium betrachtet».

Le maître de l'animation qu'est Norman McLaren définit l'animation comme étant l'art du mouvement dessiné, et non pas l'art des dessins animés. Par ailleurs, Marshall McLuhan affirme que la télévision est un média requérant une forte participation, qui ne peut être reléguée au rang d'un épiphénomène, constatation qui vaut également pour les cartoons, qui ne mettent qu'un volume d'informations très restreint à la disposition du spectateur. Or, l'animation au service de la TV (particulièrement en séries) dément l'un et l'autre de ces auteurs en proposant au téléspectateur des messages pauvres en mouvement, mais riches en informations verbales. En fait, l'animation partielle ou systématique à la télévision nord-américaine a mis en route un processus socioculturel encourageant le public à participer aux aspects non visuels, auditifs et tactiles du langage parlé. En Europe, par contre, l'animation, même à la TV, a toujours mis l'accent sur l'invention de personnages animés et d'ambiances visuelles déterminées, ce qui crée le phénomène inverse: les Européens traditionnellement audio-tactiles voient se développer, grâce à la télévision, leur pouvoir d'appréciation visuelle.

Etant donné l'interdépendance de fait de ces deux approches contraires, on peut prévoir que la capacité de synthèse propre à l'animation — l'animateur roumain Ion Popescu ne disait-il pas en 1966 qu'elle s'introduit dans le cerveau du téléspectateur pratiquement sans donner lieu à une analyse? — la recommandera dans une mesure croissante comme forme d'expression convenant le mieux au média électronique de la TV, ce véhicule privilégié du toucher, qui prolonge les facultés tactiles de l'homme, surtout si l'on considère qu'une demi-minute télévisée équivaut à trois minutes de jeu théâtral.

L'effet implosif de l'avènement de la télévision requiert d'urgence la recherche de contenus nouveaux propres à restituer au spectateur son équilibre alphabétique et visuel. Or, l'animation télévisée peut apporter une contribution importante à l'identification et à la mise en forme de ces nouveaux contenus, étant donné le degré de maturité qu'elle a atteint. Ce serait l'occasion de donner un tour positif à une situation que John Halas, président de l'ASIFA, déplorait dans le Manifeste de l'Animation publié fin 1975 en ces termes: en général, «le film d'animation attend encore d'être reconnu à sa juste valeur contributive par l'industrie de la télévision, dont les représentants ont une fâcheuse tendance à la considérer comme un média encore en pleine adolescence».

Television Films
Fernsehfilme
L'Animation télévisée

451–460 *How to Make Your Child Schizophrenic.* Sequence and colour drawing from a three-minute animated cartoon forming part of a two-hour film broadcast by TV Globo, Rio. The cartoon illustrates a modern mother's way of bringing up her son, with a background commentary by a psychiatrist. Of Polish/Russian/Spanish stock, the artist grew up in Australia and Brazil, where she is now a household word. Her style has all the flamboyance of a carnival in Rio, but her picture of humanity is pure satire. Her satire, however, is never lethal: she wants to make people laugh, and mingles cynicism with sheer mischievousness.

451–460 *Wie erziehe ich mein Kind zur Schizophrenie.* Sequenz und Farbzeichnung eines 3-Minuten-Zeichentrickfilms als Teil eines zweistündigen Films, ausgestrahlt von der TV Globo, Rio. Der Trickfilm zeigt die total verfehlten Erziehungsmethoden einer Mutter, mit einem Begleitkommentar eines Psychiaters. Die Künstlerin, von polnisch-russisch-spanischer Abstammung, wuchs in Australien und Brasilien auf. Ihr Stil widerspiegelt die ganze Farbenpracht eines Karnevals in Rio, ihr Bild der Menschheit hingegen ist reine Satire. Das Ergebnis ist jedoch nie zynisch, denn sie will vor allem die Leute zum Lachen bringen.

451–460 *Comment faire de votre enfant un schizophrène.* Séquence et illustration couleur d'un dessin animé de 3 mn faisant partie d'une émission filmée de 2 h de la TV Globo à Rio. Le dessin animé illustre les méthodes d'éducation moderne, la voix d'un psychiatre commentant les scènes familiales. D'origine polonaise-russe-espagnole, l'artiste a passé sa jeunesse en Australie et au Brésil. Son style a tout le dynamisme, toute l'exubérance du carnaval de Rio, mais sa vision de l'humanité est purement satirique. Toutefois, sans être cynique, car elle veut faire rire les gens, sa malice est alliée à une gaieté de cœur.

ARTIST / KÜNSTLER / RÉALISATION:
451–460 Marguerita Bornstein

DIRECTOR / RÉGISSEUR:
451–460 Marguerita Bornstein

PRODUCTION / PRODUKTION:
451–460 TV Globo, Rio de Janeiro

460

ARTIST / KÜNSTLER / RÉALISATION:

461—464 Maurice Sendak

DIRECTOR / RÉGISSEUR:

461—464 Maurice Sendak

PRODUCTION / PRODUKTION:

461—464 Sheriss Productions, New York for CBS,
New York/Weston Woods Studios

462

463

461

461—464 *Really Rosie.* Maurice Sendak, master of children's book illustration, is responsible for the scenario, lyrics and key drawings of this CBS TV Colour Special of 30 minutes' duration, with music by Carole King. Rosie (Fig. 461) is the star of the show and quite a personality for a ten-year-old. She has decided to make a film about her life, not forgetting to feature her friends, the Nutshell Kids. Kathy, a shy and clumsy little girl, the bookish Johnny, Alligator (who really is an alligator) and even don't-care Pierre all love her and do as she directs. They introduce themselves with songs all except one who happens to be missing, viz. the fat, cheerful little boy Chicken Soup, who is devoted to Rosie and is always hungry. When it begins to rain outside, they all go down to the cellar, which provides the perfect dramatic setting for Rosie's performance as "the star from afar". In spite of some alarming intermezzos—as in the story of Pierre who was eaten by a lion because he didn't care whether he was or not, but was later shaken out of the animal again by his parents—the day ends happily, even Chicken Soup turning up and consoling them all with a month-by-month story about Chicken Soup and Rice. Finally they all go home for the night. Maurice Sendak's characters have a knack of winning the affection of viewers.

464

461—464 *Really Rosie*. Maurice Sendak, ein Meister der Kinderbuchillustration, schuf das Drehbuch, die Texte und Vorlagen für diesen 30minutigen Farbfilm, der vom CBS-Spezialprogramm ausgestrahlt wurde. Die Musik komponierte Carole King. Rosi (Abb. 461), der Star dieser Show, ist für ihre 10 Jahre bereits eine Persönlichkeit. Sie entschliesst sich, zusammen mit ihren Freunden einen Film über ihr Leben zu drehen. Kati, das scheue und unbeholfene kleine Mädchen, Hans, der Bücherwurm, Alligator und sogar der gleichgültige Klaus, sie alle bewundern Rosi und spielen mit. Alle stellen sich mit einem Lied vor, alle ausser dem fröhlichen, etwas dicklichen und immer hungrigen kleinen Jungen Hühnersuppe, der Rosi sehr zugetan ist. Wie es zu regnen beginnt, begeben sich alle in den Keller, der ein perfektes Dekor bildet für Rosis Vorstellung als «der Star, der von weit her kommt». Ausser einigen aufregenden Zwischenfällen – Klaus wird von einem Löwen gefressen, weil es ihm völlig gleichgültig ist, was mit ihm geschieht, wird später aber von seinen Eltern wieder aus dem Löwenmagen geschüttelt – nimmt der Tag ein glückliches Ende. Sogar Hühnersuppe taucht wieder auf und tröstet alle mit einer Geschichte über Hühnersuppe und Reis. Nach der Vorstellung gehen alle zufrieden nach Hause.

461—464 *Really Rosie*. Maurice Sendak, le chef de fil des illustrateurs de livres d'enfant, est responsable du scénario, des textes ainsi que des illustrations clé de ce film couleur émis par CBS Télévision dans le cadre d'un programme spécial. La musique a été composée par Carole King. Rosie (fig. 461), la vedette de ce show, est une jeune fille de dix ans déjà assez résolue. Elle décide de tourner un film sur sa vie avec la participation de tous ses amis: Kathy, la petite fille timide et maladroite, Johnny, le bouquineur, Alligator et même Pierre, l'impassible. Ils adorent Rosie et jouent le rôle qu'elle leur attribue avec enthousiasme. Ils se présentent tous par une chanson, sauf Crème de volaille, le gros gamin gai qui a toujours faim. Quand il commence à pleuvoir, le spectacle est transféré à la cave – un cadre qui crée la parfaite atmosphère dramatique pour l'entrée en scène de Rosie, «la vedette qui vient de loin». Sauf quelques incidents excitants – dû à son indifférence, Pierre est avalé par un lion, mais lorsqu'on secoue l'animal il le rend – le spectacle est mené à bonne fin: Crème de volaille réapparaît à la fin de la journée et afin de reconforter ses amis il leur raconte l'histoire de Crème de volaille au Riz. A la tombée de la nuit, les protagonistes rentrent tout contents de leur film.

ARTIST / KÜNSTLER / RÉALISATION:

465–472 Maurice Sendak

DIRECTOR / RÉGISSEUR:

465–472 Maurice Sendak

PRODUCTION / PRODUKTION:

465–472 Sheriss Productions, New York for CBS,
New York/Weston Woods Studios

465–472 *Really Rosie* (see preceding spread). Further frames from this delightful television musical, which is entertainment not only for the children but for the whole family. Moral values are conveyed with charm and imagination, and the drawings have the quality that has made Sendak famous. Television with its colour, immediacy and mass audience is no doubt the ideal medium for this kind of show.

A book version of this film has been published by Harper & Row, New York, under the same title, and a German version is now in preparation and will be published by Diogenes, Zurich, in the course of 1976.

465–472

465–472 *Really Rosie* (s. vorangehende Doppelseite). Weitere Bilder aus diesem reizenden Fernsehmusical, welches nicht nur für Kinder, sondern auch zur Unterhaltung der ganzen Familie gedacht ist. Die Zeichnungen, wie auch die auf subtile Art eingeflochtenen moralischen Aspekte zeugen einmal mehr von Sendaks aussergewöhnlichem Können. Dank seiner Unmittelbarkeit und Verbreitung ist das Fernsehen hier das ideale Medium.

Zeichnungen und Texte zu diesem Film sind bei Harper & Row in New York unter dem selben Titel in Buchform erschienen. Eine deutsche Version ist in Vorbereitung und wird im Laufe des Jahres 1976 im Diogenes Verlag in Zürich herauskommen.

465–472 *Really Rosie* (v. page précédente). Autres images de la ravissante comédie musicale, d'un film TV savoureux pour le divertissement des enfants aussi bien que de toute la famille. Les aspects moraux que Sendak fait ressortir avec une subtilité exceptionnelle ainsi que ses dessins témoignent une fois de plus de sa virtuosité. La TV couleur, grâce à sa grande portée et son immédiateté, est sans doute le médium idéal.

Les dessins et textes de ce film ont paru sous forme de livre chez Harper & Row à New York. Une version allemande est en préparation et paraîtra au cours de l'année 1976 chez les Editions Diogenes à Zurich.

473–484

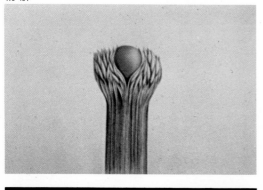 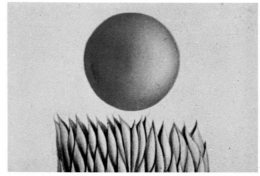 

DIRECTOR / RÉGISSEUR:

473–484 Ken Brown
485–487 Hilary Hayton/Graham McCallum
488–493 Pavel Prochazka

PRODUCTION / PRODUKTION:

473–487 Colin Cheeseman/BBC Television, London
488–493 M. Schliesser und P-Trick/Südwestfunk,
          Baden-Baden

485–487

473–484 *The Gardener.* A sequence from a BBC fifteen-minute pilot film for a proposed animated drama series.
485–487 *Crystal Tipps and Alistair,* a series of 50 five-minute animated films in colour shown on BBC 1, intended for a child audience.
488–493 *Wer hat Angst vorm kleinen Mann?* (Who's Afraid of the Little Man?). A little boy has no chance of measuring up to his elders, who all laugh at him. Only his grandfather understands his problems and encourages him to look out for himself.

473–484 *The Gardener* (Der Gärtner). Sequenz aus einem 15minutigen Probefilm der BBC für eine geplante Trickfilmserie.
485–487 *Crystal Tipps and Alistair,* aus einer Serie von fünfzig fünfminutigen Farbtrickfilmen, die BBC 1 in ihrem Kinderprogramm ausstrahlte.
488–493 *Wer hat Angst vorm kleinen Mann?* Ein kleiner Junge hat keine Chance, sich mit den Älteren zu messen, jeder macht sich lustig über ihn. Nur sein Grossvater hat Verständnis für seine Probleme und ermutigt ihn, sich selber zu helfen.

473–484 *The Gardener* (Le Jardinier). Séquence d'un film pilote de 15 mn pour une série de films d'animation projetée par BBC.
485–487 *Crystal Tipps and Alistair,* une série de cinquante films d'animation en couleur, d'une durée de 5 mn, émis par la BBC 1 dans le cadre d'un programme pour enfants.
488–493 *Wer hat Angst vorm kleinen Mann?* (Qui a peur du petit bonhomme?). Un gamin n'a aucune chance de se mesurer avec les aînés qui se moquent de lui. Ce n'est que son grand-père qui le comprend et qui l'encourage à se débrouiller.

488–493

494

ARTIST / KÜNSTLER / RÉALISATION:

494–496 John Worsley
497, 498 Christine Chagnoux

DIRECTOR / RÉGISSEUR:

494–496 John Worsley
497, 498 Henri Gruel

PRODUCTION / PRODUKTION:

494–496 Paul Honeyman/Anglia Television, Norwich/GBR
497, 498 Editions Dargaud/ORTF, Paris

494 *A Christmas Carol,* a TV Special based on Charles Dickens's well-known story. With his superb descriptive style Dickens brought to life the poverty, the cruelty and sometimes the happiness of the London he knew so well. This was a natural choice for the Anglia production team. The one-hour programme was made in 1970 and required 150 paintings from John Worsley. It was acclaimed by the critics when shown throughout England at Christmas 1970.

495, 496 *The Wind in the Willows.* Kenneth Graham's classic story of Toad and Badger, Ratty and Mole was Anglia's first children's serial. It consists of 18 quarter-hour episodes and required a total of 550 paintings which were completed by John Worsley in six months. One picture may be held on the screen for anything from a few seconds to a minute.

497, 498 *Le petit Potam,* a series on French TV suggested by Christine Chagnoux's delightful children's books. Her drawings are naive in inspiration, but her naiveté lies only in the dew-fresh imagination with which she describes the magic world of childhood.

495

496

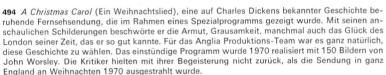

494 *A Christmas Carol* (Ein Weihnachtslied), eine auf Charles Dickens bekannter Geschichte beruhende Fernsehsendung, die im Rahmen eines Spezialprogramms gezeigt wurde. Mit seinen anschaulichen Schilderungen beschwörte er die Armut, Grausamkeit, manchmal auch das Glück des London seiner Zeit, das er so gut kannte. Für das Anglia Produktions-Team war es ganz natürlich, diese Geschichte zu wählen. Das einstündige Programm wurde 1970 realisiert mit 150 Bildern von John Worsley. Die Kritiker hielten mit ihrer Begeisterung nicht zurück, als die Sendung in ganz England an Weihnachten 1970 ausgestrahlt wurde.

495, 496 *The Wind in the Willows* (Der Wind in den Weiden). Kenneth Grahams Geschichte von Toad und Badger, Ratty und Mole war die erste Kinderserie des Anglia Studios. Sie umfasste achtzehn 15minutige Episoden, wozu 550 Bilder von John Worsley nötig waren, die er im Laufe von sechs Monaten schuf. Ein Bild kann beliebig lange auf dem Bildschirm gehalten werden.

497, 498 *Le petit Potam*, eine Serie des französischen Fernsehens, inspiriert von den reizenden Kinderbüchern Christine Chagnoux. Die subtilen Zeichnungen mögen auf naiven Vorstellungen beruhen, ihr Reiz besteht jedoch in der poetischen Umdichtung der Welt, die sie beschreiben, sowie in der Phantasie, mit der die Autorin die magische Welt des Kindes heraufbeschwört.

494 *A Christmas Carol* (Le Chant de Noël). Ce conte, l'un des plus connus de Charles Dickens, fut émis dans le cadre d'un programme spécial. Le style descriptif propre à Dickens évoque le Londres d'antan, la misère, la cruauté, parfois le bonheur qu'il a connu si bien. C'était bien évident que le choix des cinéastes du Studio Anglia se portait sur ce conte. John Worsley a créé les 150 peintures qu'il fallait pour la réalisation de ce film de 60 mn. Lors de sa présentation en Grande-Bretagne à Noël 1970 il n'y avait guère de critiques qui n'en parlaient pas avec enthousiasme.

495, 496 *The Wind in the Willows*. Dans sa première série pour enfants, Anglia a présenté l'histoire de Toad et Badger, Ratty et Mole par Kenneth Graham. Cette série en 18 épisodes de 15 mn chacune est composée de 550 peintures créées au cours de six mois par John Worsley. La durée de projection d'une image peut varier de quelques secondes jusqu'à une minute.

497, 498 *Le petit Potam*, une série réalisée par la Télévision Française. Elle s'inspire des ravissants livres d'enfant de Christine Chagnoux. Un art subtil du dessin issu d'une représentation naïve du monde. Pourtant, elle est loin de là – cette naïveté sert à la récréation poétique du monde que Christine Chagnoux s'attache à décrire dans l'imagination qu'elle a su préserver pour évoquer en magicienne le monde de l'enfant.

497

498

499

499 *Being Green*, a drawing for the famous American television series for children, *Sesame Street*. Etienne Delessert, well-known illustrator of children's books, is also an acknowledged capacity in other children's entertainment branches, such as television. He takes great pride in being associated with CBS in *Sesame Street*.

500–503 *Watch With Mother* is an old-established BBC children's programme in which various artists have been able to present their talent. The stills are from the following features: *Barnaby, The Herbs, The Wombles,* and *The Magic Roundabout*, this last being a series originally made in France and translated into English.

504–507 *Sesame Street*. Several frames from films designed by Etienne Delessert as part of the popular CBS children's programme.

499 *Being Green*, eine Zeichnung für die berühmte amerikanische Kinder-Fernsehserie *Sesamstrasse*. Etienne Delessert ist nicht nur ein bekannter Illustrator von Kinderbüchern, sondern auch ein international anerkannter Experte in anderen Medien für die Unterhaltung von Kindern, z.B. im Fernsehen. Er wirkt mit Stolz in der *Sesamstrasse* der CBS mit.

500–503 *Watch With Mother* ist eine beliebte BBC-Kindersendung, an welcher die verschiedensten Künstler mitarbeiten. Die hier gezeigten Bilder stammen aus folgenden Filmen: *Barnaby, The Herbs* (Kräuter), *The Wombles* und *The Magic Roundabout* (Das magische Karussell); dieser letzte Film stammt ursprünglich aus einer französischen Serie, die ins Englische übersetzt wurde.

504–507 *Sesamstrasse*. Einige Bilder aus einem von Etienne Delessert gezeichneten Film, der im Rahmen dieser beliebten Kindersendung der CBS gezeigt wurde.

500—503

499 *Being Green* (Etre vert), un dessin réalisé pour *Sesame Street,* une série télévisée pour enfants. Etienne Delessert, célèbre illustrateur de livres d'enfant, est reconnu sur le plan internationa en tant qu'expert dans le domaine de la production de divertissements pour enfants, p. ex. à la télévision. Il est très fier de pouvoir contribuer à cette série de CBS.
500—503 *Watch With Mother.* C'est une longue série très populaire de la BBC, réalisée chaque fois par un artiste différent. Les cases se réfèrent aux films suivants: *Barnaby, The Herbs, The Wombles* et *The Magic Roundabout* (Le Carrousel magique); ce dernier était initialement réalisé pour une série télévisée en France, il n'était adapté et traduit en anglais qu'après coup.
504—507 *Sesame Street.* Cases de divers films créés par Etienne Delessert pour ce programme populaire de CBS pour les petits.

ARTIST / KÜNSTLER / RÉALISATION:

499, 504—507 Etienne Delessert

DIRECTOR / RÉGISSEUR:

499, 504—507 Etienne Delessert

PRODUCTION / PRODUKTION:

499, 504—507 Carabosse SA, St.-Sulpice for CBS, New York
500—503 BBC Television, London

504—507

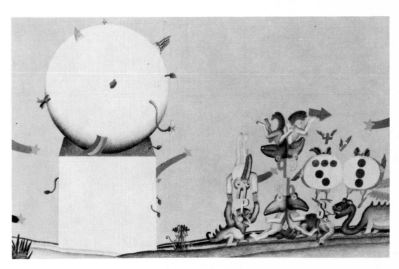

508–510 *Katerfamilie* (Tomcat Family) is by S. Prochazkova, a Czech artist living in Germany. It is a series of brief funny cat stories that are sandwiched between the advertising spots of South-West German Television.

511–516 *Kasparek, Honza and the Dragon* is a series in seven instalments produced by Czechoslovak Television in the paper cut-out technique. It is intended for young children and shown in the regular bedtime fairy-tale programme.

517–522 *Der Traum vom Fahren*. These six frames are taken from one of the twelve instalments of a series about everything that floats. The series forms part of a family programme broadcast by South-West German Television.

523 *Treasure Island*, painted by John Worsley for Anglia Television. It is made up of six half-hour episodes and required 350 paintings. The fact that still pictures are used does not detract from the pace of the action.

508–510 *Katerfamilie* wurde von S. Prochazkova, einer in der Bundesrepublik lebenden tschechischen Künstlerin realisiert. Es ist eine Serie von kurzen Katzengeschichten, die zwischen den Werbespots des Südwestfunks ausgestrahlt werden.

511–516 *Kasparek, Honza and the Dragon*, eine Serie des tschechischen Fernsehens in sieben Folgen, in Collage-Technik realisiert. Die Serie ist für kleine Kinder bestimmt und wird im regulären abendlichen Kinderprogramm gesendet.

517–522 *Der Traum vom Fahren*. Diese sechs Bilder stammen aus einer der 12 Folgen einer Serie über alles «was auf dem Wasser schwimmt». Sie ist Teil des Südwestfunk-Familienprogramms.

523 *Treasure Island* (Schatzinsel). John Worsley hat die 350 Bilder für die aus sechs halbstündigen Episoden bestehende Serie von Anglia Television geschaffen. Die Tatsache, dass Bilder ohne Bewegung verwendet werden, hat keinen Einfluss auf den Fluss der Geschichte.

508–510 *Katerfamilie* (La famille du matou), réalisé par S. Prochazkova, une artiste tchèque qui vit en Allemagne fédérale. Cette série d'histoires amusantes de chats est diffusée entre les télé-spots de la Télévision du Sud-Ouest de l'Allemagne.

511–516 *Kasparek, Honza and the Dragon,* une série en sept suites diffusée par la Télévision Tchèque. La technique appliquée était celle du collage. Cette série fait partie du programme du soir pour enfants.

517–522 *Der Traum vom Fahren*. Ces six cases figurent dans l'une des 12 suites d'une série consacrée à «tout ce qui flotte». Elle fait partie du programme de famille diffusé par la Télévision du Sud-Ouest de l'Allemagne.

523 *Treasure Island* (Ile au trésor) peint par John Worsley pour Anglia Television. Cette série de six épisodes de 30 mn est composée de 350 peintures. Le fait qu'il s'agit d'images immobiles n'a aucun effet nuisible quant au déroulement de l'action.

523

ARTIST / KÜNSTLER / RÉALISATION:

508–510 Stanislava Prochazkova
511–516 Bohuslav Šrámek
517–522 Tony Munzlinger
523 John Worsley

DIRECTOR / RÉGISSEUR:

508–510 Pavel Prochazka
511–516 Bohuslav Šrámek
517–522 Tony Munzlinger
523 John Salway

PRODUCTION / PRODUKTION:

508–510, 517–522 Südwestfunk, Baden-Baden
511–516 Czech Television, Bratislava
523 Paul Honeyman/Anglia Television, Norwich/GBR

ARTIST / KÜNSTLER / RÉALISATION:

524–531 Stefan Lemke
532, 533 Emanuele Luzzati
534–541 Tony Munzlinger
542, 543 Jan W. Habarta

DIRECTOR / RÉGISSEUR:

524–531 Janos Meszaros
532, 533 Giulio Gianini/Emanuele Luzzati
534–541 Tony Munzlinger
542, 543 Jan W. Habarta

PRODUCTION / PRODUKTION:

524–531 Westdeutscher Rundfunk, Köln
532, 533 Gianini/Luzzati for RAI TV Italiana
534–541 Südwestfunk, Baden-Baden
542, 543 Jan W. Habarta, Landshut/GER

524–531 *Die Geschichte vom Huhn und dem Auto* (The Story of the Chicken and the Car) forms part of West German Television's Series with the Mouse, a popular children's programme. The Lemke-Pricken team designs regularly for this and other TV series. This is the story of a chicken that doesn't quite know how to escape when it is nearly run over by a car. Finally it sits down on the road in despair, with the car wildly hooting at it. Only when the car stops hooting does the chicken get up and strut proudly over to its companions in the ditch.

532, 533 Two frames from *Turandot* with Luzzati's sumptuous colouring. This filming of C. Gozzi's work is divided into two 12-minute parts.

534–541 "Expression" is part of a six-part series about means of communication entitled The Dream of Understanding *(Der Traum von der Verständigung).* The chapters are devoted to places, expressions, signs and signals, language, writing, forms and agreements. The film, made by West German Television, is a combination of live action and animation.

542, 543 *Rummelplatz* (Playground) is the work of Czech artist Jan Habarta now living in Germany, where he has been a regular contributor to children's television. This film was produced entirely by Habarta himself. He uses a cut-out technique. The "playground" with its shows and amusements symbolizes our modern environment, through which a little man moves, carelessly and thoughtlessly having a good time at his own—and the world's—expense.

532

533

 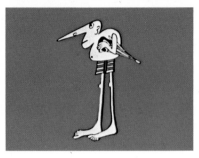  

524–531 *Die Geschichte vom Huhn und dem Auto* ist ein Teil der WDR-*Sendung mit der Maus,* ein beliebtes Programm für Kinder. Das Lemke-Pricken Team arbeitet regelmässig für diese Sendung, wie auch für eine Reihe anderer Fernseh-Sendungen. Die Geschichte erzählt, wie ein Huhn auf der Strasse von einem Auto aufgescheucht wird und vergebens versucht, sich zu retten. Schliesslich setzt es sich verzweifelt vor den hupenden Wagen. Erst als dieser aufhört zu hupen, steht das Huhn auf und stolziert würdevoll zu seinen Kameraden am Strassenrand.
532, 533 Zwei Bilder aus *Turandot*, der von Luzzati in herrlichen Farben gemalt wurde. Diese Verfilmung von C. Gozzis Werk besteht aus zwei 12minutigen Teilen.
534–541 *Der Traum von der Verständigung.* «Ausdruck» ist ein Teil der Serie in sechs Folgen über verschiedene Verständigungsmittel. Der Stoff wird in folgenden Kapiteln zusammengefasst: Ort, Ausdruck, Zeichen und Signale, Sprache, Schrift, Formen und Vereinbarungen. Das Programm ist eine Kombination von Real- und Trickfilm.
542, 543 *Rummelplatz* ist das Werk von Jan Habarta, einem in der Bundesrepublik lebenden tschechischen Künstler. Seit sechs Jahren arbeitet er an Fernsehprogrammen für Kinder mit. Diese Serie produzierte er selber. Er bedient sich der «Legetrick»-Technik mit ausgeschnittenen Teilen. Der Rummelplatz, halb Wunschtraum, halb Realität, symbolisiert unsere Umwelt, in welcher sich ein Männchen vergnügt, mit grenzenloser Sorglosigkeit sich und seiner Umwelt gegenüber.

524–531 *Die Geschichte vom Huhn und dem Auto* (L'Histoire de la poule et de la voiture) fait partie de la Série avec le souris, programme populaire pour enfants. Le team Lemke-Pricken réalise régulièrement des films pour cette série et nombre d'autres. On y raconte l'histoire de la poule effrayée par une voiture. Elle essaie de se sauver mais en réalisant sa situation désespérée elle se place droit devant la voiture claxonnante. Ce n'est qu'au moment où la voiture cesse de claxonner qu'elle se lève et se pavane vers l'accotement.
532, 533 Deux cases de *Turandot*, somptueusement coloriées par Luzzati. Cette adaptation cinématographique de l'œuvre de C. Gozzi est diffusée en deux parties de 12 mn chacune.
534–541 *Der Traum von der Verständigung* (Le rêve de la communication). Six suites consacrées aux moyens de communication, dont l'une est intitulée «Expression». Le matériel est réuni dans les chapitres: lieu, expression, signes et signaux, langue, écriture, formes et accords. Ce film réalisé par la TV de l'Ouest de l'Allemagne est un mélange de dessin animé et de film à acteurs.
542, 543 *Rummelplatz* (Champ de Foire) est l'œuvre de Jan Habarta, artiste tchèque résidant en Allemagne fédérale, où il réalise régulièrement des programmes TV pour enfants. Il a été produit entièrement par lui-même. Technique: papiers découpés et collages. Le champ de foire, un lieu de plaisir entre la réalité et le rêve, devrait symboliser notre environnement où s'amuse un petit bonhomme tout à fait insouciant quant à sa personne et son environnement.

542

543

544 *The New Beginning.* A frame from one of a series of ten-minute films retelling stories from the New Testament.
545–556 *Geschichten vom Warten* (Stories about Waiting). From a partly animated Christmas programme for children, in which a man who has been waiting for something to happen ever since his childhood sits and waits for Santa Claus to bring him the fulfilment of all his wishes, and is once more disappointed.
557–565 Drawing and sequence from *Dr. Katzenbergers Badereise* (Dr. Katzenberger's Bathing Trip), a mixture of animated and live film based on a story by Jean Paul. When it was adapted as a television play, both drawn characters and live actors were used as dramatis personae against the drawn backgrounds.

544 *The New Beginning* (Der neue Anfang). Bild aus einem der 10-Minuten-Filme einer Serie, die Geschichten aus dem neuen Testament erzählt.
545–556 *Geschichten vom Warten,* eine teilanimierte Bildergeschichte für das Kinderprogramm an Weihnachten. Sie handelt von einem Mann, der seit seiner Kindheit darauf wartet, dass etwas geschehen würde. Er sitzt und wartet auf den Weihnachtsmann und erhofft von ihm die Erfüllung seiner Wünsche – doch auch diesmal wartet er vergebens.
557–565 *Dr. Katzenbergers Badereise,* nach Jean Pauls gleichnamiger Geschichte gedreht. In diesem Fernseh-Theaterstück, einer Kombination von wirklichem Theater und Zeichentrickfilm, wirken sowohl wirkliche Schauspieler wie auch gezeichnete Figuren mit. Die Szenen spielen alle vor gezeichnetem Hintergrund.

544 *The New Beginning* (Le Recommencement). Image de l'un des films de 10 mn qui fait partie d'une série consacrée à des histoires du Nouveau Testament.
545–556 *Geschichten vom Warten* (Histoires de l'attente). Une histoire en partie animée, réalisée dans le cadre d'un programme de Noël pour enfants. Ce film raconte l'histoire d'un homme qui s'attend depuis son enfance à ce que quelque chose arrive. Il attend le Père Noël, espérant que celui-ci exaucera ses vœux – mais hélas, il attend en vain, cette fois aussi.
557–565 *Dr. Katzenbergers Badereise* (Le voyage balnéaire du Dr Katzenberger), un mélange de dessin animé et de film réel, réalisé d'après une histoire de Jean Paul. Des scènes dessinées constituent le fond pour les personnages dessinés et réels.

544

545–556

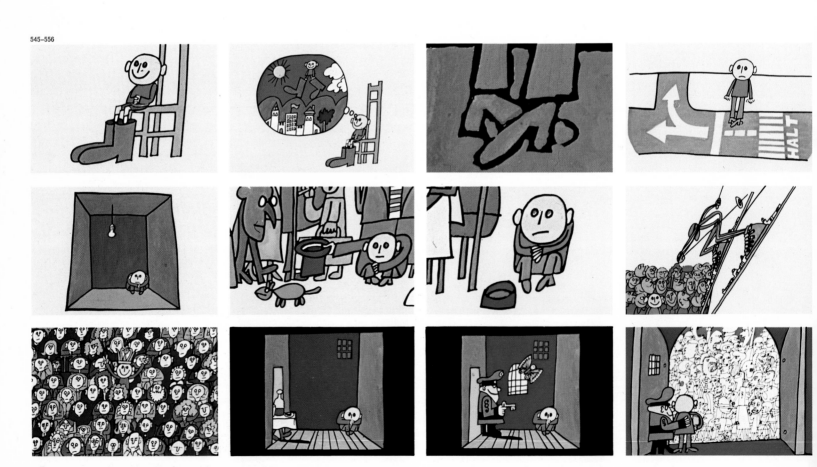

557

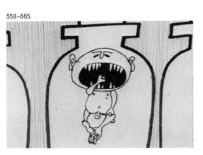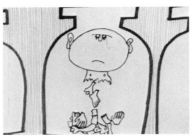

558–565

ARTIST / KÜNSTLER / RÉALISATION:

544 Paul Birkbeck
545–556 Tony Munzlinger

DIRECTOR / RÉGISSEUR:

544 Molly Cox
545–556 Tony Munzlinger
557–565 Norbert Schulze

PRODUCTION / PRODUKTION:

544 BBC Television, London
545–556 Südwestfunk, Baden-Baden
557–565 Sender Freies Berlin, Berlin

566–574 *When Roobarb Made a Spike.* Roobarb the dog is the hero of a new series directed by Bob Godfrey, and thus takes his place beside Gene Deitch's *Nudnik* and Bosustow's *Mr. Magoo.* The films are wittily drawn and can be limited to essentials since they are directed at a public accustomed to the comic strip. Here Roobarb watches absorbed how birds pull long things out of the ground. He wants to join in the game, but lands, like a modern Icarus, on his artificial beak.

575–577 *Zagor and the Musical Grass.* Frames from a 6½-minute episode from the television series *Toffsy.* The wizard Zagor has hypnotized the occupants of a castle in order to steal their treasures. Toffsy catches him out and forces him to play the musical grass as a sign of repentance. First prize for an animated film forming part of a TV series in Zagreb, 1974.

578–589 *Le Chat Caméléon* (The Chameleon Cat), part of the 39-episode international TV series *European Fables.* produced by Corona Cinematografica. Every effort is made to ensure that the local character and style of the folk tales is preserved. This is a fable from the Swiss mountains. Little Hansi's chameleon cat possesses magic powers and helps the oppressed inhabitants of a town to regain their freedom from the evil governor.

566–574 *When Roobarb Made a Spike* (Roobarb landet auf der Nase). Roobarb, der Hund, ist der Held einer neuen Serie von Bob Godfrey – eine neue Figur nach Deitchs *Nudnik* und Bosustows *Mr. Magoo.* Die einzelnen Filme sind witzig gezeichnet und können sich, dank den an Comic-Strips «geschulten» Zuschauern, auf das Wesentliche beschränken. Hier beobachtet Roobarb, wie die Vögel komische lange Dinger aus der Erde ziehen. Er versucht es auch, landet jedoch – ähnlich einem modernen Ikarus – auf seinem künstlichen Schnabel.

575–577 *Zagor and the Musical Grass* (Zagor und das musikalische Gras), eine Episode aus der Fernsehserie *Toffsy.* Der Zauberer Zagor hat die Bewohner eines Schlosses hypnotisiert, um ihren Schatz zu stehlen. Toffsy erwischt ihn dabei und zwingt ihn, als Zeichen der Reue die Grasmusik zu spielen.

578–589 *Le Chat Caméléon* (Die Chamäleon-Katze). Dieser Film ist Teil der 39 Episoden umfassenden internationalen TV-Serie *Europäische Sagen.* Es wird darauf geachtet, dass der lokale Charakter und Stil der Volkssagen beibehalten wird. Diese Sage spielt in den Schweizer Bergen: Hansis Chamäleon-Katze hat magische Kräfte und hilft den Bewohnern einer Stadt, sich von einer übelgesinnten Regierung zu befreien.

566–574 *When Roobarb Made a Spike* (Le Jour où Roobarb tomba sur son bec). Le chien Roobarb est la vedette d'une nouvelle série produite par Bob Godfrey, qui prend le relais de *Nudnik,* par Gene Deitch, et de *Monsieur Magoo,* par Bosustow. Les dessins sont très spirituels. S'adressant à des spectateurs déjà «rodés», ils se limitent à l'essentiel. Ici, Roobarb observe avec intérêt des oiseaux qui extraient de longs machins du sol. Il veut se joindre à eux, mais tombe sur son bec artificiel comme un nouvel Icare.

575–577 *Zagor and the Musical Grass* (Zagor et l'Herbe mélodieuse). Images d'un épisode de la série TV *Toffsy.* Le magicien Zagor a hypnotisé les habitants d'un château pour leur ravir leurs trésors. Toffsy l'attrape et le force à jouer un air sur un brin d'herbe mélodieuse en signe de repentir. 1er prix du film d'animation faisant partie d'une série TV, Zagreb 1974.

578–589 *Le Chat Caméléon.* Ce film fait partie d'une série TV internationale de 39 *Fables Européennes.* On s'efforce à conserver le caractère et le style locaux. Cette fable-là se passe dans les Grisons. Le chat Caméléon du petit Hansi a le pouvoir de se transformer quand on lui joue un air de flûte. Il fait appel à tous ses pouvoirs magiques pour débarasser le pays du bailli.

ARTIST / KÜNSTLER / RÉALISATION:

566–574 Bob Godfrey/Grange Calveley
575–577 Pierluigi Demas/Gianandrea Garola
578–589 Gisèle & Ernest Ansorge

DIRECTOR / RÉGISSEUR:

566–574 Bob Godfrey
575–577 Pierluigi Demas
578–589 Ernest Ansorge/Max Massimino-Garnièr

PRODUCTION / PRODUKTION:

566–574 Bob Godfrey Films Ltd. for BBC Television, London
575–577 Audiovisivi Demas S.r.l., Milan for RAI TV Italiana, Rome
578–589 Ezio Gagliardo/NAG Film, Etagnières/Corona Cinematografica

578–589

590–595 *3 x C. Dupin,* a series of animated films, also used on Czech television, based on three tales by Edgar Allan Poe. Šalamoun's pictures enter into league with the text, extending its imaginative, informative or humourous content. The descriptive element, often inspired by old prints, has been reinstated. The accumulation of objects, provided with signs and numbers and a veneer of scientific accuracy, heightens the sense of absurdity. For children the impression is one of adventure, while adults sense the irony of our age behind the grotesquely magnified objects. Poe's blend of fantasy and objective detail suits Šalamoun well and is unified by his own logic.

590–595 Zeichnungen aus der Trickfilm-Serie *3 x C. Dupin,* die auch am tschechischen Fernsehen gezeigt wurde. Den Filmen liegen drei Erzählungen von E. A. Poe zugrunde. Šalamouns Bilder stehen in enger Beziehung zum Wort und erweitern so dessen informativen Gehalt. Seine Darstellungen verraten, dass er sich von alten Drucken inspirieren liess. Oft akkumuliert der Künstler die Gegenstände, versieht sie mit Zeichen und Nummern, um mit solch scheinbar wissenschaftlichem Anstrich eine absurde Welt zu katalogisieren. Während die Bilder bei den Kindern den Eindruck von Abenteuer und Romantik erwecken, spüren die Erwachsenen hinter der grotesken Vergrösserung der Dinge die Ironie unserer Zeit. Šalamoun wird besonders angesprochen vom unerschöpflichen Einfallsreichtum Poes und der sachlichen Ausgestaltung der Details, die er durch seine Logik zu einer Einheit werden lässt.

590–595 Cartoons tirés de trois dessins animés présentés en série sous le titre de *3 x C. Dupin* et montrés entre autres par la Télévision Tchécoslovaque. Ces films sont basés sur trois récits de Poe. L'image s'allie au texte dont elle prolonge et élargit le contenu imaginatif, informatif et humoristique. Šalamoun s'est inspiré dans beaucoup de ses dessins de vieilles estampes. Il dessine des entassements d'objets en les dotant d'inscriptions, de numéros, avec un souci méticuleux de l'exactitude scientifique qui augmente la sensation de l'absurde. Pour l'enfant ce sont des histoires aventureuses, alors que, pour le lecteur adulte, il s'y dévoile aussi le caractère ironisant de notre époque. L'art subtil d'Edgar Allan Poe, mélangeant l'imaginaire et le détail objectif, s'est déjà combiné à la perfection avec les propres tendances de Šalamoun.

590

591

592

593

594

595

ARTIST / KÜNSTLER / RÉALISATION:
590–595 Jiri Šalamoun

DIRECTOR / RÉGISSEUR:
590–595 Martin Holly

PRODUCTION / PRODUKTION:
590–595 Filmove Studio Koliba/Czech Television, Bratislava

John Halas

Animation offers many advantages for industrial, scientific and educational films. It can make use of every type of graphic style and presentation to illuminate its messages, from the wholly symbolic approach to the simplest diagrammatic explanation. It also adds an aesthetic factor to the purely intellectual content.

This raises it to the level at which the powers of suggestion begin to operate and the imagination is brought into play, a quality that is often particularly useful in industrial films intended for general audiences, where the basic principle is more important than the details.

Animation also has the advantage of colour, which can be used to pick out certain lines of action and thereby to convey instantaneously to the eye things which it would be laborious to explain in words. Colour can also be employed to set a mood or create psychological implications.

While movements can be accelerated or slowed down in live-action films, this can be done with greater flexibility and variety in animation techniques. It is often more economical to present important phases in emphatic slow time while the less important can be speeded up or flashed by.

The basic principle of animation technique is the superimposition of transparent celluloid sheets, each bearing only one element of the composite image. Consequently it is easy to break down a complex process by peeling off layer after layer, and one element can be isolated while others are kept in abeyance. Animation can also be superimposed on living images to reveal underlying principles.

Much of the technical equipment used today is highly complex. Where animation is used to explain it, it can be graded from the simplest form of demonstration to the fullest and most elaborate to suit a particular audience. For the purposes of technical instruction, animated films have proved easier to memorize than live-action films supplying comparable information.

Scientists are today making very extensive use of animated graphics. Some theoretical aspects of quantum physics can only be demonstrated with moving diagrams aided by computers. Companies have adopted film graphics to explain their organizations, governments to disseminate information. But some of the most interesting applications have been in the educational field, where CBS for instance has used animation to teach children to read and write and to understand the world around them.

Die Animation bietet dem Industrie-, Wissenschafts- und Lehrfilm unendlich viele Vorteile. Das ganze Spektrum der graphischen Gestaltung, von der symbolischen Aussage bis zur diagrammatischen Erklärung, kann für die Darlegung des Themas ausgewertet werden. Auch gibt er dem rein intellektuellen Inhalt einen ästhetischen Anstrich.

Dies hebt ihn auf die Ebene, auf welcher die Suggestionskräfte aktiviert werden und die Vorstellungskraft zu spielen beginnt, was besonders für Industriefilme, die sich an ein breites Publikum richten, wichtig ist, weil dort die Darlegung der Grundprinzipien mehr zählt als das Detail.

Der Animationsfilm bietet auch durch die Farbe einen Vorteil, da bestimmte Handlungsabläufe hervorgehoben und visuell schneller vermittelt werden können, als wenn sie umständlich in Worten erklärt werden müssten. Farbe wird auch eingesetzt, um eine bestimmte Atmosphäre zu schaffen oder psychologische Implikationen zu evozieren.

Während Bewegungen im Realfilm beschleunigt oder verlangsamt werden können, ist dies beim Animationsfilm mit grösserer Flexibilität und Vielfalt möglich. Es ist oft wirtschaftlicher, wichtige Phasen in Zeitlupe zu zeigen, während unwichtigere beschleunigt oder gerafft abgespielt werden.

Grundprinzip der Animationstechnik ist das Übereinanderlegen transparenter Zelluloidfolien, wobei jede nur je ein Element des Gesamtbildes enthält. Es ist somit leicht, einen komplexen Handlungsablauf zu zerlegen, indem Schicht um Schicht abgehoben und jede Phase einzeln gezeigt wird. Zur Verdeutlichung von Einzelheiten können Animations- und Realfilm übereinanderkopiert werden.

Ein Grossteil der modernen technischen Ausrüstung ist äusserst komplex, und der Animationsfilm kann diese Komplexität auf einfachste Art verständlich machen, oder aber, je nach Publikum, auf sehr detaillierte Weise. Auf dem Gebiet des technischen Unterrichts haben sich Animationsfilme als dem Gedächtnis einprägsamer erwiesen als Realfilme, die eine vergleichbare Information liefern.

Wissenschafter machen heute ausgiebigen Gebrauch von Animationsgraphiken. Einige theoretische Aspekte der Quantenphysik können nur anhand von beweglichen, von Computern gesteuerten Diagrammen dargelegt werden. Die Filmgraphik wird von Firmen zur Erklärung ihrer Organisation oder von Regierungen für die Verbreitung von Informationen genutzt. Besonders interessant scheint der Einsatz von Animationsfilmen im Bildungsbereich, z. B. für den Lese- und Schreibunterricht etc.

L'animation présente de nombreux avantages lorsqu'il s'agit de réaliser des documentaires industriels, des films scientifiques et éducatifs. On peut y faire appel à n'importe quel style et mode de présentation pour la mise en relief des messages, du symbolisme jusqu'au diagramme élémentaire. L'animation ajoute également un facteur esthétique à la démonstration purement intellectuelle.

C'est par le biais de l'animation qu'est activée la puissance de suggestion et que l'imagination entre en scène, ce qui est particulièrement utile dans les films à l'intention du grand public, où l'exposé des principes de base compte plus que les détails.

L'animation présente également l'avantage de la couleur employée pour mettre l'accent sur des éléments déterminés et transmettre ainsi directement à l'œil des données qu'il serait malaisé de traduire en mots. La couleur sert en outre à créer l'atmosphère et à évoquer des prolongements psychologiques.

L'accéléré resp. le ralenti du mouvement exploités au cinéma peuvent l'être avec bien plus de souplesse et de variété grâce à l'animation. Il s'avère souvent plus économique de présenter des phases importantes au ralenti, ce qui donne toute l'importance voulue, alors que les éléments secondaires peuvent être traités en accéléré ou défiler à un rythme rapide.

Le principe de base des techniques d'animation est la superposition de feuilles transparentes (cels) d'acétate de cellulose, chaque cel ne comportant qu'un élément de l'image composite. Il est donc facile de décomposer un processus complexe en isolant les différents éléments et en les présentant successivement. Les dessins animés peuvent aussi être superposés à des images cinématographiques ordinaires pour en révéler la constitution intime.

L'animation fait pleine justice à la complexité de la plupart des équipements techniques d'aujourd'hui, qu'elle peut présenter sous une forme élémentaire aussi bien que sous une forme très élaborée destinée à des spécialistes. Dans l'instruction technique, les films d'animation s'avèrent plus simples à mémoriser que des documentaires en prise de vues réelle.

Le film scientifique connaît de nos jours un essor prodigieux. Certains aspects de la physique quantique ne peuvent être démontrés que par des diagrammes animés créés à l'aide d'ordinateurs. Les entreprises adoptent la création graphique filmée pour expliquer leur organisation, les gouvernements pour diffuser l'information. Au nombre des applications les plus fascinantes figurent les films réalisés pour les programmes d'alphabétisation CBS.

Sponsored Films

Patronatsfilme

Films institutionnels

Industrial Films
Scientific Films
Educational Films
Social Films
Institutional Films

Industriefilme
Wissenschaftsfilme
Lehrfilme
Soziale Filme
Institutionelle Filme

Documentaires
Films scientifiques
Films éducatifs
Films sociaux
Films institutionnels

596–601 Stills from a 9½-minute film produced by the Hubley Studio, New York, for the Institute for World Order and entitled *Voyage to Next*. Mother Earth and Father Time observe the state of life on planet Earth. Mother Earth has intended humans to share their brains and resources, but this unfortunately has not happened. Humankind has shut itself off in a system of nationalistic boxes. After considering the present, Father Time projects the future to twenty years from now. Both try to understand how things have gone amiss, pointing out the wrong choices the humans have made. When they recover from their depression, it appears that discussions are starting all over the world, people are becoming aware of each other and thinking of new possibilities. They begin to conjure up their imaginary worlds. Father Time asks Mother Earth if she thinks they will succed and she tentatively suggests they might. He responds: "But in time?"

602–610 Stills from WOW, *Women of the World*, a 10-minute film produced for the World Council of Churches in honour of International Women's Year 1975. It presents a global view of the changing relationship between male and female in world history. Beginning in the distant past, it explores the role of women in the early creation myths and the art surviving from matriarchal society, depicting women in positions of leadership, women as goddesses, women in chariots. The men revolt and matriarchal life is destroyed, the goddesses attacked and humbled, and patriarchy is established. Women are put in cages, humiliated, left voiceless and without franchise. Dominated by male governments which fail to solve basic problems, the globe becomes overpopulated and resources dwindle—until women rebel, open their cages, achieve and organize, reaching out towards a real relationship between the sexes and genuine human liberation.

596–601 Stills aus dem Film *Voyage to Next* (Reise in die Zukunft), vom Hubley Studio, New York, im Auftrag des Institute of World Order produziert. Mutter Erde und Vater Zeit überprüfen das Leben auf der Erde. Mutter Erde hatte gehofft, die Menschen würden ihre körperlichen und geistigen Kräfte vereinen, um eine gemeinsame Welt aufzubauen – doch leider kam es anders. Die Menschen kapselten sich in kleinen nationalistischen Systemen ab. Nachdem er die Gegenwart betrachtet hat, wendet Vater Zeit den Blick in die Zukunft. Beide versuchen zu verstehen. warum alles fehlschlug, warum die Menschen schlecht gewählt hatten. Sie schöpfen jedoch neue Hoffnungen, weil sie sehen, dass überall diskutiert und geplant wird, um eine Verständigung unter den Völkern herbeizuführen. Vater Zeit zweifelt daran, ob die Menschen es diesmal schaffen werden, Mutter Erde ist etwas zuversichtlicher. Vater Zeit fragt sich bekümmert: «Wird die Zeit dafür noch reichen?»

602–610 Stills aus dem Film WOW, *Women of the World* (Frauen der Welt), einer Auftragsproduktion des Weltkirchenrates für das Jahr der Frau. Der Film gibt einen historischen Überblick über die wechselnden Beziehungen zwischen Mann und Frau. Er erforscht die Rolle der Frau, wie sie in archaischen Schöpfungsmythen oder Kunstgegenständen aus matriarchalischen Gesellschaften zum Ausdruck kommt – die Frau als Göttin, Herrscherin, Kriegerin. Doch die Männer beginnen zu rebellieren und stürzen die bestehende Gesellschaftsordnung. Die Göttinnen werden verhöhnt und die Frauen mit der Einführung des Patriarchats zu rechtlosen Gefangenen degradiert. Es zeigt sich jedoch, dass unter männlicher Staatsherrschaft grundlegende Probleme ungelöst bleiben – die Überbevölkerung nimmt zu, die Rohstoffquellen versiegen. Die Frauen erheben sich, reissen die gesellschaftlichen Barrieren nieder und suchen eine neue Grundlage der zwischenmenschlichen Beziehungen.

596–601 Cases du film *Voyage to Next* (Voyage à l'avenir), produit par le Hubley Studio, New York, pour l'Institute of World Order. La Mère Terre et le Père Temps surveillent la situation sur la planète Terre. La Mère Terre s'attendait à ce que les hommes prétendraient à un rapprochement des peuples en vertu de leurs facultés intellectuelles. Malgré les espoirs mis en l'homme, il instaure un système qui tente à renfermer les peuples dans des boîtes dites nationalistes. Tout compte fait de la situation actuelle, le Père Temps se dévoue aux 20 ans à venir. Tous les deux cherchent à comprendre pour quelle raison les hommes ont failli à leur tâche et, en méditant sur la situation chaotique, ils s'aperçoivent que les hommes se mettent à discuter leurs problèmes afin d'ouvrir de nouvelles voies vers un rapprochement des peuples. Le Père Temps s'en doute du succès, tandis que la Mère Terre est plus confiante. Le Père Temps redoute qu'ils rattrapent le temps gaspillé à la légère.

602–610 Cases du film WOW, *Women of the World* (Femmes du monde entier), réalisé pour le Conseil œcuménique des Eglises à l'occasion de l'Année internationale de la femme. Il retrace l'historique des relations entre les sexes. Les recherches remontent aux mythes archaïques et aux objets d'art de périodes de matriarcat dans lesquels se projette le rôle de la femme: la femme en tant que déesse, en tant qu'autorité, en tant que guerrier. Mais l'ordre social en vigueur est renversé par la révolution des hommes qui, en raillant les déesses, instaurent le patriarcat. Les femmes sont contraintes à mener une vie de captive sans aucun droit. Cependant, ils s'est avéré à la longue que les hommes ont failli à résoudre les problèmes fondamentaux, ce qui a abouti au surpeuplement et à l'épuisement des ressources naturelles. Après une longue période de répression et de discrimination, les femmes se sont enfin organisées et tentent d'ouvrir la voie à de nouveaux rapports et à la libération.

596–601

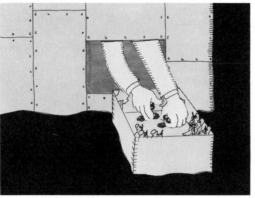

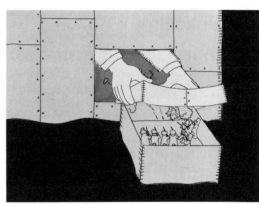

ARTIST / KÜNSTLER / RÉALISATION:

596–601 John Hubley
602–610 Faith Hubley

DIRECTOR / RÉGISSEUR:

596–601 John Hubley
602–610 Faith Hubley

ART DIRECTOR / DIRECTEUR ARTISTIQUE:

596–610 John & Faith Hubley

PRODUCTION / PRODUKTION:

596–610 The Hubley Studio, New York

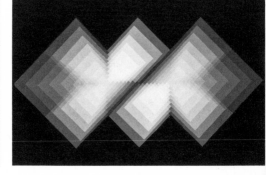

ARTIST / KÜNSTLER / RÉALISATION:

611–619 Faith & John Hubley
620–625 Ishu Patel

DIRECTOR / RÉGISSEUR:

611–619 John Hubley
620–625 Ishu Patel

ART DIRECTOR / DIRECTEUR ARTISTIQUE

611–619 John & Faith Hubley
620–625 Ishu Patel

PRODUCTION / PRODUKTION:

611–619 The Hubley Studio, New York
620–625 National Film Board of Canada, Montreal

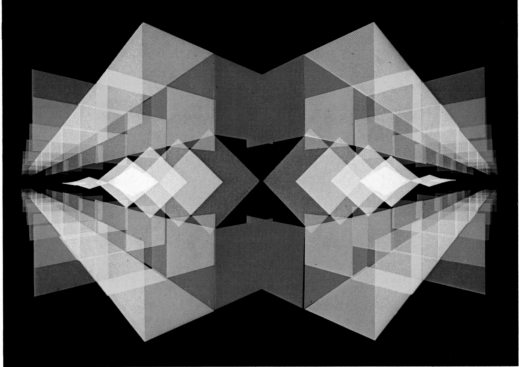

625

611–619 *Everybody Rides the Carousel.* This 72½-minute film was prepared in collaboration with Kenneth Keniston and The School of Art Film Seminar of Yale University. It is a dramatization of Erik H. Erikson's concept of the eight stages of the human life cycle and depicts the growth of the human being through a series of challenges and conflicts inherent in each stage of development. The struggle between opposing inner forces at each stage is symbolized by animated characters which are seen to exist and to compete for hegemony within the individual. The major part of the film's sound track consists of improvisations illustrating successful resolutions or failures to resolve the essential conflict at each stage of life.
620–625 *Perspectrum.* The film explains the basic principles used in creating perspectives. With the use of these techniques and various combinations of perspective principles, it was possible to structure a complex pattern of visual effects. Each programme was shot with a computer-operated camera.

611–619 *Everybody Rides the Carousel.* Der Film wurde in Zusammenarbeit mit Kenneth Keniston und der School of Art Film Seminar der Yale-Universität realisiert Diese Verfilmung basiert auf Erik H. Eriksons Konzept der acht Lebensabschnitte des Menschen, dessen Entwicklung von einer Reihe von Herausforderungen und Konflikten in jedem Lebensstadium gekennzeichnet ist. Der innere Kampf, von zwei widerstreitenden Kräften ausgelöst, wird durch Figuren symbolisiert, die um die Herrschaft über den Einzelnen wetteifern. Der grösste Teil der Vertonung besteht aus Improvisationen, die Erfolg und Versagen des Einzelnen bei der Lösung dieses Grundkonflikts in jeder Lebensphase untermalen sollen.
620–625 *Perspectrum.* Dieser Film erklärt das Grundprinzip der Anwendung von Perspektiven. Anhand dieser Techniken und verschiedener Kombinationen von perspektivischen Prinzipien wurde ein komplexes System visueller Effekte erzielt. Der Film wurde mit einer computergesteuerten Kamera aufgenommen.

611–619 *Everybody Rides the Carousel.* Ce film a été réalisé en collaboration avec Kenneth Keniston et The School of Art Film Seminar de l'Université de Yale. C'est une adaptation du concept d'Erik H. Erikson dans lequel se projettent les huit phases de la vie humaine. Il y discute le passage de l'être humain à travers une série d'épreuves et de conflits inhérents à chaque stade de développement. Le conflit moral inhérent à chaque stade est symbolisé par des caractères animés qui semblent se disputer l'hégémonie de chaque individu. La plus grande partie du film est sonorisée à l'aide d'improvisations illustrant les efforts – réussis ou échoués – que chaque individu fait afin de résoudre ce conflit.
620–625 *Perspectrum.* Ce film explique les principes fondamentaux de la création de perspectives. A l'aide de ces techniques combinées avec différents principes regardant la perspective on a réussi à créer un système complexe d'effets visuels. Chaque programme a été réalisé avec une caméra computerisée.

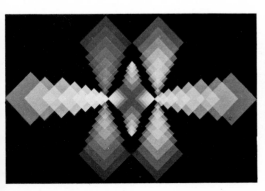

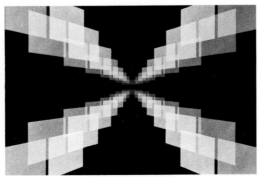

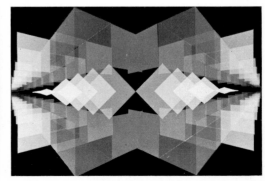

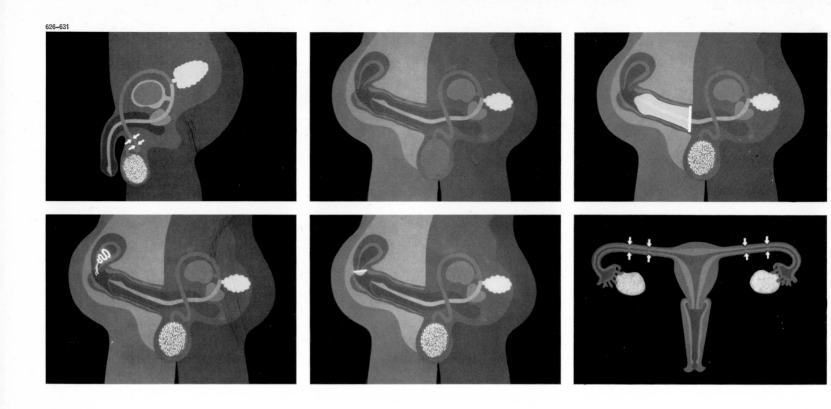

ARTIST / KÜNSTLER / RÉALISATION:

626–632, 636–641 Ishu Patel
633–635 Lynn Smith

DIRECTOR / RÉGISSEUR:

626–632, 636–641 Ishu Patel
633–635 Lynn Smith

ART DIRECTOR / DIRECTEUR ARTISTIQUE:

626–632, 636–641 Ishu Patel
633–635 Lynn Smith

PRODUCTION / PRODUKTION:

626–632, 636–641 National Film Board of Canada, Montreal
633–635 Education Development Center, Cambridge, Mass.

632

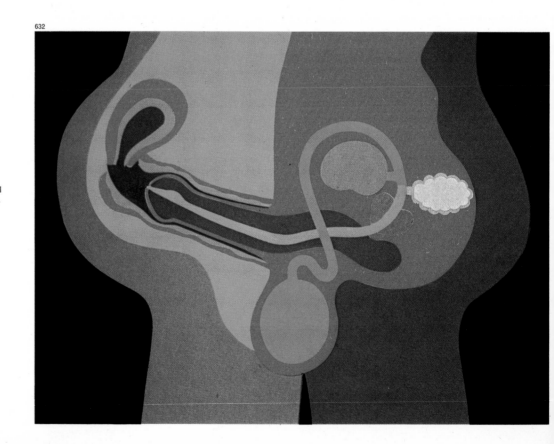

626–632 *Conception and Contraception* is the title of this educational film which, in simple and clear drawings, sets out the principles of its subject matter. It is intended as additional information for courses and conferences.

633–635 *Teacher, Lester bit me,* a colour film of 9 minutes' duration, made for the Education Development Center in Cambridge, Massachusetts.

636–641 *About Puberty and Reproduction.* As in Figs. 626–632, Ishu Patel's work is again distinguished by its clarity.

626–632 *Conception and Contraception* ist ein Aufklärungsfilm, der anhand einfacher Zeichnungen Empfängnis und Empfängnisverhütung veranschaulicht. Er wird als zusätzliches Informationsmaterial bei Kursen und Tagungen verwendet.

633–635 *Teacher, Lester bit me* (Herr Lehrer, Lester hat mich gebissen), ein 9minutiger Farbfilm, der für das Education Development Center in Cambridge, Mass., gedreht wurde.

636–641 *About Puberty and Reproduction.* Auch dieser Film zeichnet sich durch seine Klarheit aus.

626–632 *Conception et Contraception,* c'est le titre d'un film éducatif qui explique à l'aide de dessins simplifiés et faciles à comprendre les principes fonctionnels. Il sert d'information complémentaire pour des cours et des conférences.

633–635 *Teacher, Lester bit me* (Maître, Lester m'a mordu). Film couleur de 9 mn produit pour l'Education Development Center à Cambridge, Massachusetts.

636–641 *About Puberty and Reproduction* (Puberté et reproduction). Film qui se distingue par la simplicité des dessins.

633–635

636–641

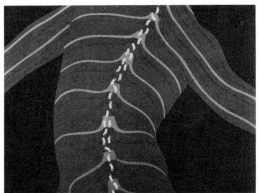
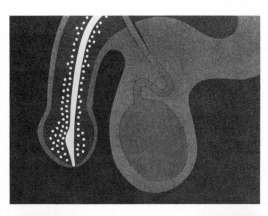

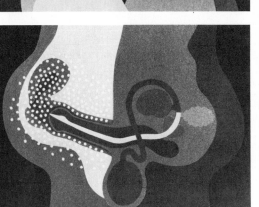
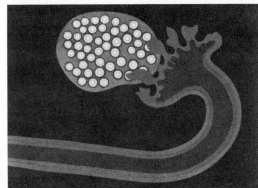
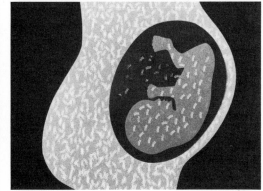

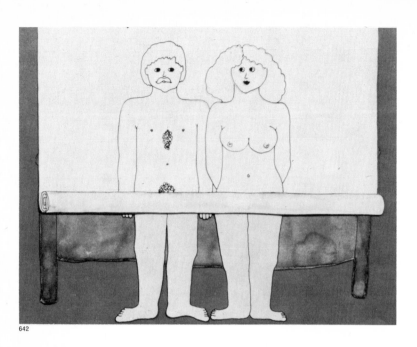

642

642–654 *Kinder wachsen nicht auf Bäumen* (Children don't grow on trees), a sex education film for schools commissioned by the West German authorities.
655–662 *Das Wahlrecht in der Bundesrepublik* (Franchise in the Federal Republic of Germany). Commissioned by the government of Nordrhein-Westfalen, the film explains the voting and election system in this West German state.
663–670 *Zwischen Mehrheitswahl und Verhältniswahl* (Between the majority and the proportional vote), another government-commissioned film explaining to the man in the street the two principal voting systems.

642–654 *Kinder wachsen nicht auf Bäumen*. Dieser Aufklärungsfilm wurde von der Bundeszentrale für gesundheitliche Aufklärung für die Vorführung in Schulen in Auftrag gegeben.
655–662 *Das Wahlrecht in der Bundesrepublik*. Dieser Lehrfilm für politische Bildung wurde von der Landeszentrale für politische Bildung Nordrhein-Westfalen herausgegeben. Er erklärt das Stimm- und Wahlsystem in diesem Bundesland.
663–670 *Zwischen Mehrheitswahl und Verhältniswahl*. Dies ist wiederum ein Lehrfilm für politische Bildung, der von der Landeszentrale für politische Bildung in Auftrag gegeben wurde. Er soll dem Mann auf der Strasse auf einfache und leicht verständliche Weise den Unterschied zwischen diesen beiden Wahlsystemen erklären.

642–654 *Kinder wachsen nicht auf Bäumen* (Les enfants ne poussent pas sur les arbres). Ce film pour l'éducation sexuelle est distribué aux écoles. Il a été commandité par la centrale fédérale pour l'éducation sexuelle de la jeunesse.
655–662 *Das Wahlrecht in der Bundesrepublik* (Le droit de vote en République fédérale d'Allemagne). Ce film, produit pour le compte de l'autorité du Land de la Rhénanie-du-Nord-Westphalie, discute le mode de scrutin en vigueur dans ce Land.
663–670 *Zwischen Mehrheitswahl und Verhältniswahl*. C'est un autre film commandité par une autorité officielle (la centrale pour l'éducation politique du Land de la Rhénanie-du-Nord-Westphalie). Il discute de façon compréhensible la différence entre les deux modes de votation, soit le vote majoritaire et le vote proportionnel.

643–654

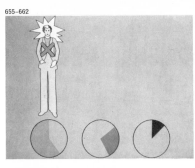
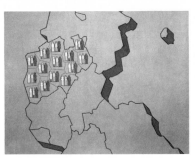
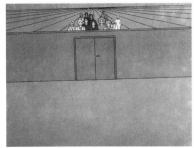

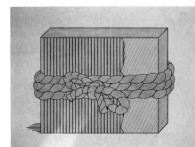

ARTIST / KÜNSTLER / RÉALISATION:

642–654 Jule Steinbach
655–670 Albrecht Ade/Peter Fischer

DIRECTOR / RÉGISSEUR:

642–670 Albrecht Ade

ART DIRECTOR / DIRECTEUR ARTISTIQUE:

642–654 Albrecht Ade/Jule Steinbach
655–670 Albrecht Ade/Thomas Haegele

PRODUCTION / PRODUKTION:

642–670 Studio Ade, Wuppertal

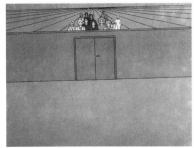

671–682 A film for The Open University.
683–690 *If* the dirt of all the skies and all the waters in Europe comes together—why don't we come together? If we can hear each other quite clearly up there (in Europe), why don't we listen to each other down here (in Europe)? If the insects are international, why don't we think internationally? Let us keep it international all the way.
691–702 *Voeding* (Food). In this Dutch film children and grown-ups give their "animated" opinion on food. Good and bad opinions alternate with brief statements made by food experts, which are also animated.

671–682 Ein Film über die Open University.
683–690 *If* (Wenn) sich der Schmutz in der Luft und in allen Gewässern Europas zusammentut – warum können wir uns nicht zusammentun? Wenn wir uns hier oben (in Europa) so gut verständigen können – warum bringen wir es hier unten (in Europa) nicht fertig? Wenn alle Insekten international sind – warum denken wir nicht international? Lasst uns unsere Probleme auf internationaler Ebene lösen.
691–702 *Voeding* (Nahrung). In diesem Film zeigen Kinder und Erwachsene ihre «getrickte» Meinung über Ernährung. Positive und negative Meinungen wechseln mit kurzen Feststellungen und Erklärungen von Ernährungsspezialisten.

671–682 Un film sur l'Open University (L'Université ouverte).
683–690 *If* (Si) la pollution de l'air et de toutes les eaux de l'Europe se réunit – pourquoi nous ne réunissons-nous pas? Si nous nous entendons si bien là-haut (en Europe) – pourquoi nous n'entendons-nous pas ici en bas (en Europe)? Si tous les insectes sont internationaux – pourquoi ne subordonnons-nous pas nos intérêts particuliers aux intérêts internationalistes?
691–702 *Voeding* (Alimentation). Dans ce film des enfants et des adultes donnent leurs opinions «animées» sur les problèmes d'alimentation. Des opinions positives et négatives alternent avec les constatations et explications faites par des experts d'alimentation.

ARTIST / KÜNSTLER / RÉALISATION:

671–682 Ken Gay/Stewart Hardy Films
683–702 Roy Pfaff/Ida & Kalman Kozelka

DIRECTOR / RÉGISSEUR:

671–682 Andrew Crilly
683–702 Harrie Geelen

ART DIRECTOR / DIRECTEUR ARTISTIQUE:

671–682 Ronald Jackson/Charles McGhie
683–702 Harrie Geelen

PRODUCTION / PRODUKTION:

671–682 BBC Television, London
683–702 Toonder Studio's B.V., Nederhorst
den Berg/NLD

671–682

691–702

Harold Friedman

There is a general consensus of opinion – at least among people such as Bob Godfrey, Morton Goldsholl, Arnold Levin and Lee Savage, with whom an exchange of opinions took place before these lines were written – that the advertising agency holds the dominant position in the television commercial world today, at least in the United States. It is the agency that provides the basic concept, which has been pre-sold to the client in the form of a storyboard. It also screens and selects the animation studios, heads production and supervises the making of the film up to the final optical.

The animation studio is first asked to make a bid for a commercial on the basis of the agency's storyboard. There will usually be three animation studios in the running. If it is given the assignment, it will be expected to turn out, say, a thirty-second spot in a production time of about six weeks.

Most of the significant new work today comes from small teams, and the general artistic standards in animation have never been higher. The artist-animator now paints in movement, not in technique.

There is also a widespread feeling that animated commercials work better than live action because animation can make an incredible statement real. The heaviness of live action does not allow a situation to evolve except in real time. In animation strong, sweeping moves are totally acceptable and even desirable. Repeatedly shown over a long period, live action becomes boring, trite and wholly unbelievable. With animation you can get information across quicker, commercials can be funnier and they can be kept under absolute control.

The USA and Britain are today emerging as the creative centres of television animation. Countries like Australia and Canada, where the American influence is strong, or those without any marked sense of national identity, may tend to imitate the Americans, who of course have by far the largest output. Japan would like to compete in the world market but has some difficulty in understanding what constitutes Western entertainment.

There has recently been some attempt to adapt the charm and fantasy that have always been the strong points of animation to what is called "live animation" (rotoscoping) and electric light graphics as used in the spectacular, big-budgeted *7Up*, *Levi's* and *Remington Razor* spots. This in itself is a sincere form of flattery and an acknowledgement of animation's continued attraction.

Man ist sich allgemein darüber einig – zumindest unter Leuten wie Bob Godfrey, Morton Goldsholl, Arnold Levin und Lee Savage, mit denen ein Meinungsaustausch stattfand, ehe diese Zeilen geschrieben wurden – dass die Werbeagentur heute auf dem Gebiet der Fernsehwerbung eine dominierende Rolle innehat, vor allem in den Vereinigten Staaten. Die Agentur erarbeitet das Grundkonzept, das dem Kunden in Form eines Storyboard unterbreitet wird. Sie überprüft und wählt auch die Animationsstudios, leitet die Produktion und überwacht die Herstellung bis zur allerletzten Aufnahme.

Das Studio wird vorerst beauftragt, aufgrund des Agentur-Storyboards ein Angebot für einen Werbespot zu unterbreiten. Gewöhnlich werden Angebote von drei Studios eingeholt. Ist der Auftrag einmal erteilt, erwartet man, dass z. B. ein 30-Sekunden-Spot in rund sechs Wochen fertiggestellt wird.

Die bedeutendsten Arbeiten kommen heute von kleinen Teams, und es muss anerkennenderweise gesagt werden, dass das allgemeine künstlerische Niveau noch nie so hoch war. Der Filmanimator hat den Akzent mehr und mehr auf die Bewegung verlegt, die angewandte Technik spielt nunmehr eine untergeordnete Rolle.

Weitverbreitet ist auch die Ansicht, dass der Zeichentrickfilm als Werbespot beim Publikum besser ankommt als der Realfilm, da er die unwahrscheinlichsten Aussagen glaubhaft präsentieren kann. Der Realfilm wirkt schwerfälliger, da der Handlungsablauf an die wirkliche Zeit gebunden ist. Im Animationsfilm dagegen sind schnelle Situationswechsel durchaus akzeptabel, ja sogar wünschenswert. Wird der Realfilm über längere Zeit gezeigt, wirkt er bald abgedroschen und völlig unglaubwürdig. Der Trickfilm hingegen vermittelt die gewünschte Information rascher, ist unterhaltsamer, leichter kontrollierbar und zielgerichteter.

Als eigentliche Zentren des Fernsehtrickfilms gelten heute die USA und Grossbritannien, deren Einflussbereich sich auch auf Australien und Kanada ausdehnt. Japan möchte gern mithalten, hat aber einige Schwierigkeit, den im Westen üblichen Unterhaltungsstil zu verstehen.

Es hat in jüngster Zeit Versuche gegeben, durch Real-Animation (Rotoscopie) oder elektronische Graphik den Charme und die Phantasie, die dem Animationsfilm aneignen, auf den Realfilm zu übertragen, so etwa bei den spektakulären und aufwendigen Spots für *7Up*, *Levi's* und *Remington*-Rasierapparate. Damit anerkennt man indirekt die Vorzüge des Animationsfilms.

Commercial Films

Werbefilme

Films commerciaux

On s'accorde généralement à constater le rôle déterminant que joue l'agence publicitaire dans le monde de la télévision commerciale de nos jours, du moins en ce qui concerne les Etats-Unis. C'est ce qui ressort d'un échange de vues avec des spécialistes du rang d'un Bob Godfrey, d'un Morton Goldsholl, d'un Arnold Levin et d'un Lee Savage, lors de la préparation de cet article. C'est en effet l'agence qui prépare la conception de base dans le storyboard remis au client. C'est encore elle qui choisit le studio d'animation, organise la production et surveille l'exécution du film.

Le studio d'animation se voit tout d'abord demander un devis pour un film commercial sur la base du storyboard de l'agence, qui sollicite généralement les devis de trois studios différents. Le studio remportant la commande devra produire p. ex. un spot de 30 secondes dans les six semaines.

La plupart des travaux de qualité proviennent aujourd'hui de petites équipes. Jamais le niveau artistique du cinéma d'animation n'a été aussi élevé. L'artiste-animateur a désormais déplacé l'accent créateur sur l'effet cinétique, le mouvement comptant plus à ses yeux que la technique employée.

Une opinion assez généralisée veut que la publicité faisant appel au film d'animation a de meilleures chances de réussir que celle utilisant le film à acteurs, étant donné qu'elle peut rendre vraisemblables les messages les plus incroyables. Un film «live» est plus lourd parce qu'il est lié au temps réel. Dans l'animation, par contre, les renversements de situation rapides sont parfaitement tolérés, sinon souhaités. Le film à acteurs souffre aisément de l'ennui et du manque de crédibilité vu la répétition au fil des semaines. L'animation aide à transmettre plus rapidement le message, elle le rend divertissant et permet d'en contrôler l'effet à tout moment.

Les grands centres de l'animation au service de la TV sont aujourd'hui les Etats-Unis et la Grande-Bretagne et leurs pays satellites, Australie et Canada en tête. Le Japon aimerait s'imposer sur le marché mondial, mais se heurte au handicap d'une conception différente du divertissement.

On a assisté récemment à une tentative d'adaptation du charme et de l'imagination propres à l'animation, sous forme de «live animation» (rotoscopie) et de création graphique lumineuse. Les meilleurs exemples en sont les spots spectaculaires à grand budget pour *7Up, Levi's* et les rasoirs *Remington.* On peut y voir un hommage sincère en même temps que la reconnaissance de l'attrait permanent qu'exerce le film d'animation.

ARTIST / KÜNSTLER / RÉALISATION:

703–708, 715–720 Bill Littlejohn
709–714 Georges Lemoine

ART DIRECTOR / DIRECTEUR ARTISTIQUE:

703–708, 715–720 Lester Feldman
709–714 André Chante

AGENCY / AGENTUR / AGENCE – STUDIO:

703–708, 715–720 Doyle Dane Bernbach, Inc., New York
709–714 Hollenstein Création, Paris

PRODUCTION / PRODUKTION:

703–708, 715–720 Uniroyal, New York
709–714 Hollenstein Création, Paris

703–708, 715–720 Sequences from two black-and-white television commercials intended to popularize British *Uniroyal* car tyres in the United States and referring to the tiger-like grip of their tread.
709–714 Sequence from an audio-visual commercial for *Gebr. Schmidt,* manufacturers of printing inks, which was shown at the *Drupa* printing exhibition in Dusseldorf in 1972.

703–708, 715–720 Bildfolgen aus zwei Schwarzweiss-Werbefilmen über *Uniroyal*-Pneus und die ausgezeichnete Haftung auf der Strasse, dank ihrer Profile, die in diesen Spots mit Tigerkrallen verglichen werden.
709–714 Sequenz aus einem audio-visuellen Werbefilm für die Druckfarbenfabrik Gebr. Schmidt GmbH. Der Film wurde an der *Drupa '72* in Düsseldorf gezeigt.

703–708, 715–720 Séquences de deux émissions publicitaires en noir et blanc pour les pneus *Uniroyal,* vantant l'adhérence formidable grâce au profil, dont les propriétés sont comparées aux griffes du tigre.
709–714 Séquence d'un film des Frères Schmidt, fabricants d'encres d'imprimerie, présenté à l'exposition de l'imprimerie, la *Drupa* de Dusseldorf, 1972.

703–708

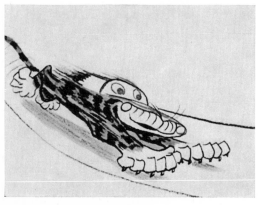  

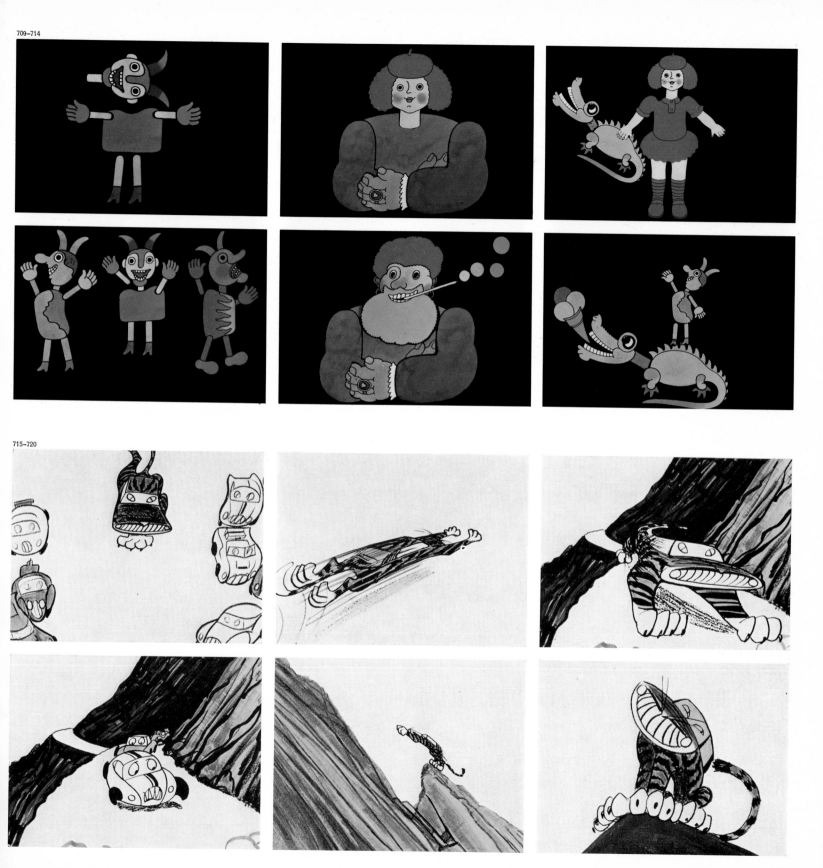

715–720

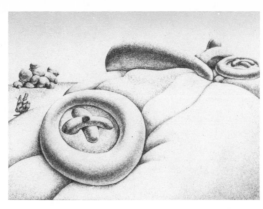

ARTIST / KÜNSTLER / RÉALISATION:

721–726 Bob Peluce
727–732 Jerry Lieberman
733–738 Guy Billout

ART DIRECTOR / DIRECTEUR ARTISTIQUE:

721–726 Bob Kurtz
727–732 Herb Jager
733–738 Jim Burton

AGENCY / AGENTUR / AGENCE – STUDIO:

721–726 Sack's Finley & Kaye
727–732 Gaynor & Ducas, New York
733–738 N.W. Ayer International, New York

PRODUCTION / PRODUKTION:

721–726 Kurtz & Friends, Hollywood
727–732 Ovation Films, Inc., New York
733–738 Linda Kligman/Perpetual Motion, New York

727–732

721–726 Three frames each from two television commercials for *Sparklett's* table waters.
727–732 *Whitman's Dance*, a 30-second commercial which shows dancing throughout the ages up to the present day. It utilizes a graph and a little man also used in the package design, incorporating a needle-point motif.
733–738 *Incredible Machine* is a 60-second colour TV commercial for the American Telephone & Telegraph Co. The objective is to tell people that the telephone company is an intricate system made up of nearly a million people who keep 116 million telephones in working order.

721–726 Je drei Bilder aus zwei verschiedenen Fernsehwerbe-filmen für das Mineralwasser *Sparklett's.*
727–732 *Whitman's Dance*, ein Werbespot von 30 Sekunden, der die Tänze der verschiedenen Jahrhunderte bis heute zeigt. Die Zeichnungen auf Millimeterpapier, mit Kreuzstich-Motiven, zeigen einen kleinen Mann, der auch auf Verpackungen erscheint.
733–738 *Incredible Machine* (Die unglaubliche Maschine), ein Werbespot in Farbe für eine Telephongesellschaft. Er soll dem Zuschauer das komplizierte System einer Telephongeselllchaft vor Augen führen, wo eine Million Angestellte für das Funktio-nieren von 116 Millionen Anschlüssen verantwortlich ist.

721–726 Cases extraits de deux films publicitaires télévisés pour l'eau minérale *Sparklett's.*
727–732 *Whitman's Dance*, spot publicitaire présentant les danses des siècles écoulés jusqu'à nos jours. Dessins sur papier millimètre. Le petit bonhomme est utilisé aussi pour des em-ballages. Motifs s'inspirant de la broderie au point de croix.
733–738 *Incredible Machine.* Emission publicitaire en couleurs de l'AT&T, visant à expliquer au téléspectateur le méchanisme extrêmement compliqué de la compagnie de télécommunication. Le fonctionnement des 116 millions de téléphones est assuré par un million d'employés environ.

743–746

747–750

   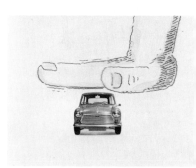

ARTIST / KÜNSTLER / RÉALISATION:

739–742 Pagot Film
743–746 Jean Massé
747–750 Harold F. Mack
751–754 Hal Silvermintz
755–758 Mordi Gerstein
759–764 Walbercy Ribas Camargo

ART DIRECTOR / DIRECTEUR ARTISTIQUE:

739–742 Pagot Film
743–746 Jean Massé
747–750 Harold F. Mack
751–754 Bob Walker
755–758 John Caggiano
759–764 Walbercy Ribas Camargo

AGENCY / AGENTUR / AGENCE – STUDIO:

739–742 Dr. Perissinotto, Rome
743–746 J. Walter Thompson Co., New York
747–750 Wiener, Deville & Wälchli, Küsnacht-Zürich
751–754 Batten, Barton, Durstine & Osborn, Inc., New York
755–758 Doyle Dane Bernbach, Inc., New York
759–764 Eternit do Brasil SA, Sao Paulo

PRODUCTION / PRODUKTION:

739–742 Flli Barbieri, Padua
743–746 Phillips 66, New York
747–750 Anglo-Dutch Group, Amstelveen
751–754 Perpetual Motion Pictures, New York
755–758 Acrilan Carpets, New York
759–764 Start Desenhos Animados, Sao Paulo

759–764

   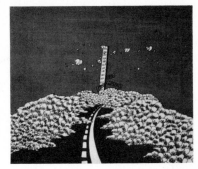

  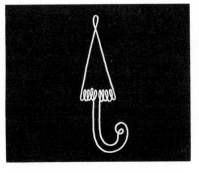 

739–742 *Aperol*. Frames from a colour television commercial for an apéritif.
743–746 *Phillips 66*. Frames from a television commercial for *Phillips 66* tyres which are, it is claimed, tough enough for anything that's waiting for them.
747–750 *British Leyland Mini*. Frames from a story about an Eastern potentate who finds himself stuck while driving his large car and his elephant, whereas his wives can easily pass him in comfort and safety in their *Minis*.
751–754 Frames from a colour television commercial for *The Wall Street Journal*. It refers to the paper's covering of the story of an invasion of America by voracious Formosan termites.
755–758 Frames from a television commercial for *Acrilan* carpets, illustrating the advantages of the various types of fibre.
759–764 Frames from a 30-second television commercial about *Eternit* tiles, made for Eternit do Brasil SA.

739–742 *Aperol*. Sequenz aus einem Fernsehwerbefilm in Farbe.
743–746 Bilder aus einem Werbespot für die Autoreifen *Phillips 66*, von welchen behauptet wird, dass sie jedes Hindernis, das ihnen in den Weg gelegt wird, spielend überwinden.
747–750 Aus einem Werbefilm für *British Leyland*. Die Geschichte handelt von einem orientalischen Herrscher, der mit seinem Strassenkreuzer und seinem Elephanten stecken bleibt, während ihn seine Frauen im *Mini* spielend überholen.
751–754 Sequenz aus einem Fernsehwerbefilm für das *Wall Street Journal*. Die farbigen Zeichnungen beziehen sich auf eine Reportage über eine Termiteninvasion in Amerika.
755–758 Bilder aus einem Fernsehwerbefilm für *Acrilan*-Teppiche, der die Vorteile der verschiedenen Fasern illustrieren soll.
759–764 Bilder aus einem 30 Sekunden dauernden Fernsehwerbespot in Farbe für *Eternit*-Ziegel der für Eternit do Brasil SA produziert wurde.

739–742 *Aperol*. Séquence d'un film publicitaire télévisé en couleurs.
743–746 Images d'une émission publicitaire télévisée pour les pneus *Phillips 66*, dont on prétend qu'ils résistent à tout obstacle qui barre leur chemin.
747–750 D'un film publicitaire pour *British Leyland*. C'est l'histoire d'un potentat oriental qui reste en panne avec sa grande voiture et son éléphant, tandis que ses femmes le dépassent sans difficulté grâce à la *Mini* qu'elles conduisent.
751–754 Séquence d'un film publicitaire pour le *Wall Street Journal*. Les dessins couleur se réfèrent à un reportage sur une invasion de l'Amérique par les termites de Formose.
755–758 Cases d'une émission publicitaire télévisée pour les tapis *Acrilan*, illustrant les avantages des fibres synthétiques.
759–764 Images figurant dans un spot publicitaire télévisé en couleur pour les tuiles en *Eternit*. Film produit pour Eternit do Brasil SA.

765–770 Sequence from an instructional colour film used at an international sales promotion conference on newspapers and magazines.
771–773 Frames from an animated television spot using a skating motif for the *Schweppes* soft drink *Cresta*.
774–779 Sequence from another spot for the soft drink *Cresta*.
780–785 A TV colour commercial for the *American Cancer Society* advising people to have regular medical check-ups even when things seem rosy.

765–770 Sequenz aus einem Informationsfilm in Farbe, der anlässlich einer internationalen Konferenz über Verkaufswerbung für Zeitungen und Zeitschriften gezeigt wurde.
771–773, 774–779 Bilder aus zwei Fernsehwerbespots für *Cresta*, ein Fruchtgetränk von *Schweppes*.
780–785 Aus einem farbigen Fernsehwerbefilm der amerikanischen Krebsliga, die die Zuschauer informiert, dass regelmässige ärztliche Kontrolluntersuchungen unumgänglich sind, auch wenn man sich bei bester Gesundheit wähnt.

765–770 Séquence figurant dans un film informatif en couleurs qui a été montré lors d'une conférence internationale sur l'auto-promotion des journaux et magazines.
771–773, 774–779 Cases de deux spots publicitaires différents pour la limonade *Cresta* de *Schweppes*.
780–785 D'un film couleur de la Ligue américaine pour la lutte contre le cancer, prévenant les téléspectateurs de l'importance des examens médicaux réguliers même s'ils se croient en parfaite santé.

ARTIST / KÜNSTLER / RÉALISATION:

765–770 Graham Clarke
771–773 Richard Williams
774–779 Chris Baker
780–785 Warren A. Kass

ART DIRECTOR / DIRECTEUR ARTISTIQUE:

765–770 Clarke/Clements/Hughes
771–773 Richard Williams
774–779 John Webster
780–785 Sam Cooperstein

AGENCY / AGENTUR / AGENCE – STUDIO:

765–770 Peter Masson & Partners, London
771–779 Boase Massimi Pollitt, London
780–785 Young & Rubicam International, Inc., New York

PRODUCTION / PRODUKTION:

765–770 Clarke/Clements/Hughes, Maidstone/GBR
771–779 Richard Williams Animation Ltd., London
780–785 American Cancer Society, New York

It's frothy man.

ARTIST / KÜNSTLER / RÉALISATION:
786–801, 802–822 Seymour Chwast

ART DIRECTOR / DIRECTEUR ARTISTIQUE:
786–801, 802–822 Bill Alderisio

AGENCY / AGENTUR / AGENCE – STUDIO:
786–801, 802–822 Ogilvy & Mather, Inc., New York

PRODUCTION / PRODUKTION:
786–801, 802–822 Schweppes (USA) Ltd., New York

786–797, 801 Sequence from a television commercial for *Schweppes,* one of eight spots showing how ancestors and kinsmen of Commander Whitehead—a British figure used for *Schweppes* advertising in the USA—played a part (with the aid of *Schweppervescence*) in famous episodes from British history. Here Orville Whitehead brings down an enemy plane by rather unorthodox means in the Battle of Britain.
798–800 Single frames from a series of eight television commercials for *Schweppes.*

786–797, 801 Sequenz aus einem Fernsehwerbefilm für *Schweppes.* Acht farbige Werbespots zeigen die grossen Taten der Vorfahren und Verwandten des illustren Kommandanten Whitehead – eines typischen Engländers –, die in berühmt gewordenen Ereignissen der englischen Geschichte eine ruhmvolle Rolle gespielt haben sollen. Diese Sequenz zeigt, wie Orville Whitehead in der Schlacht um England ein feindliches Flugzeug zum Absturz bringt.
798–800 Szenen aus verschiedenen Fernsehwerbefilmen für *Schweppes.*

786–797, 801 Séquence d'un film publicitaire télévisé pour *Schweppes.* Huit spots en couleur retracent l'histoire des membres de la famille Whitehead qui a eu une part décisive dans les grands événements de l'histoire anglaise et dont les prouesses contribuèrent à la gloire de l'Angleterre – à en croire à cette série! Dans cette séquence avec Orville Whitehead en vedette on apprend des faits nouveaux sur la Bataille d'Angleterre.
798–800 Images extraites de différents films publicitaires télévisés réalisés pour *Schweppes.*

798

799

800

801

157

802

802 Single frame from *Beau Reggie*, a *Schweppes* film which explains the origin of the stiff upper lip.
803–810 Sequence from the television commercial *Lawrence of Arabia*, the hero of which is once more a member of the Whitehead family (see Figs. 786–797). This time it is a Whitehead who stages the party at which Lawrence's camel laps up a party-size bottle of *Schweppes* tonic and is thus primed for the hazardous desert crossing that brought Lawrence fame.
811–822 Sequence from a television commercial recounting how Captain Cook was saved by *Schweppervescence*.

802 Image tirée du film publicitaire de *Schweppes* intitulé *Beau Reggie*. Il explique l'origine de l'intrépidité britannique.
803–810 Séquence du spot publicitaire télévisé intitulé *Lawrence d'Arabie*. Le héros en est une fois de plus un membre de la grande famille Whitehead. Ici, on le voit organiser la soirée au cours de laquelle le chameau de Lawrence avale tout rond une grosse bouteille de tonique *Schweppes*, ce qui le met en état de tenir bon pendant la périlleuse chevauchée dans le désert qui devait valoir la gloire à Lawrence.
811–822 Séquence du film publicitaire télévisé narrant le sauvetage du capitaine Cook grâce à *Schweppes*.

802 Bild aus dem *Schweppes*-Werbefilm *Beau Reggie*, der den Ursprung der «steifen Oberlippe» erklären soll.
803–810 Bildfolge aus einem anderen *Schweppes*-Fernsehwerbespot – *Lawrence von Arabien*. Wiederum spielt ein Mitglied der berühmten Familie Whitehead die Hauptrolle. Der Film zeigt, wie er die Party organisiert, an welcher das Kamel von Lawrence eine Party-Flasche *Schweppes*-Tonic trinkt und sich auf diese Art für die gewagte Wüstendurchquerung, die Lawrence grossen Ruhm einbrachte, aufs Beste versorgt.
811–822 Diese Sequenz zeigt, wie *Schweppes* dem berühmten *Captain Cook* das Leben rettete.

Credits on previous page
Künstlerlisten auf vorangehender Seite
Liste d'artistes à la page précédente

  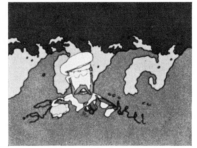 

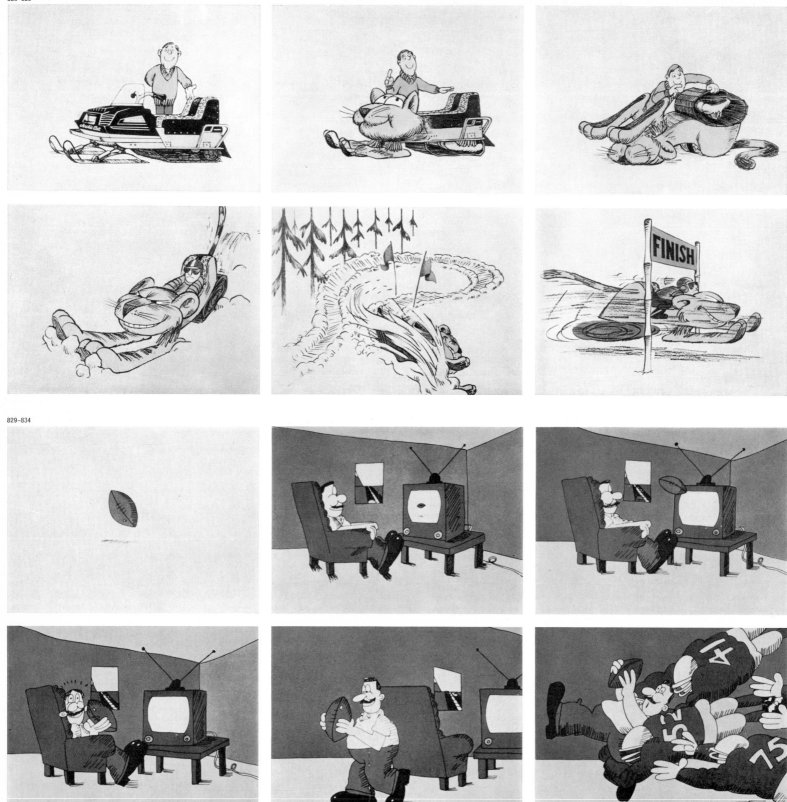

823–828 Sequence from a television commercial about the qualities of *Arctic Cat* snowmobiles.
829–834 Sequence from a 2-minute colour teaser to promote CBS sports programmes. It is without voice tracks, so that a live voice can be introduced on each programme.
835–840 Sequence from a television commercial about *Bonduelle* tinned vegetables. The wheelbarrow—suggesting garden-fresh vegetables—is widely used in the company's publicity.
841–843 *Detefon-Mata-Tudo*, a 30-second colour commercial for an insecticide. A whole theatre full of insects is destroyed by the powerful powder.

ARTIST / KÜNSTLER / RÉALISATION:

823–828 M. Lind/Richard Pantano/Stavros Cosmopulos
829–834 Len Glasser/Lou Dorfsman
835–840 Tomi Ungerer
841–843 Daniel Messias

823–828 Bildfolge aus einem Fernsehwerbefilm für *Arctic Cat*-Schneemobile.
829–834 Bildfolge aus einem farbigen 2-Minuten-«Anreger» zur Förderung der Sportprogramme des CBS-Fernsehens.
835–840 Sequenz aus einem Fernseh-Werbespot für *Bonduelle*-Gemüsekonserven. Der Schubkarren wird in der Werbung dieser Firma häufig verwendet: er spielt auf frisches Gemüse an.
841–843 Bilder aus einem farbigen Fernsehspot für das Insektizid *Detefon-Mata-Tudo*. Der Film zeigt, wie die ganze «Insekten»-Zuschauermenge eines Theaters durch Besprühen mit diesem Mittel ausgerottet wird.

AGENCY / AGENTUR / AGENCE – STUDIO:

823–828 Hill, Holliday, Connors, Cosmopulos, Inc., Boston
829–834 CBS Broadcast Group, New York
835–840 Robert Pütz GmbH & Co., Köln
841–843 McCann Erickson, Sao Paulo

823–828 Séquence d'un film publicitaire télévisé pour les véhicules de neige *Arctic Cat*.
829–834 Spot publicitaire couleur déstiné à éveiller la curiosité du spectateur au sujet des programmes sportifs CBS.
835–840 Séquence d'un film TV pour les conserves de légumes *Bonduelle*. La société fait un usage intense de la brouette afin d'évoquer les légumes frais du jardin.
841–843 Cases d'un spot publicitaire en couleurs pour l'insecticide *Detefon-Mata-Tudo*. Tous les insectes spectateurs réunis dans le théâtre seront anéantis après avoir été aspergés de cet insecticide.

PRODUCTION / PRODUKTION:

823–828 Jack Zander
829–834 Harold Friedman/Directors' Circle, Inc., New York
835–840 TV Cartoons, London
841–843 Daniel Messias Studios, Santana/BRA

841–843

ARTIST / KÜNSTLER / RÉALISATION:

844–851 Tom Ballenger
852–855 Marv Newland
856–863 Peter Helbling
864–875 Paul Vester

ART DIRECTOR / DIRECTEUR ARTISTIQUE:

844–851 Mike Lawlor
852–855 Marv Newland
856–863 Peter Schreiner
864–875 Karl Klein

AGENCY / AGENTUR / AGENCE – STUDIO:

844–851 Doyle Dane Bernbach, Inc., New York
852–855 Cole & Weber, Seattle
856–863 B + W AG, Zürich
864–875 Synergie/Synodis, Paris

PRODUCTION / PRODUKTION:

844–851 Kim & Gifford Productions, Inc., New York
852–855 International Rocketship Ltd., Vancouver
856–863 Piraud AG, Thalwil/SWI
864–875 Chloe Walters/Halas & Batchelor Animation Ltd., London

844–851 *The Hare and the Tortoise.* In this variation on the old theme the tortoise gets so far ahead that he checks into a hotel for a nap. When he awakes he is so far behind that he has to buy some very fast *Keds Sneakers* in order to win the race and a *Keds* whistle.
852–855 *Western Washington Fair.* A commercial made to announce the opening of a fair.
856–863 Sequence from a television commercial for a product called *Tannspray* to prevent pine needles falling from Christmas trees.
864–875 Sequence from a Halas & Batchelor television commercial for *Antar* petrol. The purpose is to show how research and development help the petrol-station attendant.

844–851 *The Hare and the Tortoise.* Die Schildkröte ist dem Hasen so weit voraus, dass sie ein Nickerchen macht. Unterdessen überrundet sie der Hase. Sie realisiert, dass sie nur mit *Keds Sneakers* gewinnen kann. Der Preis: eine Pfeife, nicht für den Sieg, sondern als Werbegeschenk.
852–855 Aus einem TV-Spot, der die Eröffnung der *Western Washington Fair* anzeigt.
856–863 Bildfolge aus einem Fernsehwerbefilm für *Tannspray*, ein Produkt, das bei Christbäumen den frühzeitigen Nadelregen verhindert.
864–875 Sequenz aus einem Fernsehwerbefilm für *Antar*-Treibstoffe. Die Bilder sollen zeigen, wie Forschung und Entwicklung zur Erleichterung der Arbeit des Tankwarts beitragen können.

844–851 *The Hare and the Tortoise.* La tortue a distancé le lièvre de loin et se met à faire un petit somme. En se réveillant elle réalise que le lièvre l'a doublée et que ce n'est qu'avec des *Keds Sneakers* que la course peut être gagnée. Elle arrive la première et remporte un sifflet non pas en tant que prix mais en tant que cadeau publicitaire.
852–855 Spot télévisé annonçant l'ouverture de la *Western Washington Fair.*
856–863 Séquence d'un film publicitaire télévisé en faveur de *Tannspray*, un produit empêchant la chute des aiguilles des sapins de Noël.
864–875 Séquence d'un film publicitaire TV réalisé par Halas & Batchelor pour les pétroles *Antar.* On y montre l'influence de la recherche et du développement sur le travail du pompiste.

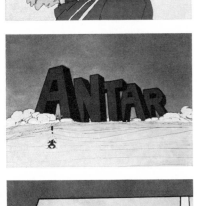

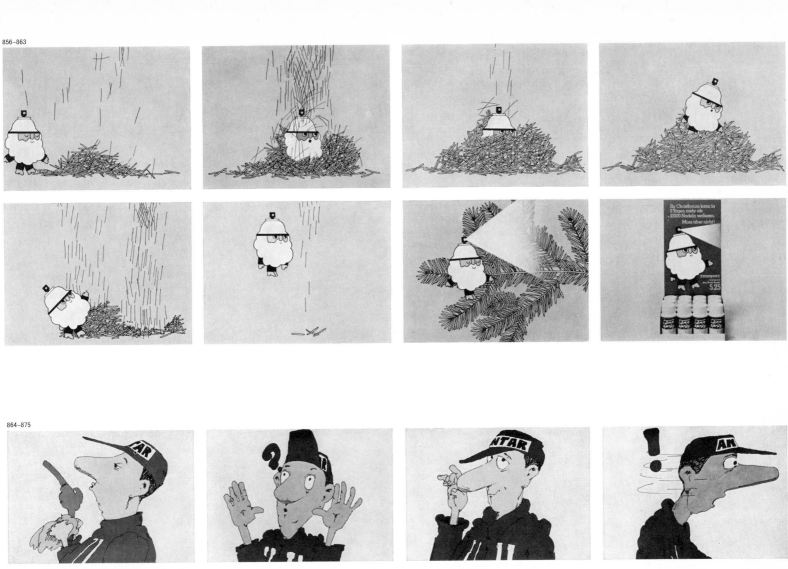

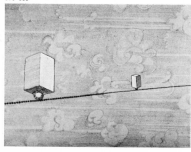

876–883 Sequence from a colour television commercial for AT&T to encourage personal weekend telephone calls.
884–891 From a 60-second colour cinema commercial about the *7Up* soft drink *Hippies* which has won a number of international prizes.
892–899 Sequence from a colour television commercial about the *Volkswagen,* showing that the "beetle" successfully resists all efforts to destroy it.
900–907 Sequence from a television commercial showing how the *Pan-Am* freight service can help clients to save.

876–883 Bildfolge aus einem farbigen Fernsehwerbefilm der Telephongesellschaft AT&T. Er soll die Zuschauer dazu anregen, vermehrt über das Wochenende zu telephonieren.
884–891 Sequenz aus einem Kino-Werbefilm in Farbe für *Hippies,* eine neues Mineralwasser von *7Up.* Der Film wurde mit verschiedenen internationalen Preisen ausgezeichnet.
892–899 Bildfolge aus einem farbigen Fernsehwerbefilm über den *Volkswagen.* Die Bilder zeigen, wie der «Käfer» allen auf ihn abzielenden Zerstörungsversuchen mit Erfolg widersteht.
900–907 Sequenz aus einem Fernsehwerbefilm, der zeigt, wie der Frachtdienst der *Pan Am* dem Kunden helfen kann, Kosten einzusparen.

  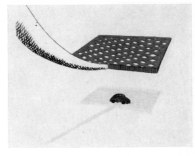

876–883 Séquence d'un film publicitaire télévisé en couleur d'une compagnie de télécommunications encourageant les téléspectateurs à faire leurs appels téléphoniques pendant le week-end.
884–891 Séquence d'un film publicitaire TV en couleur pour *Hippies,* une eau minérale de *7Up.* Ce film a remporté de nombreux prix internationaux.
892–899 Séquence d'une émission publicitaire en couleurs sur la *Volkswagen.* Elle démontre que la «Coccinelle» défie toute tentative visant à la détruire.
900–907 Séquence d'un spot publicitaire télévisé montrant comment les services de fret de *Pan Am* permettent à leurs clients de réduire les frais.

ARTIST / KÜNSTLER / RÉALISATION:

876–883 Faith & John Hubley
884–891 Harold F. Mack
892–899 Richard Bairstow
900–907 Robert O. Blechman/Bruce Colson

AGENCY / AGENTUR / AGENCE – STUDIO:

876–883 N.W. Ayer & Son, New York
884–891 PRAD B.V., Amsterdam
892–899 Doyle Dane Bernbach GmbH, Düsseldorf/Richard Williams, London
900–907 Tatham-Laird & Kudner, Inc., New York

ART DIRECTOR / DIRECTEUR ARTISTIQUE:

876–883 Jim Cherry
884–891 Harold F. Mack
892–899 Richard Bairstow
900–907 Bruce Colson

PRODUCTION / PRODUKTION:

876–883 The Hubley Studio, New York
884–891 Anglo-Dutch Group B.V., Amstelveen/Holland
892–899 Volkswagenwerk GmbH, Wolfsburg
900–907 Pan American World-Airways, New York

 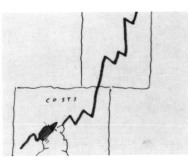  

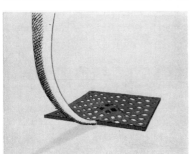   

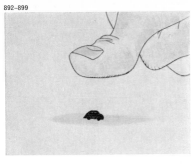

908–916 Frames from a series of American TV commercials based on fairy tales for *Jack in the Box* drive-in restaurants.
917–922 Sequence from a French *Esso* film on oil refining processes entitled *Raffiner Toujours*.
923–925 Frames from a television commercial about indoor temperatures for the American Gas Association.

908–916 Bilder aus einer Serie von Fernsehwerbefilmen mit Neufassungen von Märchen, für Drive-in-Restaurants.
917–922 Sequenz aus einem Film von *Esso* über die Ölraffinierung, mit dem Titel *Raffiner Toujours*.
923–925 Bildfolge aus einem Fernsehwerbefilm der amerikanischen Gasversorgungsgesellschaft. Thema: Innentemperaturen.

908–916 D'une série de films publicitaires télévisés avec des extraits de contes pour une chaîne de restaurants américains.
917–922 Séquence tirée du film *Raffiner Toujours* de l'*Esso*, qui présente les techniques de raffinage du pétrole.
923–925 Cases d'une émission publicitaire d'une compagnie de gaz américaine traitant des températures à l'intérieur.

908–916

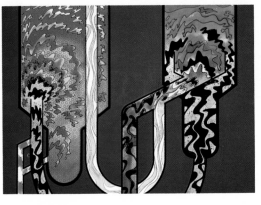

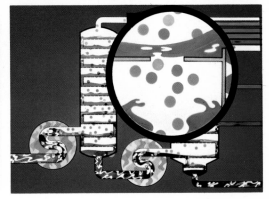

ARTIST / KÜNSTLER / RÉALISATION:

908–916, 923–925 André François
917–922 Studio Arcady

ART DIRECTOR / DIRECTEUR ARTISTIQUE:

908–916, 923–925 André François
917–922 J. Aurence

AGENCY / AGENTUR / AGENCE – STUDIO:

908–916 Doyle Dane Bernbach, Inc., Los Angeles
923–925 J. Walter Thompson Co., New York

PRODUCTION / PRODUKTION:

908–916 Jenkyns, Shean & Elliott, Inc., Los Angeles
917–922 Ph. Landrot/Esso, Paris
923–925 American Gas Association, New York

926–933 This film was designed to explore and project the new *7Up* graphics as applied to the bottle carriers for sugar-free products.

934–941 Sequence from a television commercial for *Olivetti* entitled *The Fruitstore*. Pompeo and Zeno, proprietors of the P & Z fruitstore, have an argument. They decide to separate and to divide their inventory with the aid of a calculator. After dividing everything evenly they are left with a problem: who is to get the calculator? Zeno proposes that they divide that also. He is to use it on Monday, Wednesday and Friday, and Pompeo can use it on Tuesday, Thursday and Saturday. But who is to use it on Sunday? Unable to solve this problem, and reluctant to part with their calculator even for a day, they decide to resolve their differences and to remain in business together.

942–957 Sequence from the television commercial *The Message*, for *Olivetti*, based on an idea by Giorgio Soavi.

926–933 Zweck dieses Filmes war, das neue graphische Symbol der zuckerfreien Produkte von *7Up*, wie es auf Flaschenträgern und Lieferwagen erscheint, einzuführen.

934–941 Sequenz aus einem Fernsehwerbefilm (Die Obsthandlung) von *Olivetti*. Nach einer Auseinandersetzung entschliessen sich Pompeo und Zeno, die Besitzer der Obsthandlung, sich zu trennen. Mit Hilfe einer Rechenmaschine teilen sie ihren Besitz in zwei gleiche Teile – doch, was soll mit der Rechenmaschine geschehen? Zeno schlägt vor, dass sie auch diese teilen, der eine kann sie Montag, Mittwoch und Freitag, der andere Dienstag, Donnerstag und Samstag brauchen. Wer aber soll sie am Sonntag brauchen? Da sich keiner auch nur für einen Tag von der Rechenmaschine trennen will, beschliessen sie zu guter Letzt, den Streit zu begraben und das Geschäft gemeinsam weiterzuführen.

942–957 Aus dem TV-Spot *Le Message* für *Olivetti*, nach einer Idee von Giorgio Soavi.

926–933 Ce film vise à introduire le symbole graphique pour les produits *7Up* pauvres en sucre, symbole récemment créé et utilisé pour les portes-bouteilles et les fourgonnettes.

934–941 Séquence d'un film publicitaire *Olivetti* (La Fruiterie). Après une querelle, Pompeo et Zeno, les propriétaires de la fruiterie, décident à se séparer. A l'aide d'une calculatrice ils partagent minutieusement tout ce qu'il y a dans le magasin – mais que faut-il faire de la calculatrice? Zeno propose qu'ils la partagent aussi, de manière que l'un peut s'en servir le lundi, le mercredi et le vendredi, l'autre le mardi, le jeudi et le samedi. Mais qui s'en servira alors le dimanche? Puisque ni l'un ni l'autre n'est prêt à y renoncer même pour un seul jour, ils se mettent finalement d'accord d'enterrer ce différend et de reprendre ensemble le commerce de fruits.

942–957 Séquence d'un film publicitaire télévisé intitulé *Le Message*. Il a été réalisé pour *Olivetti* d'après la conception de Giorgio Soavi.

ARTIST / KÜNSTLER / RÉALISATION:

926–933 Morton Goldsholl/Dick Greenberg
934–941 Robert O. Blechman
942–957 Jean Michel Folon

ART DIRECTOR / DIRECTEUR ARTISTIQUE:

926–933 Morton Goldsholl
934–941 Robert O. Blechman
942–957 Jean Michel Folon

AGENCY / AGENTUR / AGENCE – STUDIO:

926–933 J. Walter Thompson Co., New York
942–957 Gianini/Luzzati, Rome

PRODUCTION / PRODUKTION:

926–933 Goldsholl Associates, Inc., Northfield, Ill.
934–941 Robert O. Blechman, Inc., New York
942–957 Gianini/Luzzati, Rome

942–957

958

959

960–963

964–967

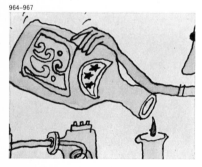

ARTIST / KÜNSTLER / RÉALISATION:

958, 959 Wayne Anderson
960–963 Harold F. Mack
964–967 René Fehr
968 Suzan Pitt Kraning
969–971 Etienne Delessert
972–975 Horst Piehler

ART DIRECTOR / DIRECTEUR ARTISTIQUE:

958, 959 Geoff Dunbar/Fritz de Jonge
960–963 Harold F. Mack
964–967 Ruedi Külling
969–971 Ivan Horwath

AGENCY / AGENTUR / AGENCE – STUDIO:

958, 959 Franlen Hey & Veltman, Amsterdam
960–963 PRAD B.V., Amsterdam
964–967 Advico Werbeagentur, Gockhausen-Zürich
969–971 Ogilvy & Mather, Inc., New York

PRODUCTION / PRODUKTION:

958, 959 Halas & Batchelor Animation, New York
960–963 Anglo-Dutch Group B.V., Amstelveen/NLD
964–967 Topic, Gockhausen/Jean Zippèr, Küsnacht
968 Whitney Museum of American Art/
Film Production, Inc., New York
969–971 Ivan Horwath/Tom Brennan/Electra, New York
972–975 Deutsche Dokumentar- und
Werbefilm GmbH, Berlin

972–975

958, 959 Two frames from a colour television commercial for *Dessa* margarine.
960–963 *7Up Cameleons*. Frames from a prize-winning commercial for the soft drink.
964–967 Sequence from a television commercial for the fruit drink *Sinalco*, executed in the typical pop style adopted by this company.
968 A frame from the *Whitney Commercial*, a film about the New York museum, often shown at festivals.
969–971 Frames from a television commercial in colour for *Pepperidge Farm* bakery products.
972–975 From a commercial for the illustrated German magazine *Der Stern*.

958, 959 Bilder aus einem farbigen Fernsehwerbespot für *Dessa*-Margarine.
960–963 Bilder aus dem preisgekrönten Werbespot *7Up Chamäleon* für das beliebte Tafelgetränk.
964–967 Sequenz aus einem Fernsehwerbefilm für das Fruchtgetränk *Sinalco*. Auch dieser Film wurde in dem für die *Sinalco*-Werbung verwendeten Pop-Stil gezeichnet.
968 Bild aus einem farbigen Fernsehwerbespot des *Whitney Museums* in New York, der über die Filmvorführungen des Museums informiert.
969–971 Sequenz aus einem farbigen Fernsehwerbefilm für *Pepperidge Farm*-Backwaren.
972–975 Bildfolge aus einem Fernsehwerbefilm für die Zeitschrift *Der Stern*.

958, 959 Deux cases d'un spot publicitaire télévisé en couleurs pour la margarine *Dessa*.
960–963 Séquence d'un film plusieurs fois couronné – *7Up Caméléon* – pour une boisson de table.
964–967 Séquence d'un film publicitaire télévisé pour le mélange de jus de fruits *Sinalco*. Le film est dessiné dans le style pop qui caractérise la publicité pour cette boisson.
968 Image d'un spot publicitaire télévisé en couleurs pour le *Whitney Museum* à New York. Il annonce le programme des manifestations culturelles.
969–971 Séquence d'un film publicitaire en couleurs pour la pâtisserie *Pepperidge Farm*.
972–975 Séquence d'un film publicitaire télévisé pour le magazine *Der Stern*.

968

969–971

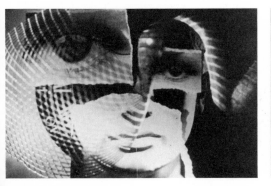
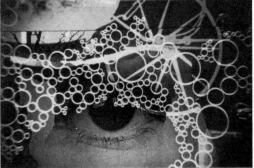

Louis Dorfsman

The early fifties saw the beginning of a design explosion in the Western world. One of the new departures at that time was the application of thoughtful, provocative visual design to motion pictures in the shape of "titling" or "openings". Saul Bass was in the forefront of this development, inspiring and stimulating those who came after. Naturally enough, the impact of cinema film titling soon spilled over into that youngest and most voracious consumer of moving images, television.

Titling might be compared in function to a book jacket or the packaging—one must go inside for the contents. The object, here too, is to catch the eye, to arouse interest and to impart some hint of what is to come. This calls for concept design, graphic drama, style and often the imaginative use of sound. With this range of instrumentation, the possibilities inherent in film and tape are infinite. Television titling differs from cinema film titling in calling for a more rigid synthesis. Cinema titling can occupy leisurely minutes to make its statement. Television offers only seconds: anything from 3½ to 30 is normal. The cinema's titles serve as a curtain raiser or give the audience time to settle in their seats. Its titling art can also be more specific, for by its nature a motion picture is unique to itself. In television, by contrast, titling for a weekly series cannot be done in very specific terms, since the titles must serve for all episodes, week after week. The problem is rather one of maintaining interest and provocativeness over long periods without going stale or wearing out one's welcome. On the one hand TV titling should act as a recognition signal for the viewer—"here comes my favourite show"; yet on the other there is the ever present pitfall of monotony through frequency of exposure—or even of generating public annoyance by constant repetition. For this reason the TV medium calls for a degree of invention and enterprise that is perhaps more challenging than in the cinema film.

Today cinema film titling is near a fully realized state, while TV titling is just awakening to its potential. Cinema films play to captive audiences, while TV is a continuous stream of programmes in which the need to stimulate audience expectation is much more pronounced.

The graphic designer who has only worked in print and has never experienced the rigorous but heady world of sight, sound and motion is today an acutely underprivileged designer.

Die westliche Welt erlebte in den frühen fünfziger Jahren eine wahre Designexplosion, die sich auch in einer durchdachten und provokativen Gestaltung von Filmtitel und Vorspann manifestierte. Grosses Verdienst, neue Marksteine gesetzt zu haben, kommt dabei Saul Bass zu, an welchem sich bald eine ganze Reihe Graphiker orientierte. Wie selbstverständlich griff die neue Welle von Titel- und Vorspanngestaltung auf das jüngste und auf bewegte Bilder versessenste Medium über: das Fernsehen.

In seiner Funktion ist der Titelvorspann mit einem Bucheinband oder einer Verpackung zu vergleichen — man muss hineinschauen, will man den Inhalt kennen. Hier wie dort will man ins Auge fallen, will das Interesse wecken und das zu Erwartende andeuten. Dies erfordert ein auf das Gesamtkonzept ausgerichtetes Design, zündende Ideen sowie eine phantasiereiche Vertonung. Die Möglichkeiten, die sowohl der Film wie das Videoband bieten, sind schlechthin unbegrenzt. Fernsehvorspanne unterscheiden sich dabei von Titelvorspannen für Kinofilme durch eine strengere Synthese. Das Fernsehen erlaubt nur Sekunden – 3½–30 durchschnittlich –, während Kinotitel mehrere Minuten lang auf der Leinwand erscheinen. Filmtitel dienen als kurzes Vorspiel und geben dem Kinobesucher Zeit, seinen Platz einzunehmen. Die Titelgestaltung kann auch spezifischer sein, da der Film an sich ein einmaliges Ereignis ist. Im Gegensatz dazu wird ein Titel im Fernsehen für eine wöchentliche Sendung nie so spezifisch wirken, da er Woche für Woche auf dem Bildschirm erscheint. Das Problem liegt eher darin, das Interesse des Zuschauers zu wecken; er dient als Aufhänger für die Sendung und darf über längere Zeit nicht abstumpfen. Der Titel soll dem Zuschauer einerseits als Erkennungszeichen dienen – «ah, da kommt meine Lieblingssendung!» – andererseits birgt aber schon die Tatsache der ständigen Wiederholung die Gefahr der Monotonie und Langeweile in sich. Aus diesem Grund verlangt das Fernsehen einen höheren Grad an Erfindungsgeist als der Kinofilm.

Der Vorspann für Kinofilme hat heute beinahe den Höhepunkt der Entwicklung erreicht, während sein TV-Pendant eben erst dabei ist, sein Potential zu entdecken. Kinofilme spielen vor einem gebannten Publikum, während das Fernsehen einen unablässigen Programmstrom bietet, so dass das Bedürfnis nach Zuschauer-Stimulierung ausgeprägter ist.

Der Graphik-Designer, der nur für die Presse gearbeitet hat und nie die rauhe, aber berauschende Welt von Bild, Ton und Bewegung kennenlernte, ist heute beinahe ein unterprivilegierter Designer.

Le monde occidental a connu dès le début des années 50 une véritable explosion graphique, qui s'est matérialisée dans le domaine de la création de titres et génériques de films par une approche réfléchie et provocatrice à la fois. Le mérite d'avoir frayé cette voie revient à Saul Bass, qui inspira bientôt nombre de graphistes. Inévitablement, les titres et génériques nouvelle vague ne tardèrent pas à envahir un média nouveau, consommateur vorace d'images animées: la télévision.

Le titre exerce la même fonction que l'emballage ou la jaquette de livre – il faut se reporter à l'intérieur pour connaître le contenu. Il s'agit ici aussi d'accrocher le regard, de susciter de l'intérêt et d'évoquer de manière générale ce qui va suivre. Il y faut un design axé sur le concept, un graphisme dramatique, du style et souvent l'emploi imaginatif du son. Les possibilités inhérentes à la pellicule et à la bande vidéo deviennent alors proprement illimitées. Le titrage TV diffère du titrage cinéma par une rigueur de synthèse plus poussée. Il ne dispose que de secondes – 3½ à 30, en moyenne – là où le cinéma peut occuper des minutes entières. Les génériques du cinéma servent de lever de rideau ou donnent aux spectateurs le temps de s'installer dans leurs fauteuils. L'art du titrage peut être plus spécifique, un film étant un événement unique en soi. A la TV, le titrage d'un feuilleton ne peut être poussé jusqu'à la spécificité, puisqu'il doit servir des semaines durant. Le problème consiste alors plutôt à soutenir l'intérêt et à assurer l'effet d'accrochage pendant des périodes assez longues sans lasser le téléspectateur ni épuiser sa capacité d'accueil. Le titrage TV sert d'une part de repère – «ah, voilà mon émission préférée!»; d'autre part, le fait même de sa répétition risque de le faire tomber dans le piège de la monotonie et de l'ennui sources d'irritation pour le téléspectateur. C'est pourquoi la création graphique pour la TV requiert une part plus grande d'inventivité et d'audace et impose un défi peut-être plus difficile à relever qu'au cinéma.

La confection de génériques pour le grand écran semble avoir aujourd'hui atteint sa vitesse de croisière, alors que son homologue TV n'en est qu'à une prise de conscience de ses potentialités propres. Le flux continu de programmes TV impose par ailleurs un plus grand effort de singularisation que le film de cinéma, pour mobiliser l'attention.

Ces considérations font pressentir l'intérêt que revêt pour tout graphiste la création dans le domaine combiné du visuel, du son et de l'animation, domaine exigeant, mais capiteux où s'éprouve le vrai talent.

Film Titles and Captions

Titelgestaltung

Titres et génériques

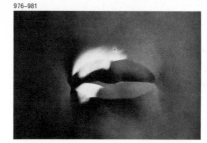
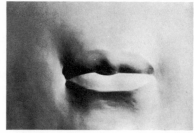

976–981 Titling sequence for *Omnibus*, a programme on the arts regularly broadcast in Britain by the BBC.
982–987 From the storyboard of *1975 on BBC 1*, an annual retrospect of the previous year's programmes broadcast by the BBC.
988–993 Titling sequence for a programme entitled *Password*, a series regularly broadcast in Britain by the BBC.
994 A typographically treated title for a television play presented by the Canadian Broadcasting Corporation.
995 ABC day-of-the-week logo, a 3-second effect used to introduce the programmes of ABC Television for the various days of the week. The three-dimensional effect is obtained by modulating the light source in the course of a time exposure.
996 Typographically treated title for a film magazine programme presented regularly on Canadian television.

976–981 Vorspann zur Sendung *Omnibus*, ein vom britischen Fernsehen regelmässig ausgestrahltes Kunstprogramm.
982–987 Sequenz aus dem Storyboard für die Sendung *1975 on BBC*, einem Jahresrückblick des britischen Fernsehens.
988–993 Vorspann zu einer Sendereihe mit dem Titel *Password* (Kennwort), die vom britischen Fernsehen ausgestrahlt wird.
994 Typographische Gestaltung des Titels für ein Theaterstück, das am kanadischen Fernsehen gezeigt wurde.
995 Logo für das ABC-Fernsehen. Dieses Signet wird für 3 Sekunden eingeblendet und kündigt die Programmvorschau für den entsprechenden Tag an. Der dreidimensionale Effekt wurde erzielt, indem die Lichtintensität bei einer Zeitaufnahme moduliert wurde.
996 Typographische Gestaltung des Titelvorspanns für ein Filmprogramm, das regelmässig vom kanadischen Fernsehen gesendet wird.

976–981 Générique introduisant le programme *Omnibus* de la télévision britannique, programme consacré aux beaux-arts.
982–987 Séquence du storyboard pour un programme de la télévision britannique intitulé *1975 à la BBC*.
988–993 Générique d'introduction pour une série intitulée *Password* (Mot de passe), série diffusée par la télévision britannique.
994 Présentation typographique extraite d'un générique d'introduction d'une émission dramatique au réseau français de la télévision canadienne.
995 Logo de ABC que cette station de télévision fait apparaître pour annoncer les prochaines émissions. L'effet tridimensionnel a été obtenu par la modulation de la lumière pendant une pose prolongée.
996 Présentation typographique extraite du générique d'introduction pour un programme culturel au réseau français de la télévision canadienne.

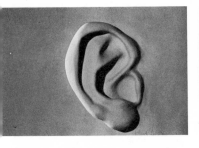  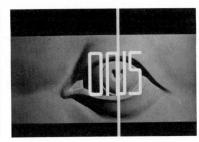 

996

ARTIST / KÜNSTLER / RÉALISATION:

976–981 Bob Blagdon
982–987 Peter Clayton
988–993 Bernard Lodge
994, 996 André Theroux
995 Robert Abel/Con Pederson

ART DIRECTOR / DIRECTEUR ARTISTIQUE:

976–981 Bob Blagdon
982–987 Peter Clayton
988–993 Bernard Lodge
994, 996 Robert Sarrazin
995 Harry Marks/Robert Abel

PRODUCTION / PRODUKTION:

976–993 British Broadcasting Corporation, London
994, 996 Société Radio-Canada, Montréal
995 American Broadcasting Companies, Inc., New York

1004–1006

997–1002 Titling sequence for a programme shown on Rediffusion Television in Britain.
1003 Promotion slide for a series entitled *Action 72* shown on Granada Television.
1004–1006 Captions for various occasions—end of cartoons, fashion and stamp-collecting—from a series of women's programmes broadcast by Monte Carlo television under the title *Boutique de Valérie*.
1007–1012 Titling sequence for a BBC documentary about the Red Cross organization.

997–1002 Titelfolge für ein Programm, das von einer britischen Fernsehgesellschaft ausgestrahlt wurde.
1003 Voranzeige für das Programm *Action 72*, eine Sendereihe der Fernsehgesellschaft Granada.
1004–1006 Aus einer Serie von Voranzeigen für verschiedene Sendungen: Ende des Comics-Programms; Mode und Philatelie aus der Sendereihe für Frauen *Boutique de Valérie*. Alle Programme wurden von Télé Monte Carlo ausgestrahlt.
1007–1012 Sequenz aus dem Titelvorspann für einen Dokumentarfilm des britischen Fernsehens über das Rote Kreuz.

997–1002 Séquence extraite du générique pour un programme diffusé par Rediffusion Television en Angleterre.
1003 Diapositive publicitaire pour une série de la télévision Granada, intitulée *Action 72*.
1004–1006 Exemples d'une série de diapositives publicitaires utilisées par Télé Monte Carlo pour divers programmes: fin du programme de dessins animés; mode et philatélie de l'émission féminine intitulée *Boutique de Valérie*.
1007–1012 Séquence du générique pour un documentaire de la télévision britannique sur la Croix Rouge.

1003

ARTIST / KÜNSTLER / RÉALISATION:

997–1002 Tony Oldfield/David Gill
1003 Keith S. Aldred
1004–1006 Geneviève Strina
1007–1012 Richard Bailey

ART DIRECTOR / DIRECTEUR ARTISTIQUE:

997–1002 Tony Oldfield/David Gill
1003 Keith S. Aldred
1004–1006 R. Bricoux
1007–1012 Richard Bailey

PRODUCTION / PRODUKTION:

997–1002 Rediffusion & Television, London
1003 Granada Television, Manchester
1004–1006 Télé Monte Carlo, Monte Carlo
1007–1012 Paul Watson/BBC Television, London

1007–1012

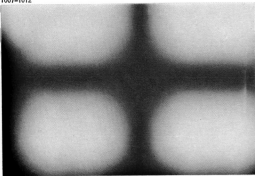

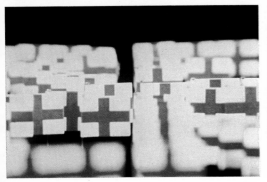

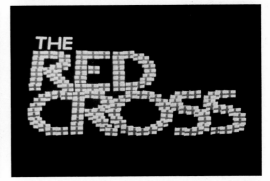

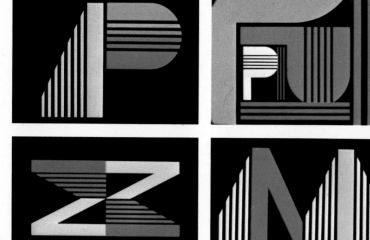
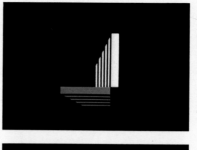
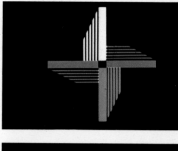
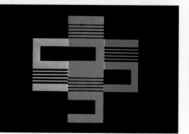

1013–1020 Typographic titling sequence for *Prisme*, a regular programme broadcast on the French-speaking network of Canadian television.
1021, 1022 *Chinaventure* and *Cornered*, captions used for two programmes of Yorkshire Television.
1023–1030 *Bobino*. Titling sequence for a children's programme shown on the French network of Canadian television.
1031 *News Headlines*. Caption for a press review on Yorkshire Television.
1032 *In Broad Daylight*. Promotion slide for a Granada television programme. Green face, orange reflection in glasses.
1033, 1034 Slides (in colour) for musical programmes of the Canadian Broadcasting Company.

PRODUCTION / PRODUKTION:

1013–1020, 1023–1030, 1033, 1034 Société Radio Canada, Montréal
1021, 1022, 1031 Yorkshire Television, Leeds/GBR
1032 Granada Television, Manchester/GBR

1013–1020 Typographisch gestaltete Titelsequenz für die Sendung *Prisme*, die im französisch-sprachigen Programm des kanadischen Fernsehens gezeigt wurde.
1021, 1022 Diapositive, die zwei verschiedene Sendungen von Yorkshire Television ankündigen.
1023–1030 Aus dem Vorspann zu einer Kindersendung mit dem Titel *Bobino*, die im französisch-sprachigen Programm des kanadischen Fernsehens gezeigt wurde.
1031 Voranzeige für die Presseschau von Yorkshire Television.
1032 Voranzeige für ein Programm von Granada Television. Grünes Gesicht, orange Spiegelung in der Brille.
1033, 1034 Ankündigungen für musikalische Programme, ausgestrahlt vom kanadischen Fernsehen.

1013–1020 Conception typographique du générique d'introduction d'une émission de la télévision canadienne.
1021, 1022 Diapositives annonçant deux émissions de Yorkshire Television.
1023–1030 Extraits du générique d'une émission pour enfants, intitulée *Bobino*, au réseau français de la télévision canadienne.
1031 Diapositive publicitaire pour la revue de la presse de Yorkshire Television.
1032 Diapositive publicitaire pour un programme de la TV Granada. Visage vert, réflexion orange dans les lunettes.
1033, 1034 Diapositives annonçant des programmes musicaux de la télévision canadienne.

1021

CHINA VENTURE

1022

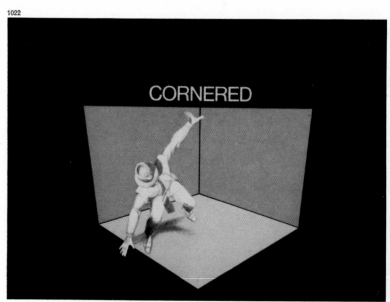

CORNERED

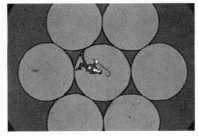
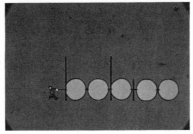

ARTIST / KÜNSTLER / RÉALISATION:

1013–1020 André Theroux
1021, 1022 Garth Bell
1023–1030 Graeme Ross
1031 Ed Bailey
1032 J.G. Adshead
1033, 1034 Dave Strang

ART DIRECTOR / DIRECTEUR ARTISTIQUE:

1013–1020 André Theroux
1021, 1022 Brian Beardmore
1031 Ed Bailey
1032 J.G. Adshead
1033, 1034 Dave Strang

1031

1032

1033

1034

ARTIST / KÜNSTLER / RÉALISATION:

1035 Burckhard Labowski
1036, 1037 Heinz Ebel
1038, 1039 Klaus Finger
1040 Klaus Meisegeier
1041 Regine Schulz
1043, 1044 Trevor Hodgson
1045, 1046 Pierre-Yves Pelletier
1047 Yvon Laroche
1048, 1049 Tim Lewis/Bill Feigenbaum
1050 Heinrich Landauer

ART DIRECTOR / DIRECTEUR ARTISTIQUE:

1035–1041 Karl-Heinz Schäfer
1043, 1044 Frank Kilbride
1045, 1046 Pierre-Yves Pelletier
1048, 1049 John Graham
1050 Eric Sokol

PRODUCTION / PRODUKTION:

1035–1041 Fernsehen der DDR, Berlin
1043, 1044 Yorkshire Television, Leeds/GBR
1045–1047 Société Radio Canada, Montréal
1048, 1049 National Broadcasting Co., New York
1050 Österreichischer Rundfunk, Wien

1035

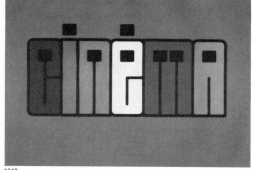

1042

1043

1044

1045

1046

1047

1036

1037

1038

1039

1040

1041

1035–1041 Colour promotion slides for several programmes broadcast by East German Television. They were designed by various artists as part of a general redesign programme for the visual image of television in the GDR.
1042 Promotion slide (in colour) for a film programme.
1043, 1044 Illustrations of nursery rhymes presented in a British programme entitled *Mr. Trimble*.
1045–1047 Promotion slide and titles for programmes shown on Canadian television.
1048, 1049 Frames from a five-minute film on special features presented by NBC Television.
1050 Promotion slide for a programme shown on Austrian television. Black and white.

1035–1041 Mehrfarbige Titel für verschiedene Sendungen des Fernsehens der DDR. Diese wurden im Rahmen einer umfassenden Neugestaltung des visuellen Erscheinungsbildes von verschiedenen Künstlern geschaffen.
1042 Voranzeige (in Farbe) für ein Filmprogramm.
1043, 1044 Titel zu Kinderprogrammen, die in der Sendereihe *Mr. Trimble* zusammengefasst sind.
1045–1047 Voranzeigen und Titel für Programme, die vom kanadischen Fernsehen ausgestrahlt werden.
1048, 1049 Bilder aus einem fünfminutigen Film über spezielle Sendungen einer Fernsehgesellschaft.
1050 Voranzeige für ein Programm, das vom Österreichischen Rundfunk gezeigt wurde.

1035–1041 Titres en couleurs pour diverses émissions de la télévision de la RDA. Ces illustrations, créées par différents artistes, font partie de la nouvelle image visuelle que cette station a mis au point récemment.
1042 Diapositive publicitaire pour un programme de cinéma.
1043, 1044 Extraits du générique de deux programmes pour enfants faisant partie de la série intitulée *Mr. Trimble*.
1045–1047 Avis préalable et titres de programmes présentés par la télévision canadienne.
1048, 1049 Stills extraits d'un film de cinq minutes sur les programmes spéciaux de la chaîne NBC.
1050 Diapositive publicitaire pour un programme de la télévision autrichienne.

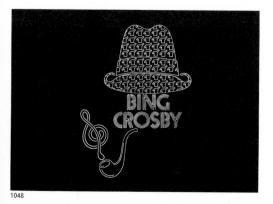

1048

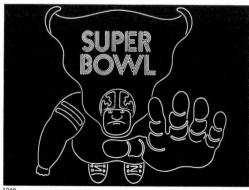

1049

1050

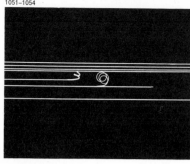 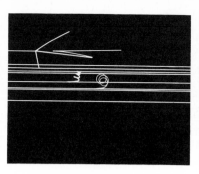 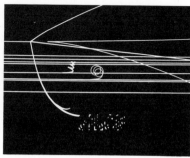 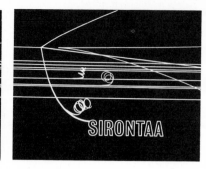

1051–1054 Titling sequence for a programme shown on Finnish television.
1055–1058 Titling sequence for *Science Fair '69,* a series of scientific programmes broadcast by the BBC for schools.
1059, 1060 Two frames from the titling sequence of a French satirical television programme in colour. Red lips, blue horizon, mauve number.
1061, 1062 Two frames from an animated sequence about the Crimean War forming part of Tony Richardson's live film *The Charge of the Light Brigade.*

1051–1054 Titelfolge für ein im finnischen Fernsehen gezeigtes Programm.
1055–1058 Titelfolge für *Science Fair '69,* eine Serie von wissenschaftlichen Programmen, die von der BBC für Schulen gesendet wurde.
1059, 1060 Zwei Bilder aus der Titelsequenz eines satirischen Fernsehprogramms in Farbe. Rote Lippen, blauer Horizont, hellviolette Zahl.
1061, 1062 Bilder aus einer Trickfilmsequenz über den Krim-Krieg, die in Tony Richardsons Live-Film *The Charge of the Light Brigade* (Der Angriff der leichten Brigade) eingebaut wurde.

1059

1060

1061

1051–1054 Extraits du générique d'un programme émis par la télévision finlandaise.
1055–1058 Générique pour *Science Fair '69*, une série de programmes scientifiques que la télévision britannique a réalisée pour les écoles.
1059, 1060 Deux images extraites du générique d'un programme satirique télévisé. Lèvres rouges, horizon bleu, numéro en mauve.
1061, 1062 D'une séquence animée qui fait partie du film à acteurs de Tony Richardson sur la guerre de Crimée, intitulé *The Charge of the Light Brigade* (La charge de la brigade légère).

1062

ARTIST / KÜNSTLER / RÉALISATION:

1051–1054 Jorma Klemi
1055–1058 Tony Geddes/John Aston
1059, 1060 Ronald Searle
1061, 1062 Richard Williams Animation

ART DIRECTOR / DIRECTEUR ARTISTIQUE:

1051–1054 Jorma Klemi
1055–1058 John Aston
1059, 1060 Maurice Dumay
1061, 1062 Richard Williams

PRODUCTION / PRODUKTION:

1051–1054 Finnish Broadcasting Co., Helsinki
1055–1058 BBC Television, London
1059, 1060 Maurice Dumay, Paris
1061, 1062 Richard Williams Animation Ltd., London

 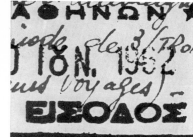  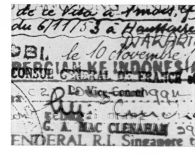

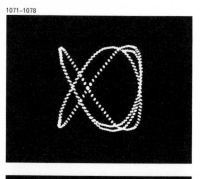  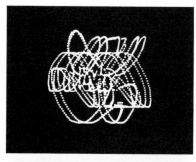 

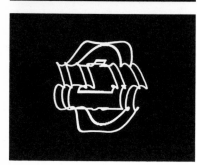   

ARTIST / KÜNSTLER / RÉALISATION:

1063–1070 Rosemary Held
1071–1078 Saul Bass/Art Goodman
1079–1086 Jacques Lamarre
1087–1094 Inni Karine Melbey

ART DIRECTOR / DIRECTEUR ARTISTIQUE:

1063–1070 Rosemary Held
1071–1078 Saul Bass/Art Goodman

PRODUCTION / PRODUKTION:

1063–1070 BBC Television, London
1071–1078 Saul Bass & Associates, Los Angeles
1079–1094 Société Radio Canada, Montréal

1063–1070 Titling sequence for *Cameron Country*, a programme shown on BBC Television.
1071–1078 Frames from a ten-second animated spot of the New York Telephone symbol which is used to introduce television commercials for the telephone company.
1079–1086 *Munich 72*. Titling sequence for a series of special reports on the Olympic Games in Munich broadcast by Canadian television.
1087–1094 Titling sequence for a children's series, *Du Soleil à cinq cents*, on Canadian TV.

1063–1070 Titelsequenz aus der von der BBC ausgestrahlten Serie *Cameron Country*.
1071–1078 Bilder aus dem 10 Sekunden dauernden Trickfilm über das Signet der New-Yorker Telephongesellschaft, der jeweils vor dem eigentlichen Werbespot dieser Firma eingeblendet wird.
1079–1086 Sequenz aus dem Vorspann für die Spezialübertragungen des kanadischen Fernsehens von den Olympischen Sommerspielen 1972 in München.
1087–1094 Titelsequenz für eine regelmässige Kindersendung des kanadischen Fernsehens.

1063–1070 Extrait du générique de la série *Cameron Country* de la télévision britannique.
1071–1078 Stills d'un dessin animé de 10 secondes sur l'emblème de la compagnie newyorkaise de télécommunication. Celui-ci précède chaque spot publicitaire de cette compagnie.
1079–1086 Extrait d'un générique d'introduction d'une série d'émissions spéciales sur les Jeux Olympiques de Munich au réseau français de la télévision canadienne.
1087–1094 Extrait du générique de présentation d'une série pour enfants de la TV canadienne.

1095–1098 Titling sequence culminating in the "graphic eye" which is the familiar symbol of CBS Television.
1099–1106 Titling sequence leading up to "72" (in blue and red) as the symbol of the CBS news campaign for election year 1972.
1107–1110 Another titling sequence culminating in the CBS "graphic eye", the design of which is subject to constant modification.
1111–1114 Titling sequence for the CBS channel TV2.
1115 Frame from a CBS titling sequence for the programme *Dinah!*

1095–1098 Bilder aus der Titelsequenz für das «Auge» der CBS, das diese Fernsehgesellschaft als Sendezeichen verwendet.
1099–1106 Sequenz aus einem farbigen Titelvorspann für eine Sendereihe der CBS über den Präsidentschafts-Wahlkampf 1972.
1107–1110 Weitere Titelsequenz in Farbe, die die CBS als Signet sendet. Das Auge als Symbol dieser Fernsehgesellschaft wird auf immer wieder neue Art graphisch abgewandelt.
1111–1114 Sequenz aus dem von der New-Yorker Station CBS-TV2 verwendeten Sendezeichen.
1115 Einzelbild aus der Titelsequenz zu einer CBS-Sendung mit dem Titel *Dinah!*

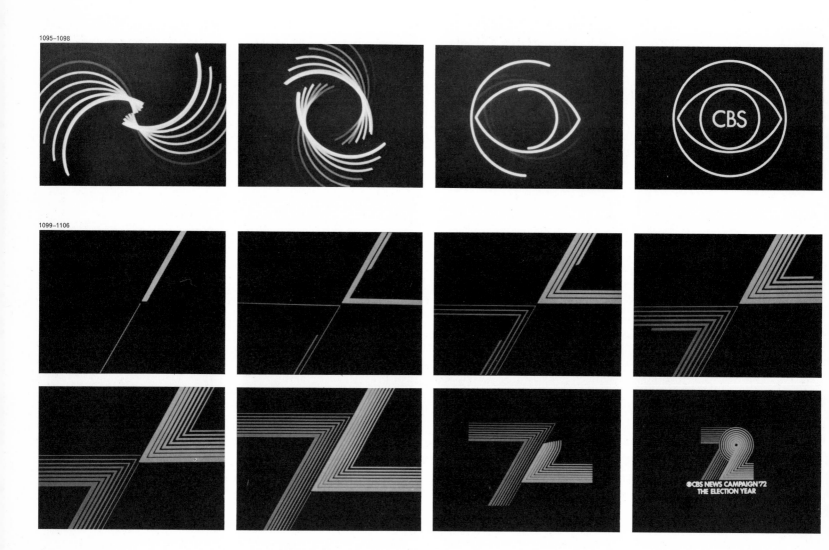

1095–1098

1099–1106

1095–1098 Images figurant dans le générique de «l'œil» de CBS, utilisé par cette compagnie en tant qu'indicatif.
1099–1106 Extrait d'un générique d'introduction en couleurs d'une série d'émissions de la CBS sur la campagne présidentielle de 1972.
1107–1110 Séquence d'un autre générique que la CBS utilise en tant qu'indicatif. La présentation graphique de l'œil, symbole de cette compagnie de télévision, est modifiée de temps à autre.
1111–1114 Extrait du générique en couleurs que la station newyorkaise WCBS utilise en tant qu'indicatif pour annoncer le programme de la chaîne 2.
1115 Images figurant dans le générique d'une émission CBS intitulée *Dinah!*

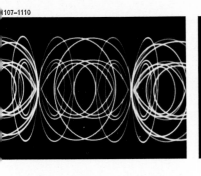
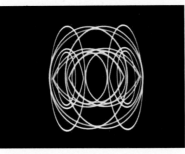
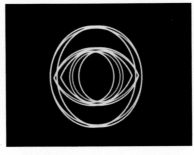
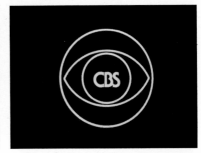

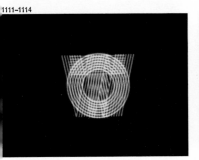
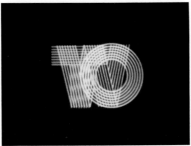

1115

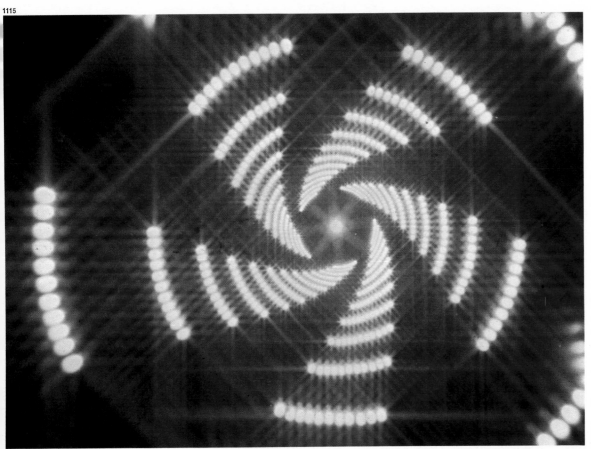

ARTIST / KÜNSTLER / RÉALISATION:

1095–1098, 1107–1114 George McGinnis
1099–1106 Akihiko Seki
1111–1114 Lou Dorfsman
1115 George McGinnis/Mark Howard

ART DIRECTOR / DIRECTEUR ARTISTIQUE:

1095–1098, 1107–1110, 1115 George McGinnis/
Lou Dorfsman
1099–1106, 1111–1114 Lou Dorfsman

PRODUCTION / PRODUKTION:

1095–1110 CBS Television/Edstan Studio,
New York
1111–1114 CBS Television/Pumpernickel,
Inc., New York
1115 CBS Television/Image Factory Inc.,
New York

ARTIST / KÜNSTLER / RÉALISATION:

1116–1124 Robert Abel/Richard Taylor/Con Pederson
1133–1140 Robert Abel/Con Pederson

ART DIRECTOR / DIRECTEUR ARTISTIQUE:

1116–1124 Robert Abel
1133–1140 Harry Marks/Robert Abel

PRODUCTION / PRODUKTION:

1116–1124 Robert Abel Films, Los Angeles/CBS Television, New York
1125–1132 Canadian Broadcasting Co., Montréal
1133–1140 Robert Abel Films, Los Angeles/ABC Television, New York

1116

1116–1124 Single frame and titling sequence for the series *CBS Bicentennial Special,* which dealt with aspects of the Bicentennial celebrations in the USA. A red, white and blue tunnel was created by a slit-scan effect, and a golden replica of the eye, well-known symbol of CBS, appeared to pass through this tunnel.
1125–1132 Titling sequence culminating in the symbol of Canadian Broadcasting Co.
1133–1140 Main titling for the series *Kung Fu* on ABC Television, New York. Streak photography was used to bring about a metamorphosis from the title to a flame-like shape and thence to the face of the star of the series.

1125–1132

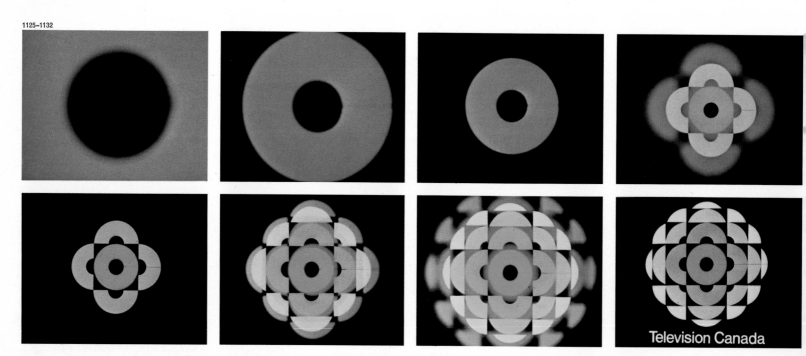

Television Canada

188

1116–1124 Einzelbild und Sequenz aus dem Sendezeichen *CBS Bicentennial*, das Spezialprogramme im Rahmen der 200-Jahrfeier ankündigte. Die Tiefenwirkung wurde durch eine spezielle Aufnahmetechnik erzielt. Eine goldene Replica des «Auges» (Symbol der CBS) scheint durch das rot-weiss-blaue Tunnel zu fliegen.
1125–1132 Sequenz aus dem Signet des kanadischen Fernsehens.
1133–1140 Sequenz aus dem Haupttitel von *Kung Fu*. Durch spezielle photographische Mittel konnte diese Metamorphose zwischen dem Haupttitel, einem flammenähnlichen Gebilde und dem Kopf des Hauptdarstellers geschaffen werden.

1116–1124 Images et séquence de l'indicatif *CBS Bicentennial* qui annonce les programmes spéciaux émis dans le cadre du bicentenaire. L'effet de profondeur a été obtenu par une technique photographique nouvelle. L'œil CBS – une réplique en or du symbole célèbre – semble voler par un tunnel en rouge, blanc et bleu.
1125–1132 Séquence extraite de l'indicatif de la Télévision Canada.
1133–1140 Extrait du titre principal de *Kung Fu.* En mettant en œuvre des techniques photographiques par stries on a créé cette métamorphose animée entre le titre principal, une forme ressemblant à une flamme et la tête du personnage principal.

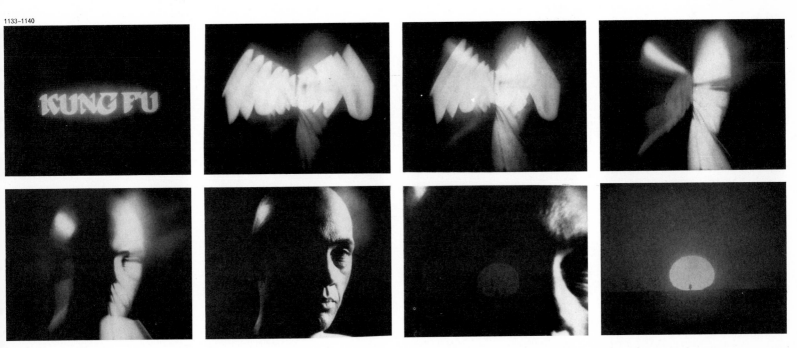

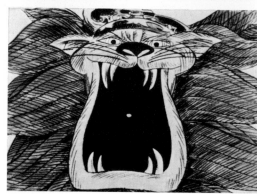
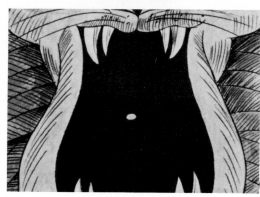

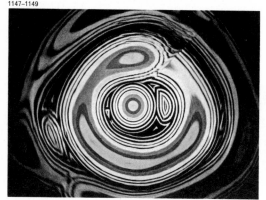
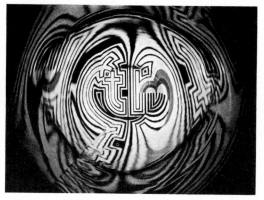

1141–1146 From the colour titling sequence of a CBS programme on the American Revolution.
1147–1149 Frames from the titling of a British television entertainment programme on ATV involving audience participation in a crossbow shooting contest.
1150–1158 Titling sequence in colour for the CBS programme *The Jensen Report*.

1141–1146 Aus der farbigen Titelsequenz für ein Programm über die amerikanische Revolution, 1770–1783.
1147–1149 Bilder aus der Titelfolge für ein Unterhaltungsprogramm der britischen Fernsehgesellschaft ATV unter Mitwirkung der Zuschauer bei einem Wettbewerb im Bogenschiessen.
1150–1158 Mehrfarbige Titelsequenz für eine von der CBS ausgestrahlte Sendung: *The Jensen Report* (Der Jensen-Bericht).

1141–1146 Extraits du générique d'introduction d'un film couleur intitulé *La Révolution Américaine: 1770–1783*.
1147–1149 Cases extraites du générique d'un programme de variété avec la participation des téléspectateurs dans un concours de tir à l'arc.
1150–1158 Générique couleur du programme CBS *The Jensen Report* (Le Rapport Jensen).

RTIST / KÜNSTLER / RÉALISATION:

141–1146 Lou Dorfsman/Karl Fischer
147–1149 George Wallder
150–1158 George McGinnis

ART DIRECTOR / DIRECTEUR ARTISTIQUE:

141–1146, 1150–1158 Lou Dorfsman
147–1149 George Wallder

PRODUCTION / PRODUKTION:

141–1146 Ron Berson/CBS Television, New York
147–1149 ATV Network Ltd, Borehamwood/GBR
150–1158 George McGinnis/CBS Television, New York

1150–1158

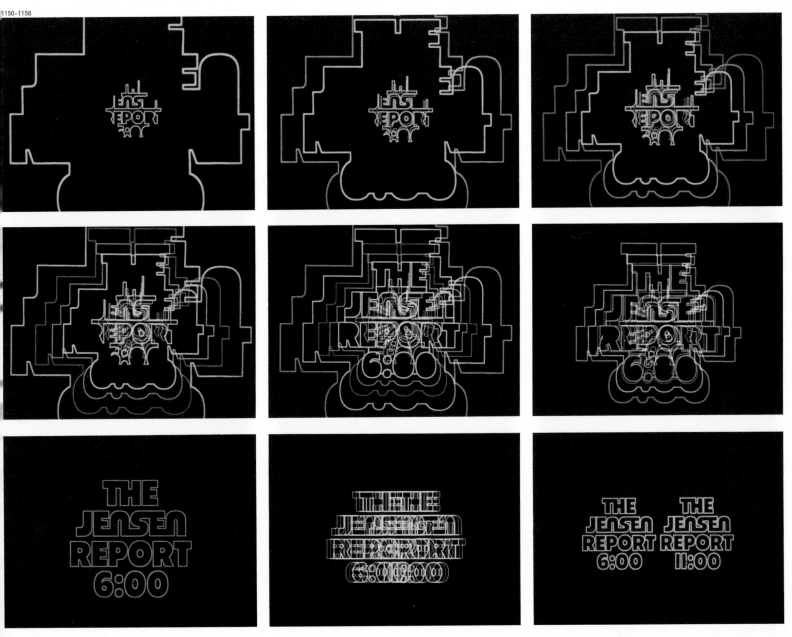

1159

1160

1161–1172

173

1174

1175

1176

1159 Announcement of a detective film in colour on Swiss television.
1160, 1173–1176 Examples of promotion slides announcing various forthcoming programmes on NBC Television, USA.
1161–1172 From a two-minute titling sequence for the series *Does the Rain have a Father?* broadcast by Dutch television.

1159 Programmhinweis für eine Krimi-Sendung im Schweizer Fernsehen. Mehrfarbig.
1160, 1173–1176 Beispiele aus einer Serie von Bildern, die jeweils vor den entsprechenden Programmhinweisen der Fernsehgesellschaft NBC eingeblendet werden.
1161–1172 Aus einer 2minutigen Titelsequenz für die Sendereihe *Does the Rain have a Father?* (Hat der Regen einen Vater?), die vom holländischen Fernsehen ausgestrahlt wurde.

1159 Annonce d'une émission de la TV suisse (film policier). En polychromie.
1160, 1173–1176 Exemples d'une série de diapositives que la chaîne NBC fait apparaître en fondu pour annoncer les émissions respectives.
1161–1172 Extraits d'un générique d'introduction de 2 mn pour la série *Does the Rain have a Father?* (La pluie, a-t-elle un père?) de la télévision néerlandaise.

ARTIST / KÜNSTLER / RÉALISATION:

1159 Paul Brühwiler
1160 John Sorjani/Orest Woronewych
1161–1172 Harold F. Mack
1173, 1174 Frank Bozzo/Orest Woronewych
1175, 1176 Tim Lewis/Orest Woronewych

ART DIRECTOR / DIRECTEUR ARTISTIQUE:

1159 Paul Brühwiler
1160, 1173–1176 John Graham
1161–1172 Harold F. Mack

PRODUCTION / PRODUKTION:

1159 Paul Brühwiler/SRG, Zürich
1160, 1173–1176 National Broadcasting Co., New York
1161–1172 Interkerkelijk Overleg in Radio en Televisie Aangelegenheden, Hilversum/Anglo-Dutch Group B.V., Amstelveen/NLD

1177

ARTIST / KÜNSTLER / RÉALISATION:
1177–1186 Jiri Šalamoun

DIRECTOR / RÉGISSEUR:
1177–1186 Jiri Šalamoun/Juraj Herz

PRODUCTION / PRODUKTION:
1177–1186 Studio Barrandov, Prague

194

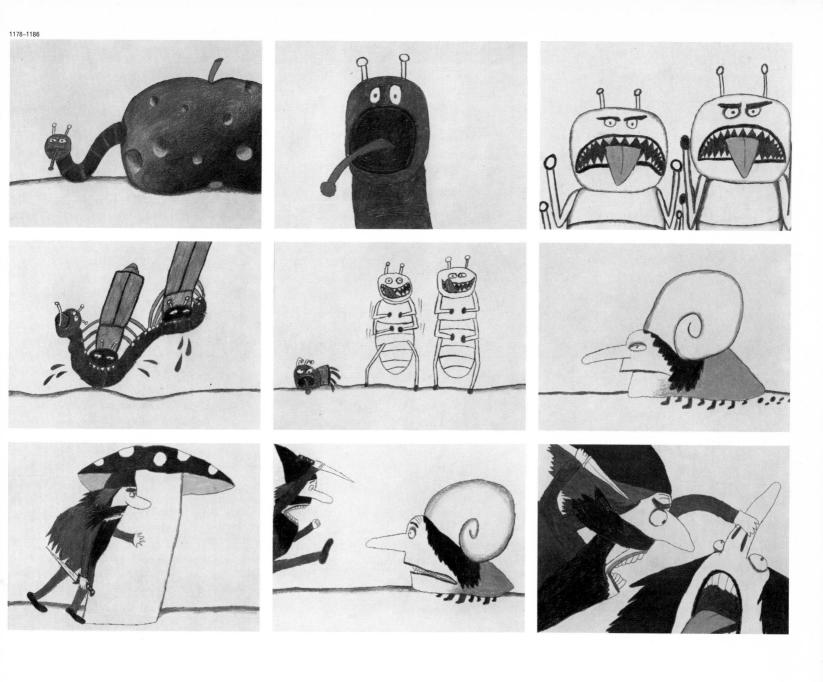

1177–1186 Single frame and opening sequence of the Czech comedy thriller *Holka na Zabiti* (A Girl to Kill). The whole sequence lasts 3 minutes and is composed of a number of static drawings together with four animated sequences and about thirty title pages. It deals with the theme of natural law and chance in a humorous vein. In colour.

1177–1186 Zeichnungen aus dem Vorspann zur tschechischen Kriminalkomödie *Holka na Zabiti* (Das Mädel zum Totschlagen). Die ganze Sequenz dauert 3 Minuten und besteht aus einer Reihe von statischen Zeichnungen, vier animierten Folgen und etwa 30 Titelblättern. Die Sequenz handelt auf eher skurrile Weise das Thema der Gesetzmässigkeit und des Zufalls ab.

1177–1186 Dessins extraits du générique d'une comédie criminelle intitulée *Holka na Zabiti* (Une jeune fille à assassiner) de la télévision tchèque. La séquence de 3 mn est constituée de dessins statiques, de quatre suites animées et d'une trentaine de frontispices. Le sujet principal qu'elle traite d'une façon comique est celui de la loi et du hasard.

Jeffrey Altshuler

Recent developments in film and television can be attributed almost as much to the scientist and engineer as to the artist. In the last few years, the computer has played an increasingly important part in the design and execution of graphics for motion pictures and television. The results have ranged from the enhancement of familiar genres to the creation of completely new visual imagery.

The application of the computer to film and television has taken many forms. By computerizeing existing film techniques, the film-maker can extend his capabilities and work in directions that were either too complex or too costly in the past. Techniques such as slit-scan and streak photography, which were developed in Stanley Kubrick's *2001: A Space Odyssey,* would have been prohibitive without the computer. In television, electronic photography coupled with computer-operated electronic editing systems allows visual information to be altered, distorted or embellished in exciting new ways. Perhaps the most intriguing developments have occurred in computer-generated graphics. These are images created by computer programming without the aid of any prepared artwork. Work in this area ranges from the simulation of realistic and recognizable forms to the creation of absolutely original imagery. Here the medium is truly the message, and here, too, lies the opportunity for the most innovative experimentation. The works created by these new tools have had much the same impact on motion picture graphics as the early works of the Abstract Expressionists had on painting. The films of computer artists such as Lillian Schwartz, whose carefully paced graphics are often accompanied by co-ordinated music tracks, generate their own audio-visual environment. In fact, they have proved to have demonstrable psychological effects on many viewers.

Computer-generated graphics are still in their infancy, and therefore hold, for the designer, a host of unexplored possibilities. However, computer operation is expensive, there is little computer time available for creative purposes, and few have the expertise needed to command the complex technology. As a result, while the field holds great promise, its growth in the foreseeable future will be limited. Whether equipped with a computer or not, the modern graphic designer/film-maker is completely immersed in moving imagery. Using techniques never before explored, he is demanding that the viewer learn to absorb more visual information and is offering exciting new approaches to perception.

Die jüngsten Entwicklungen in Film und Fernsehen können dem Wissenschafter und Techniker fast ebensosehr zugeschrieben werden wie dem Künstler. In den letzten Jahren hat der Computer in der Gestaltung und Ausführung der Film- und Fernsehgraphik eine Rolle von wachsender Bedeutung gespielt. Die Ergebnisse reichten von der Bereicherung bekannter Genres bis hin zur Schaffung einer völlig neuen Art von Bildersprache.

Die Anwendung von Computern bei Film und Fernsehen hat viele Formen angenommen. Indem existierende Filmtechniken computerisiert werden, eröffnen sich dem Filmemacher unzählige neue Möglichkeiten, die in der Vergangenheit zu kompliziert oder zu kostspielig waren. Aufnahmetechniken, wie sie für Stanley Kubricks *2001: Odyssee im Weltraum* entwickelt wurden, wären ohne Computer unerschwinglich gewesen. Elektronische Fernsehaufnahmen, gepaart mit computergesteuertem elektronischem Bildschnitt, bieten aufregende neue Möglichkeiten, visuelle Informationen zu verändern, zu verzerren oder zu bereichern. Mit am faszinierendsten aber ist die Entwicklung der computererzeugten Graphik. Es handelt sich dabei um Bilder, die von Computerprogrammen ohne vorgegebene Zeichnungen geschaffen werden. So wurde von der Simulation realistischer und erkennbarer Formen bis zur Schöpfung einer total neuen Bildersprache alles möglich. In diesem Bereich ist das Medium an sich die Botschaft und hier eröffnen sich auch ungeahnte Perspektiven für neue Experimente. Die Filme von Computerkünstlern wie Lillian Schwartz, die oft von koordinierter Musik begleitet sind, schaffen sich ihre eigene audiovisuelle Umwelt. Bei vielen Betrachtern haben sie nachweislich psychologische Auswirkungen.

Die computererzeugte Graphik steckt zwar noch in den Kinderschuhen, aber gerade deshalb bietet sie dem Designer ungeahnte Möglichkeiten. Doch der Einsatz von Computern ist teuer, es steht nur wenig Computerzeit für kreative Zwecke zur Verfügung, und nur wenige besitzen genügend Fachwissen, um die komplexe Technologie zu steuern. Deshalb wird dieser vielversprechende Bereich in absehbarer Zukunft nur in engen Grenzen wachsen. Ob mit oder ohne Computer – der Graphiker und Filmschaffende von heute ist in eine bewegte Bilderflut getaucht. Mit neuen Techniken will er den Betrachter lehren, mehr Bildinformation aufzunehmen, und gleichzeitig will er ihm eine aufregende neue Art der Sinneswahrnehmung bieten.

Les derniers développements intervenus dans les domaines du cinéma et de la télévision doivent presque autant aux chercheurs et aux ingénieurs qu'aux artistes. Ces dernières années, l'ordinateur a joué un rôle croissant dans la conception et l'exécution de créations graphiques destinées au film et à la TV, avec pour résultat la mise en valeur accrue de genres existants aussi bien que l'élaboration d'une imagerie visuelle entièrement renouvelée.

L'application de l'ordinateur aux besoins du cinéma et de la télévision a pris des formes diverses. La mise sur ordinateur des techniques cinématographiques existantes permet au réalisateur de pousser ses recherches dans des voies naguère jugées trop complexes ou trop coûteuses. Les techniques photographiques slit-scan et streak appliquées à l'œuvre de Stanley Kubrick, *2001 : Odyssée de l'Espace,* auraient coûté les yeux de la tête sans l'aide d'un ordinateur. A la TV, la photographie électronique associée aux systèmes électroniques de visualisation branchés sur ordinateur permet de modifier, de déformer ou de magnifier l'information visuelle de 1001 manières stimulantes. Les développements les plus exaltants sont probablement dus à la création graphique par ordinateur. Il s'agit d'images créées au gré d'une programmation sans aucun apport artistique préalable. Lesdits programmes vont de la simulation de formes réalistes et donc identifiables à la création d'une imagerie radicalement originale. Ici, le média est effectivement le message, et c'est bien là que gisent les chances d'une expérimentation innovatrice poussée. Les œuvres réalisées avec ces nouveaux outils ont exercé sur la création graphique animée la même influence que les premières réalisations des expressionnistes abstraits sur la peinture. Les films des tenants de l'art électronique tels que Lillian Schwartz, dont les graphismes à la chorégraphie ciselée s'accompagnent souvent de bandes sonores coordonnées, créent leur propre environnement audio-visuel. Ils ont en fait apporté la preuve d'une influence notable sur le psychisme des spectateurs.

La création graphique par ordinateur n'en est encore qu'à ses premiers pas, ce qui laisse les mains libres au designer désireux d'explorer toutes les ressources de l'invention, pour peu que le temps alloué le permette et que la compétence technique de l'utilisateur soit à la hauteur de ses aspirations — conditions qui risquent de limiter la croissance dans ce domaine. Qu'importe: le graphiste-animateur même dépourvu d'ordinateur œuvre de façon éblouissante à enrichir nos facultés de perception.

Experiments
Experimente
Films expérimentaux

Computer-Films
Audio-visual Presentations
Science Fiction

Computer-Filme
Audio-visuelle Präsentationen
Science-fiction

Créations sur ordinateur
Présentations audio-visuelles
Science-fiction

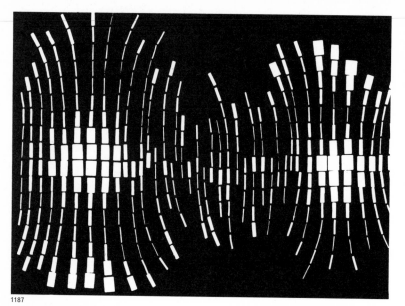

1187

1188

ARTIST / KÜNSTLER / RÉALISATION:

1187, 1188 Marie-France Molle
1189–1196 Eino Ruutsalo
1197, 1198 Eliot Noyes Jr.
1199, 1200 Georges Schwizgebel

DIRECTEUR / RÉGISSEUR:

1187, 1188 Marie-France Molle
1189–1196 Eino Ruutsalo
1197, 1198 Eliot Noyes Jr.
1199, 1200 Georges Schwizgebel

PRODUCTION / PRODUKTION:

1187, 1188 Studio Miniatur Filmowych, Warsaw
1189–1196 Eino Ruutsalo, Helsinki
1197, 1198 Cyclops Films, Inc., New York
1199, 1200 G. D. S. Carouge, Genève

1187, 1188 *L'Alouette* (The Match) was made by the young Frenchwomen Marie-France Molle while she was studying in the Studio Miniatur Filmowych in Warsaw in 1972. Inspired by the traditional French song of the same title, she set out to visualize an abstraction by animating cut-out shapes of different thickness and size which create the optical effect of an embossed surface. The enormous labour involved in such a film made it necessary to use a computer.
1189–1196 *ABC 123* (5 minutes, 1967) was one of Eino Ruutsalo's early experiments. He came to animation through his intimate knowledge of camera technique. Having to work without a camera for some time, he tried the animated film. Working a frame at a time, he was able to examine compositions and calculate rhythms. He treated unexposed, overexposed and underexposed negatives and positives by painting, scratching and typing on them. By "mutilating" the basic pictures, he expanded their function. He thus created the story of a typeface book with many stories in it.
1197, 1198 *Sandman*. Eliot Noyes Jr. moved sand on a surface which was lit from underneath. The artist also uses other materials, such as clay and superimposed "live action" pictures over animated patterns. For this film he was awarded the Critics' Prize at Annecy, 1973.
1199, 1200 *Vol d'Icare* (1974), a visualization of François Couperin's music, is made up of a number of coloured dots and depicts the legend of Icarus flying near the sun.

1189–1196

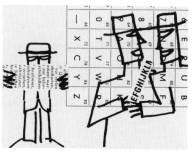

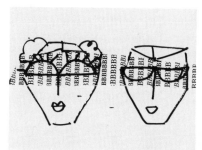

1197

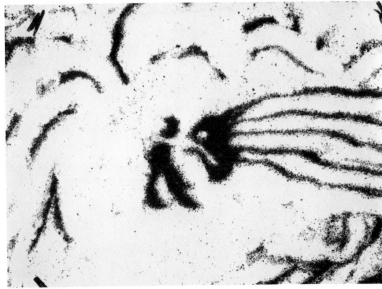

1198

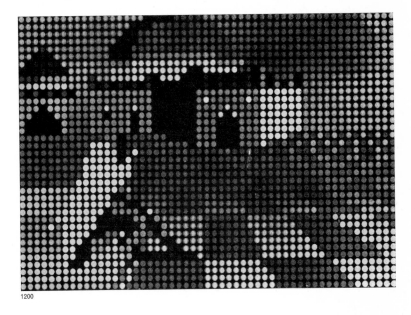

1199

1200

1187, 1188 *L'Alouette* wurde von der jungen Französin Marie-France Molle während ihres Aufenthalts im Studio Miniatur Filmowych in Warschau im Jahre 1972 gedreht. Inspiriert durch das traditionelle französische Lied, machte sie sich daran, Abstraktionen zu visualisieren durch die Animation von ausgeschnittenen Formen in verschiedenen Grössen und Dicken, womit ein plastischer Effekt erzielt wurde. Sie benützte einen Computer, um die enorme Arbeit zu bewältigen.
1189–1196 *ABC 123* (5 Minuten, 1967) ist eines von Eino Ruutsalos frühen Experimenten. Er kam zum Animationsfilm dank seinen ausgezeichneten filmtechnischen Kenntnissen und weil er für eine Weile nicht als Filmer arbeiten konnte. Da er jeweils nur an einem Bild arbeitete, konnte er sich auf die Kompositionen konzentrieren und den Rhythmus feiner abstufen. Er behandelte unbelichtete, über- und unterbelichtete Negative und Positive, indem er sie bemalte, zerkratzte oder mit Schreibmaschine auf sie schrieb. Durch diese Verstümmelung der Originalbilder erweiterte er ihre Funktion. Er schuf eine Geschichte über ein Schriftenbuch in vielen Episoden.
1197, 1198 *Sandman*. Eliot Noyes Jr. schuf auf einer von unten beleuchteten Fläche Formen aus Sand, manchmal auch aus Ton. Verschiedentlich werden Realbilder und animierte Formen übereinanderkopiert. Der Film wurde 1973 in Annecy mit dem Preis der Kritik ausgezeichnet.
1199, 1200 *Vol d'Icare* (1974), eine Visualisierung von François Couperins Musik, bestehend aus einer Anzahl farbiger Punkte, die die Legende von Ikarus' Flug zur Sonne nacherzählt.

1187, 1188 *L'Alouette* a été réalisé par la jeune Française Marie-France Molle alors qu'elle faisait un séjour d'étude au Studio Miniatur Filmowych de Varsovie en 1972. S'inspirant de la chanson du même titre, elle a tenté de visualiser une abstraction en animant des formes de dimensions et d'épaisseur différentes, découpées à l'emporte-pièce, et qui créent l'illusion d'une surface gaufrée. Seul l'emploi d'un ordinateur lui a permis de venir à bout de cette tâche.
1189–1196 *ABC 123* (5 mn, 1967) est l'une des premières expériences d'Eino Ruutsalo, un expert de la technique photographique venu à l'animation. Elaborant case après case, il eut toute opportunité d'étudier les modes de composition et de calculer les rythmes cinétiques. Il a ainsi traité par la peinture, la gravure et la frappe à la machine des négatifs et positifs vierges, sous-exposés et surexposés. En mutilant de la sorte les photos sous-jacentes, il en élargit la fonction. Le résultat est un alphabet composé de multiples récits.
1197, 1198 *Sandman* (Marchand de sable). Eliot Noyes Jr. déplace du sable sur une surface éclairée par en dessous. L'artiste fait aussi appel à d'autres matériaux, tels que l'argile et des photos de films à acteurs surimposées sur des structures animées. Pour ce film, Eliot Noyes a reçu le Prix de la Critique du Festival d'Annecy en 1973.
1199, 1200 *Vol d'Icare* (1974), visualisation de la musique de François Couperin, se compose d'une multitude de points de couleur. Le film est basé sur l'histoire de l'imprudent Icare.

1201

1201 At the Osaka Expo in 1970 the effectiveness of audio-visual communications was demonstrated on an impressive scale. All the industrialized nations employed multi-projection systems and multi-screen techniques of one kind or another. Here the Japanese Official Pavilion.
1202, 1203 Cartoon figures produced by the illumination of a pattern of small squares on a huge screen in the Canadian Pavilion at Osaka, 1970.
1204, 1205 In the Japanese Official Pavilion (Osaka, 1970) slides and films summing up life in a dazzling programme of images and figures were projected on an enormous screen made up of 120 air cushions. The projection squares could be used either individually or in groups.

1201 An der Expo in Osaka 1970 wurde die Beeinflussungskraft der audiovisuellen Kommunikation auf eindrückliche Weise demonstriert. Alle Industrienationen benutzten Multiprojektionssysteme mit Multibildschirmen aller Art. Hier der offizielle japanische Pavillon.
1202, 1203 Diese Trickfilm-Figuren im kanadischen Pavillon entstanden aus einzelnen beleuchteten Feldern, die auf riesige Bildschirme projiziert wurden. Thema: Die Umwelt der Stadt.
1204, 1205 Im japanischen Pavillon zeigten Dias und Filme das Leben in Japan in einem faszinierenden Programm von Bildern und Figuren, die auf einen riesigen Bildschirm aus 120 Luftkissen projiziert wurden. Die Projektionsquadrate konnten einzeln oder gruppenweise verwendet werden.

1201 A l'Expo d'Osaka, en 1970, l'efficacité des communications audio-visuelles a été démontrée à vaste échelle. Toutes les nations industrialisées ont fait usage de systèmes de multiprojection et de multi-écrans de divers genres. On voit ici le pavillon du Japon.
1202, 1203 Personnages de dessins animés apparaissant sur un écran géant au pavillon du Canada, à Osaka, en 1970, par combinaison d'éléments lumineux modulaires carrés.
1204, 1205 Au pavillon du Japon, à Osaka (1970), des diapositives et films résumant tous les aspects de la vie en un feu d'artifice d'images et de personnages étaient projetés sur un écran géant formé de 120 coussins d'air. Les éléments modulaires carrés de cet écran pouvaient être utilisés séparément ou groupés.

1202

1203

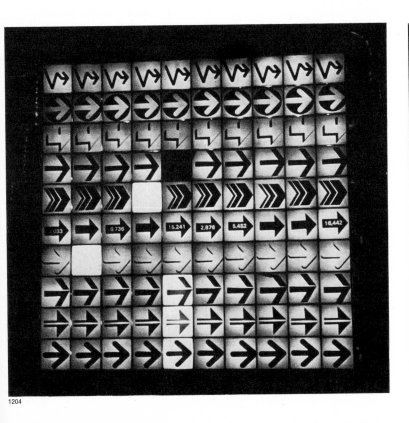

1204

1205

201

1206

1206–1212 The Czech Pavilion was one of the highlights of the Montreal Expo in 1967. The upper floor of the building accommodated a section devoted to technology in general and Czech industry in particular. It included two ingenious slide shows, *Polyvision* and *Diapolyécran*. The pictures on this spread give an impression of the latter, which presented a film by Emil Radok entitled *The Creation of the World*, an optical evocation of evolution and of the creative potential of man. Up to 15 000 slides were projected in 14 minutes by electronic control on 112 cubes forming a screen area of 20×32 ft. Each cube could be moved back and forth, creating an impression of movement and the pictures could be changed in any sequence or pattern.

1206–1212 Der tschechoslowakische Pavillon war zweifellos der erfolgreichste an der Expo Montreal 1967. Eine Abteilung war der Technik im allgemeinen und der tschechischen Industrie im besonderen gewidmet. Hier fanden die eindrücklichen Diavorführungen statt: *Polyvision* und *Diapolyécran*; von letzterem vermitteln Bilder hier einen Eindruck. Dieser «Film» von Emil Radok «Die Schöpfung der Welt», ist eine optische Beschwörung der Entwicklung der schöpferischen Möglichkeiten des Menschen. Innert 14 Min. wurden bis 15 000 elektronisch gesteuerte Dias auf 112 Würfel projiziert, die zusammen einen Bildschirm von ca. 6×10 m ergaben. Jeder Würfel liess sich vor- oder rückwärts verschieben, wodurch der Eindruck von Bewegung entstand.

1206–1212 Le pavillon tchèque a été l'une des merveilles de l'Expo de Montréal de 1967. A l'étage supérieur se trouvait une section consacrée à la technologie en général, ainsi qu'à l'effort industriel tchèque en particulier, et qui était dotée de deux systèmes ingénieux de projections de diapos, *Polyvision* et *Diapolyécran*. Les images de cette double page donnent un aperçu du second système, qui servait à présenter un film d'Emil Radok sur *La Création du monde*, une évocation de l'évolution des espèces et du pouvoir créateur détenu par l'homme. 15 000 diapos étaient projetées en 14 minutes au rythme voulu sur une surface de 6×10 m, composée de 112 cubes avancés ou reculés à souhait.

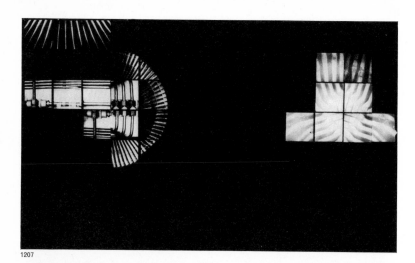

1207

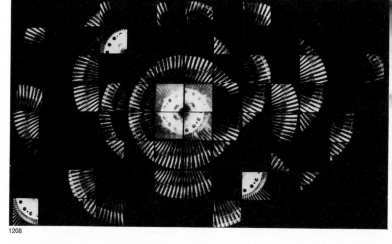

1208

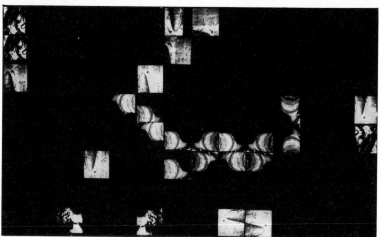

1209

1210

1211

1212

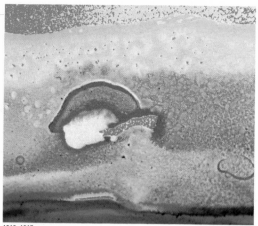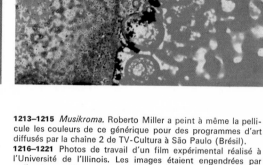

1213–1215

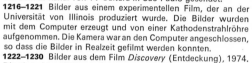

1213–1215 *Musikroma.* Roberto Miller painted the colours for this titling sequence for art programmes directly on to the film. The programmes were broadcast by Channel 2 of TV Cultura, São Paulo, Brazil.
1216–1221 Stills from an experimental film produced at the University of Illinois. The images were computer-generated and filmed off a cathode-ray tube. The camera was held by the generating computer so that the film could be made in real time.
1222–1230 Stills from a film entitled *Discovery* (1974) made in Santa Monica. The abstract images are computer-animated.

1213–1215 *Musikroma.* Roberto Miller bemalte direkt den Film für diese Titelsequenz eines kulturellen Programms. Dies wurde auf dem 2. Kanal von TV Cultura in São Paulo gesendet.
1216–1221 Bilder aus einem experimentellen Film, der an der Universität von Illinois produziert wurde. Die Bilder wurden mit dem Computer erzeugt und von einer Kathodenstrahlröhre aufgenommen. Die Kamera war an den Computer angeschlossen, so dass die Bilder in Realzeit gefilmt werden konnten.
1222–1230 Bilder aus dem Film *Discovery* (Entdeckung), 1974. Die abstrakten Bilder sind computer-animiert.

1213–1215 *Musikroma.* Roberto Miller a peint à même la pellicule les couleurs de ce générique pour des programmes d'art diffusés par la chaîne 2 de TV-Cultura à São Paulo (Brésil).
1216–1221 Photos de travail d'un film expérimental réalisé à l'Université de l'Illinois. Les images étaient engendrées par ordinateur et filmées sur l'écran de l'oscillographe cathodique où elles apparaissaient. La caméra était commandée par l'ordinateur, le film put être tourné en temps réel.
1222–1230 Photos du film *Discovery* (Découverte) réalisé à Santa Monica en 1974. Images abstraites animées par ordinateur.

1216–1221

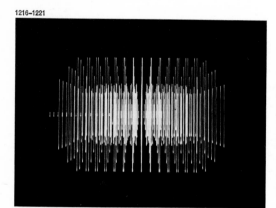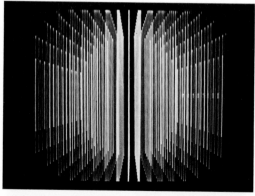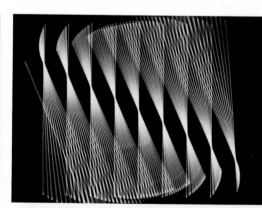

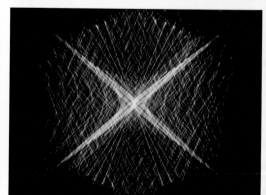

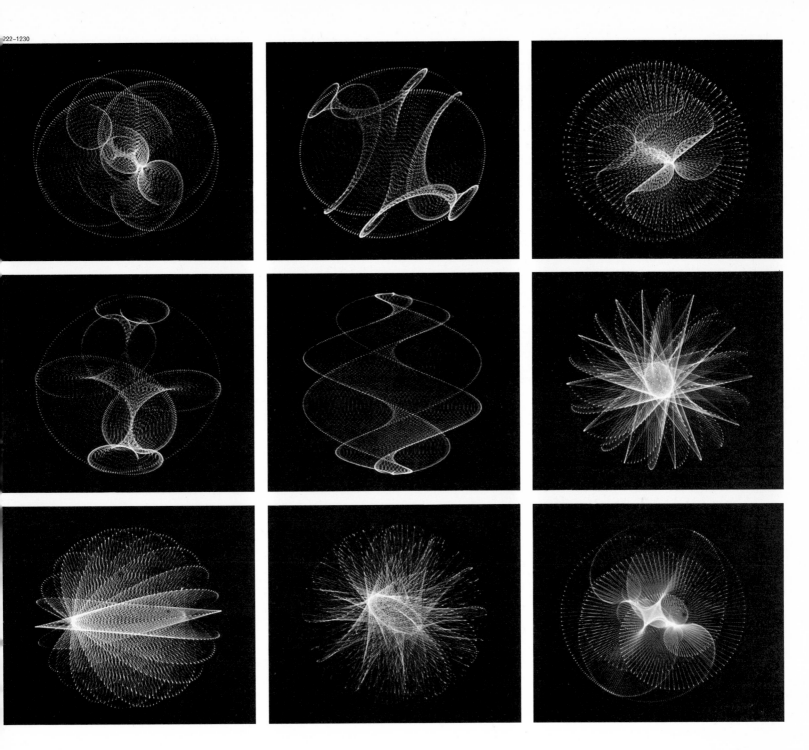

ARTIST / KÜNSTLER / RÉALISATION:

1213–1215 Roberto Miller
1216–1221 Guenther Tetz/Richard Greenberg
1222–1230 Gary Demos

DIRECTOR / RÉGISSEUR:

1213–1215 Roberto Miller
1216–1221 Guenther Tetz/Richard Greenberg
1222–1230 Gary Demos

PRODUCTION / PRODUKTION:

1213–1215 Roberto Miller/Fundacao Padre Anchieta,
           São Paulo/BRA
1216–1221 University of Illinois, Chicago
1222–1230 Pyramid Films, Santa Monica

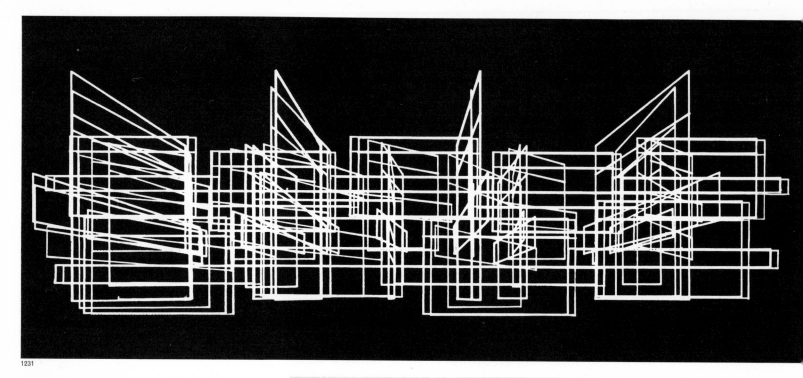

1231

1231 Computer animation drawing for the film *Energie* which the London-based company of Halas & Batchelor made for an industrial enterprise in Munich. The film combines live action and animation to explain the problems of the conservation of heat in buildings.
1232–1241 *Phenakistoscope*, a 4-minute 35-mm colour film directed, illustrated and animated by the Japanese artist Taku Furukawa. It makes use of changing, repetitive images in a concentrically organized circle.

1231 Elektronische Animations-Zeichnung für den Film *Energie*, welcher vom Londoner Studio Halas & Batchelor für F.W.U. in München aufgenommen wurde. Es ist eine Kombination von Real- und Animationsfilm, der die Probleme der Erhaltung von Wärme in Gebäuden erklärt.
1232–1241 *Phenakistoscope*, ein 4-minutiger 35-mm-Farbfilm, der vom japanischen Künstler Taku Furukawa illustriert und aufgenommen wurde. Er benützt dazu wechselnde, sich wiederholende Bilder, die in konzentrischen Kreisen angeordnet sind.

1231 Dessin animé réalisé sur ordinateur pour le film *Energie* que la société londonienne Halas & Batchelor a produit pour une entreprise industrielle munichoise. Le film combine l'animation et la prise de vues ordinaire pour expliquer les problèmes de la conservation de la chaleur dans les immeubles.
1232–1241 *Phenakistoscope*, un film de 35 mm en couleurs, de 4 mn, réalisé, illustré et animé par l'artiste japonais Taku Furukawa. Il fait usage d'images répétitives en transformation constante au sein d'un cercle organisé concentriquement.

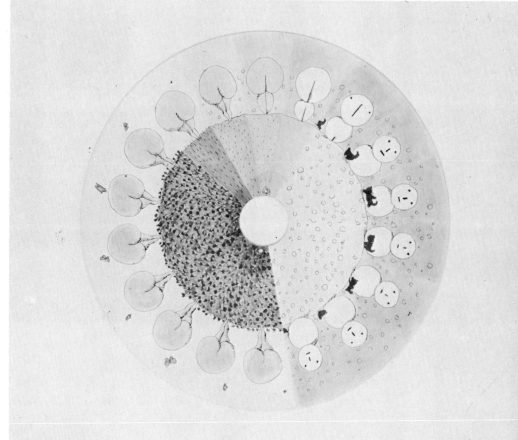

1232

ARTIST / KÜNSTLER / RÉALISATION:

1231 John Halas
1232–1241 Taku Furukawa

DIRECTOR / RÉGISSEUR:

1231 John Bandmann
1232–1241 Taku Furukawa

ART DIRECTOR / DIRECTEUR ARTISTIQUE:

1231 John Halas/Brian Borthwick
1232–1241 Taku Furukawa

PRODUCTION / PRODUKTION:

1231 Halas & Batchelor Animation Ltd., London
1232–1241 Takun Jikken Manga Box, Tokyo

1233–1241

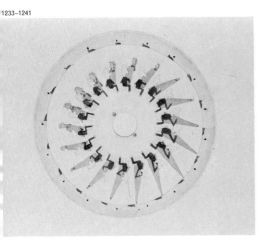

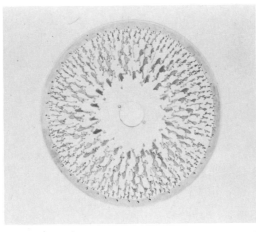

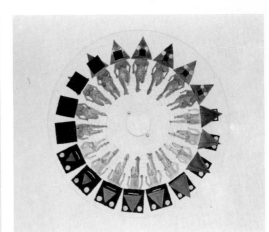

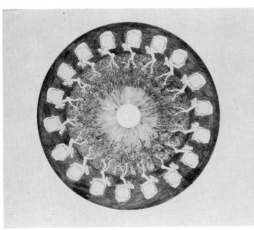

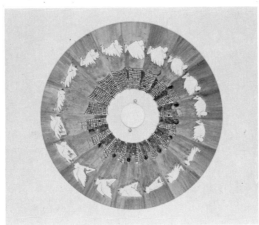

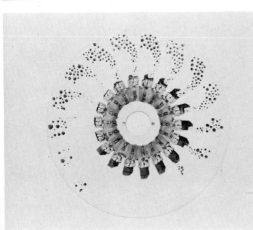

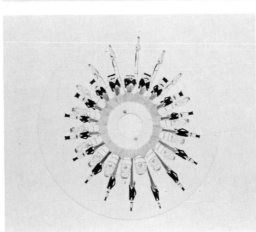

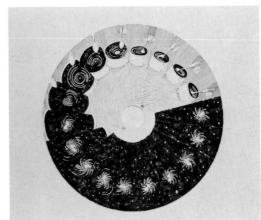

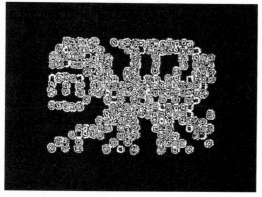
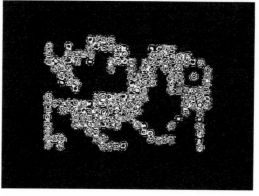
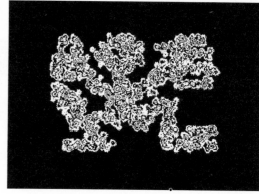

1242–1246 Art and the computer may seem a world apart, but Lillian Schwartz brings them together in her work. She is experimenting in a film technique that uses the computer as a tool. Her films—they run for only a few minutes—combine colour, motion and sound in changing patterns produced by a computer. They are so successful that they are being shown in museums and universities in the United States and abroad. "I am using the technology of today because it says what's going on in society today," she says. She is a freelance artist working with scientists and technicians (and sometimes alone) at Bell Laboratories, New Jersey, and editing her films in her studio at home. Shown here are three imaginary figures—a Mayan animal, a duck and a man; a figure built up of octagons from the 3½-minute film *Olympiad*; and a still graphic entitled *Night Scene* made on a plotting machine.

1242–1246 Kunst und Computer scheinen zwei weitauseinanderliegende Begriffe zu sein. Lillian Schwartz bringt sie in ihrem Werk zusammen, da sie mit einer Filmtechnik experimentiert, die den Computer als Hilfsmittel unerlässlich macht. In ihren Filmen kombiniert sie Farbe, Musik und Ton in wechselnden, von einem Computer produzierten Strukturen. Ihre Filme sind so erfolgreich, dass sie in Museen und Universitäten in den USA und anderswo gezeigt werden. «Ich mache mir die moderne Technologie zu eigen, da sie am besten widerspiegelt, was in unserer Gesellschaft geschieht.» Als freischaffende Künstlerin arbeitet sie mit Wissenschaftern und Technikern zusammen, schneidet und montiert aber ihre Filme im eigenen Studio. Abbildungen: drei Phantasiefiguren – Maya-Tier, Ente, Mann; aus Oktogonen bestehende Figur, aus dem Film *Olympiad*; Bild, auf einem Koordinatograph realisiert, mit dem Titel *Night Scene*.

1242–1246 Le domaine artistique et le traitement électronique de l'information ont beau être aux antipodes l'un de l'autre, Lillian Schwartz n'en a pas moins fait la synthèse dans son œuvre filmé expérimental, où elle prend l'ordinateur pour outil. Ses films – d'une durée de quelques minutes – combinent la couleur, le mouvement et le son en des structures variables produites par l'ordinateur et sont montrés dans des musées et universités aux Etats-Unis et à l'étranger. «J'ai recours à la technologie d'aujourd'hui parce qu'elle montre ce qui se passe dans notre société», nous explique-t-elle. Artiste indépendante, elle travaille avec les techniciens des Laboratoires Bell. Les images représentent trois figures imaginaires – un animal mayas, un canard, un homme; figure conçue d'octogones, d'un film intitulé *Olympiad*; une image immobile, intitulée *Night Scene*, réalisée sur un coordinatographe.

1245

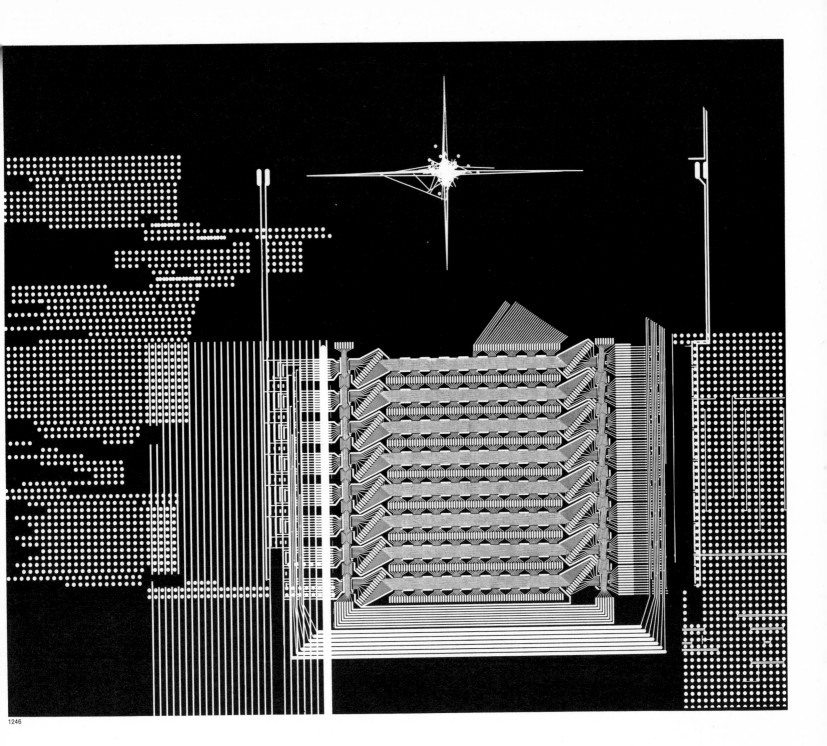

1246

ARTIST / KÜNSTLER / RÉALISATION:
1242–1246 Lillian Schwartz

DIRECTOR / RÉGISSEUR:
1242–1246 Lillian Schwartz/Ken Knowlton

PRODUCTION / PRODUKTION:
1242–1246 Lilyan Productions, Inc., Watchung, N.J.

1247

ARTIST / KÜNSTLER / RÉALISATION:
1247–1252 Wally Veevers/Douglas Trumbull/Con Pederson/Tom Howard

DIRECTOR / RÉGISSEUR:
1247–1252 Stanley Kubrick

ART DIRECTOR / DIRECTEUR ARTISTIQUE:
1247–1252 Tony Masters/Harry Lange/Ernie Archer

PRODUCTION / PRODUKTION:
1247–1252 Stanley Kubrick Production for MGM

1248

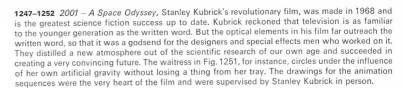

1247–1252 *2001 – A Space Odyssey*, Stanley Kubrick's revolutionary film, was made in 1968 and is the greatest science fiction success up to date. Kubrick reckoned that television is as familiar to the younger generation as the written word. But the optical elements in his film far outreach the written word, so that it was a godsend for the designers and special effects men who worked on it. They distilled a new atmosphere out of the scientific research of our own age and succeeded in creating a very convincing future. The waitress in Fig. 1251, for instance, circles under the influence of her own artificial gravity without losing a thing from her tray. The drawings for the animation sequences were the very heart of the film and were supervised by Stanley Kubrick in person.

1247–1252 *2001 – Odyssee im Weltraum*. Stanley Kubricks revolutionärer Film wurde 1968 fertiggestellt und schnell als der grösste künstlerische Filmerfolg auf dem Gebiet der Science-fiction anerkannt. Kubrick setzt voraus, dass er es mit einer Generation zu tun hat, die ebenso mit dem Fernsehen grossgeworden ist, wie mit dem geschriebenen Wort, die sich also an sichtbare Bilder hält. Die optischen Elemente dieses Films sind dem Bereich der Sprache jedoch so weit entrückt, dass den Graphikern und Special-effects-Leuten unbegrenzte Möglichkeiten offen standen. Basierend auf der modernen wissenschaftlichen Forschung schufen sie eine überzeugende Zukunftsvision. Unter Einfluss ihrer eigenen künstlichen Gravität bewegt sich z.B. die Kellnerin (Abb. 1251) im Kreis, ohne etwas von ihrem Tablett zu verlieren. Die Zeichnungen für die Animationssequenz bilden das Kernstück des Films und wurden von Kubrick persönlich überwacht.

1247–1252 *2001 – A Space Odyssey* (Odyssée de l'Espace), le film révolutionnaire de Stanley Kubrick, a été tourné en 1968 et reste à ce jour le plus grand succès du cinéma de science-fiction. Kubrick a réalisé l'importance actuelle de la TV par rapport au texte. Pourtant, les éléments optiques de son film vont bien au-delà du message écrit, ce qui a constitué une véritable aubaine pour les graphistes et les créateurs d'effets spéciaux qui purent y collaborer. Ils réussirent à évoquer une atmosphère nouvelle en partant des conquêtes scientifiques de notre époque, de manière à incarner un futur très plausible. La serveuse de la fig. 1251, p.ex., tournoie sous l'effet de sa propre pesanteur artificielle sans rien laisser échapper. Les séquences d'animation, essentielles pour le film, ont été supervisées par Kubrick lui-même.

1249

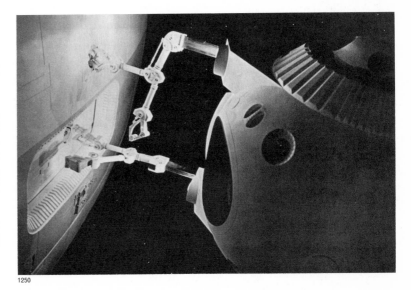

1250

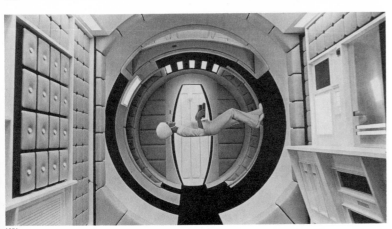

1251

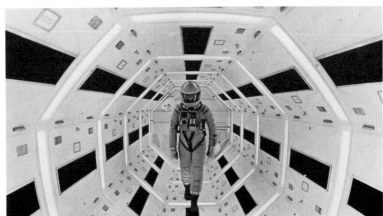

1252